READINGS ON

# THE TRAGEDIES

THE GREENHAVEN PRESS
*Literary Companion*
TO BRITISH LITERATURE

# THE TRAGEDIES

David Bender, *Publisher*
Bruno Leone, *Executive Editor*
Scott Barbour, *Managing Editor*
Bonnie Szumski, *Series Editor*
Clarice Swisher, *Book Editor*

Greenhaven Press, San Diego, CA

Library of Congress Cataloging-in-Publication Data

Readings on the tragedies of William Shakespeare / Clarice
  Swisher, book editor.
        p.     cm. — (Greenhaven Press literary companion to
  British authors)
    ISBN 1-56510-467-6 — ISBN 1-56510-466-8 (pbk.)
    1. Shakespeare, William, 1564–1616—Tragedies.
  2. Tragedy. I. Swisher, Clarice, 1933–   . II. Series.
  PR2983.R38   1996
  822.3'3–dc20                                          96-1292
                                                          CIP

Cover photo: The Bettmann Archive

*"Suit the action to the word, the word to the action: with this special observance, that you o'erstep not the modesty of nature: for ... the purpose of playing, whose end, both at the first and now, was and is, to hold, as 'twere, the mirror up to nature."*

—Hamlet
*Act 3, scene 2*

# CONTENTS

A tragedy is a serious play about the sorrows, failure, and death of a hero who occupies a highly respected, public position. In a unified drama, a tragedy tracks the hero's gradual downfall, usually brought about by his own misjudgment. The play progresses logically, showing the audience the step-by-step events that lead to destruction and death. At some pivotal point late in the play, an event, frequently a reversal of the hero's expectations, makes him recognize his dilemma and his own contribution to it. Despite the unhappy ending, a tragedy offers the audience an emotional release, or catharsis, rather than a depressing experience.

William Shakespeare is the greatest writer in the English language. He understands a wider range of human experiences and re-creates them with greater wisdom than any other writer. Moreover, Shakespeare gives apt and powerful expression to feelings of highest joy and deepest despair. Through his works, critics can discern his knowledge of nature and of human activity and his beliefs in the morality of marriage, in a divinity, and in the value of an orderly world. In *Hamlet*, Shakespeare says that a play should hold "the mirror up to nature." His mirror held up to nature indeed reflects its universal qualities.

None of the women in William Shakespeare's tragedies have the high status of tragic heroes such as Hamlet or King Lear. But Shakespeare creates women characters with distinct personalities who serve important functions in the plays. In *Romeo and Juliet*, Juliet's role is as significant as Romeo's. Women in other tragedies—Desdemona in *Othello*, Ophelia and Gertrude in *Hamlet*, Cordelia in *King Lear*, and Lady Macbeth in *Macbeth*—play supporting roles. These women are integral to the plots and have Shakespeare's "stamp of individuality."

The repetition and variety of light images in Shakespeare's *Romeo and Juliet* give the play beauty and passion. The lovers themselves are spoken of as different kinds of light, and love as a variety of light flashes. The vitality of light images intensifies the power of dark images, which accompany parting and death. Together, the light and dark images give the play a "sensation of swiftness and brilliance."

Many poets in William Shakespeare's time followed the same artistic conventions, or methods, when they wrote about love. Among the conventions are love as a religion; a proud, rejecting mistress; the poet in despair; and comparisons to famous beauties. Shakespeare uses these conventions in *Romeo and Juliet*, but the play is more than a skillful display of artistic form. *Romeo and Juliet* is a tragedy, and Shakespeare evokes the sadness of pure love destroyed and the anguish of feuding fathers' allowing it to happen.

Shakespeare's *Romeo and Juliet* has a central, unified theme: Through action and language, Shakespeare illustrates the reality that people are a blend of saint *and* villain; they are not saints *or* villains. Romeo's confidant Friar Lawrence understands this reality from the outset. Romeo learns it through two experiences: the rejection of his first false love, Rosalind, for his purer love, Juliet, and his slaying of Tybalt and Paris. Juliet learns that Romeo is not villainous simply because he is a member of an enemy family, the Montagues, nor is he a saintly lover. She accepts Romeo as both husband and her cousin's killer.

Though *Julius Caesar* fails to reach the highest sense of tragedy, it engages audiences with portrayals of politicians who appear in all ages. The play's Roman political figures exhibit opposing qualities. For example, Caesar displays arrogant public power, but private pettiness. Brutus is honest and thoughtful, but lacks the single-minded practicality to lead effectively. Antony lures the mob away from Brutus's influence, but does it with ruthless manipulation. Each character's public morality is incompatible with his private morality, and the actions that result cause disorder in Roman society.

The title character in Shakespeare's *Julius Caesar* is a great and powerful Roman ruler, but he is destined to lose a battle with fate. Because Caesar is proud and powerful, he refuses to heed warnings to stay home on the Ides of March, warnings given to him by the soothsayer and suggested by the elements. By defying both, he gave the conspirators an opportunity to kill him. For this great theme—a powerful man pitted against fate—Shakespeare wrote some of his most beautiful poetry.

mysterious one filled with questions and riddles, a world Shakespeare intentionally created that way. Throughout the play, Hamlet struggles in this world, but in the end he accepts it as it is, even though it costs his life and the ruin of the Danish kingdom.

Dialogue in plays functions in three ways: to advance the plot, to establish the setting, and to reveal character. In *Othello*, dialogue reveals qualities about Desdemona, her maid Emilia, Iago, and Othello. Both content and choice of the words show that Desdemona is a more innocent woman than her maid, that Iago is coarse and wicked, and that Othello changes, information the reader or audience learns without direct explanation.

*Othello* particularly engaged Elizabethan audiences and has appealed to audiences and readers ever since. The play appeals because it depicts emotions common to every person; it portrays a villain in Venice, a city reputed for its wickedness; it pits good against evil; and it has an exotic foreign character, a Moor. *Othello* is the perfect play, in part because it presents its theme without extraneous scenes designed to please a portion of the audience, be it the monarch or the poor paying customers standing on the ground around the stage, those called groundlings.

Splendid language and a powerful story give *Othello* its status as a masterpiece. The characters of Iago and Othello, opposites in morality, stature, and worldview, echo each other. Iago is coarse, devious, and heartless; Othello is noble, honorable, and heroic. In the beginning, the language of the two men reflects their differences. As Iago poisons Othello's mind, they begin to speak alike. Iago's is an immediate world in which he talks of cities, goats, and monkeys; Othello's is a chaste world in which he talks of stars and trumpets. Because both worlds lack human understanding and a traditional social order, one world echoes the other.

Shakespeare's *Othello* is supreme in three kinds of beauty: poetic, intellectual, and moral. Othello is an extraordinary man who speaks beautiful language—a hero like those of the ancient world, a free man who left his kin and country behind for freely chosen duties as a professional military officer. Desdemona falls in love with this military man. Othello's love for Desdemona is a "great venture of faith," which fails under Iago's calculated attacks. Structurally, all parts of the play focus on the story of Othello and Desdemona's love and its destruction. As a tragedy of fortune, the play ends heroically when Othello recovers his faith in love and in himself.

mysterious questions about the existence of suffering and good and evil, and he has the wisdom to know that he cannot answer them. The play portrays great evil, in Gloucester's son Edmund and Lear's daughters Goneril and Regan; great suffering, in Gloucester and Lear; and great good, in Cordelia, Edgar, and Kent. Shakespeare does not explain why evil, suffering, and goodness exist. He does, however, oppose evil, not by denying it, but by asserting the presence of its opposites—virtue, loyalty, and love.

Shakespeare's *King Lear* has a double plot. Both Lear and Gloucester suffer from the cruelty of their children, but their destinies differ. Gloucester, blinded and overtaken by despair, learns to "see" in a better, more feeling way. A determined Lear, who defies nature's elements, turns foolish and mad before his senses are restored when he is reunited with his daughter Cordelia. Both men die. In a terrifying way, Gloucester's blindness and death and Lear's profound anguish and death symbolize the passage of what is finite and mortal and the endurance of immortal hope and love.

The original historical story of *King Lear* has been given various treatments. In 1681, Nahum Tate rewrote the closing scenes of Shakespeare's *King Lear* to give it a happy ending and thus avoid the play's brutality. Such tampering undermines the play as a tragedy. In Shakespeare's plot and subplot, Gloucester's pain and Lear's anguish mirror each other. As a tragic hero, Lear suffers, learns patience, and dies, the only ending appropriate for Shakespeare's grand theme.

# FOREWORD

> *"'Tis the good reader that*
> *makes the good book."*
>
> Ralph Waldo Emerson

The story's bare facts are simple: The captain, an old and scarred seafarer, walks with a peg leg made of whale ivory. He relentlessly drives his crew to hunt the world's oceans for the great white whale that crippled him. After a long search, the ship encounters the whale and a fierce battle ensues. Finally the captain drives his harpoon into the whale, but the harpoon line catches the captain about the neck and drags him to his death.

A simple story, a straightforward plot—yet, since the 1851 publication of Herman Melville's *Moby-Dick*, readers and critics have found many meanings in the struggle between Captain Ahab and the whale. To some, the novel is a cautionary tale that depicts how Ahab's obsession with revenge leads to his insanity and death. Others believe that the whale represents the unknowable secrets of the universe and that Ahab is a tragic hero who dares to challenge fate by attempting to discover this knowledge. Perhaps Melville intended Ahab as a criticism of Americans' tendency to become involved in well-intentioned but irrational causes. Or did Melville model Ahab after himself, letting his fictional character express his anger at what he perceived as a cruel and distant god?

Although literary critics disagree over the meaning of *Moby-Dick*, readers do not need to choose one particular interpretation in order to gain an understanding of Melville's novel. Instead, by examining various analyses, they can gain numerous insights into the issues that lie under the surface of the basic plot. Studying the writings of literary critics can also aid readers in making their own assessments of *Moby-Dick* and other literary works and in developing analytical thinking skills.

The Greenhaven Literary Companion Series was created with these goals in mind. Designed for young adults, this unique anthology series provides an engaging and comprehensive introduction to literary analysis and criticism. The essays included in the Literary Companion Series are chosen for their accessibility to a young adult audience and are expertly edited in consideration of both the reading and comprehension levels of this audience. In addition, each essay is introduced by a concise summation that presents the contributing writer's main themes and insights. Every anthology in the Literary Companion Series contains a varied selection of critical essays that cover a wide time span and express diverse views. Wherever possible, primary sources are represented through excerpts from authors' notebooks, letters, and journals and through contemporary criticism.

Each title in the Literary Companion Series pays careful consideration to the historical context of the particular author or literary work. In-depth biographies and detailed chronologies reveal important aspects of authors' lives and emphasize the historical events and social milieu that influenced their writings. To facilitate further research, every anthology includes primary and secondary source bibliographies of articles and/or books selected for their suitability for young adults. These engaging features make the Greenhaven Literary Companion Series ideal for introducing students to literary analysis in the classroom or as a library resource for young adults researching the world's great authors and literature.

Exceptional in its focus on young adults, the Greenhaven Literary Companion Series strives to present literary criticism in a compelling and accessible format. Every title in the series is intended to spark readers' interest in leading American and world authors, to help them broaden their understanding of literature, and to encourage them to formulate their own analyses of the literary works that they read. It is the editors' hope that young adult readers will find these anthologies to be true companions in their study of literature.

# WILLIAM SHAKESPEARE: A BIOGRAPHY

By today's standards, little factual information about William Shakespeare exists; no diaries, journals, or letters remain to help biographers analyze the author's personality. By Elizabethan standards, however, more records exist concerning the events in his life than for most people like Shakespeare, a man of lesser rank than the titled nobility whose lives were often thoroughly documented. Diligent scholars have located institutional records to identify the place of his upbringing and essential events in his family life and economic records to identify some of his employment history and his economic holdings. To supplement what is known from such records, scholars have used the text of his works and their knowledge of Elizabethan history and beliefs to interpret Shakespeare as a person. Not surprisingly, interpretations differ.

## BIRTH AND FAMILY

William Shakespeare was born in Stratford (today called Stratford-on-Avon) in Warwickshire, a county in the heart of England, on April 23 or 24, 1564. The date of his birth is presumed from the record of his baptism in Holy Trinity, the Stratford Church of England, on April 26, a ceremony that, because so many children of that era died in infancy, usually occurred within two or three days of a child's birth. Shakespeare's mother, Mary Arden, came from an old county family that remained Roman Catholic well after the Church of England had become the official church. More genteel and prosperous than the Shakespeares, the Ardens provided their daughter with a dowry of land and money, which advanced the status of her husband, John Shakespeare, when the couple married in 1557. John Shakespeare was a wool dealer and glove maker in Stratford and, for a time, a prominent community leader and officeholder. His first public position was town ale taster, to which he was appointed in 1557. Subsequently, he served as burgess, a member of the town council; constable; chamberlain, a town treasurer; alderman, which allowed him to march in Sunday church processions; and bailiff, or mayor. In the early 1580s, John Shakespeare had financial troubles and lost both his wealth and his governing positions.

## EDUCATION

William was the third of eight children born to Mary and John Shakespeare; he had two older sisters, two younger brothers, and a younger sister. Two more younger siblings died in infancy. Though no school records exist, Shakespeare likely attended Stratford Grammar School, a public school typical of those children throughout England attended. Young children first spent a year in an elementary school learning their letters (alphabet), numbers, and catechism, a book in question-and-answer form summarizing the basic principles of Christianity. Between the ages of seven and sixteen or seventeen, Shakespeare probably attended grammar school, where he would have been expected to be in his seat by 6:00 A.M. in the summer and 7:00 A.M. in the winter for a school day that began and ended with Bible readings, psalm singing, and prayers. Teachers at the Stratford Grammar School had degrees from Oxford University; Simon Hunt and Thomas Jenkins, two of the headmasters during the years Shakespeare lived in Stratford, had advanced degrees. Students memorized Latin grammar and studied logic and Latin composition and literature. The curriculum included the Roman dramatists Seneca, Terence, and Plautus; the Renaissance religious text *Zodiacus Vitae,* the *Zodiac of Life;* the Roman poets Horace, Virgil, and Ovid, who retold Greek myths in his *Metamorphoses;* the complete works of satirist and moralist Erasmus, the Dutch Renaissance scholar; the works of Roman orator and philosopher Cicero; and the Roman historians Julius Caesar and Sallust. According to scholar and critic George R. Price, in *Reading Shakespeare's Plays,* "This education was at least comparable with a modern college major in classics." Playwright and contemporary Ben Jonson disparagingly called Shakespeare's learning "small Latin and less Greek," but, according to Jonson's criteria, "much" learning would have meant a five-year study of Latin, ending with a master's degree.

Shakespeare's education, however, extended well beyond the Stratford Grammar School. Since Elizabethan law required regular attendance in the Protestant Church of England, Shakespeare would have early become accustomed to readings from the Bible and the *Book of Common Prayer,* the liturgical book of the Church of England. Scholars have counted in Shakespeare's plays allusions to forty books of the Bible and many references to the commandments, quotations from Psalms, and lines from the prayer book. But Shakespeare's education extended further than what he learned in school and church. In *Shakespeare the Man,* biographer A. L. Rowse calls Shakespeare a man educated in "the university of life," whose "knowledge of human beings, of the human condition, has never been surpassed." Moreover, his plays display detailed knowledge of the entertainment, social mores, and culture of his native Warwickshire. Price says that we may

> be sure that the knowledge of hawking, hunting, and archery, of horses, dogs, and wild things, of peddlers, shepherds, and farm folk—this store of information in his plays and poems was not acquired only from books, but indicates a normal freedom to roam the countryside and enjoy himself.

Furthermore, when Shakespeare lived in Stratford, many groups of actors visited the town to present plays; though there are no records of Shakespeare's attendance, he would surely have been aware of the performances and probably attended them.

When Shakespeare was eighteen years old, he married Anne Hathaway, eight years older than he. Biographers have made much of the information that banns for the marriage were called only once, on December 1, 1582, rather than the usual three times; they assume that church officials hurried the marriage because Anne was already pregnant. However, because Elizabethan custom considered betrothal (engagement) a binding agreement and in some instances the same as marriage, her pregnancy was less unusual than modern customs might consider it. After the marriage, the couple lived with Shakespeare's family on Henley Street in Stratford. On May 26, 1583, their daughter Susanna was baptized; twenty months later the young couple had twins, baptized Hamnet and Judith on February 2, 1585. How this twenty-one-year-old man supported his family is unknown. John Aubrey, born a decade after Shakespeare died, was an English antiquarian who studied old and rare books and other objects and who kept records of facts, gossip, and anecdotes about public persons. In his journal, he says that someone told him that Shakespeare taught school and worked in his father's shop, a butcher's shop, Aubrey thought.

## FIRST YEARS IN LONDON

What prompted Shakespeare to go to London no one knows, nor are there records of any of his activities between 1585 and 1592. From poems and plays published later and records appearing in 1592, biographers have pieced together a partial picture of Shakespeare's life during the years for which there are no records. He probably went to London in 1587, a year before the English defeat of the Spanish Armada in 1588, a naval victory that launched a long era of confidence and high spirit in England. When Shakespeare came to London, attending plays was the most popular form of entertainment for all classes, from poor students to aristocrats. London boasted companies of actors and theaters; the first, built in 1576, was called simply the Theatre. Others, such as the Fortune, the Swan, Blackfriars, and the most famous, the Globe, followed. Each theater maintained a company of actors performing plays and competing with all the other theaters for popular approval. During the twelve days of Christmas, actors performed plays in Queen Elizabeth's court to entertain royal guests. In addition, touring companies performed plays in towns and cities outside London.

A common story reports that Shakespeare began his career as a dramatist by holding horses outside the theater. The story may or may not be true; more reliable information indicates that he acted in plays, many of his own. From acting, Shakespeare progressed to writing plays both for the theater and for court performances. Though attending plays was popular London entertainment, many moralists complained that the jokes were too bawdy and that young men neglected their church duties in favor of playgoing. Consequently, actors came to be looked on as riffraff at worst and men of questionable reputation at best. Price comments: "When Shakespeare became an actor, he must have deeply grieved the heart of his father and mother, and he surely gave himself cause for extreme discomfort at times." John Aubrey, however, writes: "He was a handsome, well-shap't man: very good company, and of a very readie and pleasant smoothe Witt."

Because Shakespeare was an outsider in London, a country man who lacked the sophistication and easy manners of the Cambridge and Oxford University men, he studied the ways of a gentleman, found a mentor, and read widely. Shakespeare looked to Cambridge-educated playwright Christopher Marlowe, who was the same age but who preceded Shakespeare in skillfully combining drama with poetry. In many plays throughout his career, Shakespeare paid tribute to Marlowe, though ultimately he eclipsed Marlowe as a dramatist. Shakespeare's romantic nature was influenced by the works of two British poets: Sir Philip Sidney's sonnets and a prose romance, *The Arcadia,* and Edmund Spenser's poem about glory and the queen, *The Faerie Queene.* Furthermore, Shakespeare, who loved his country and her history, read the *Chronicles* of Raphael Holinshed, a historian who came to London early in Elizabeth's reign, and the works of historian Edward Hall, who wrote about England's past royal families. Shakespeare borrowed from these works to form plots for many of his plays and used poetic techniques like those of Sidney and Spenser.

By 1592, Shakespeare had written a few plays, some of them performed on stage. His early plays mimic the form of the Roman playwrights he studied earlier. His first plays were *The Tragedy of Titus Adronicus; Henry VI, Parts I, II, and III; The Comedy of Errors;* and *Richard III.* In 1592 and 1593, a plague in London forced theaters to close. During the lull, Shakespeare wrote a series of 154 sonnets, which celebrate a young man and express powerful passion for a mysterious dark lady and the suffering caused by her rejection. (A sonnet is a fourteen-line poem with an established iambic rhythm and ten-syllable lines.) Biographer Rowse identifies the young man in the sonnets as the earl of Southampton, the patron who supported Shakespeare, who, in turn, dutifully wrote sonnets glorifying him. Rowse identifies the dark lady as Emilia Bassano, daughter of an Italian musician in the queen's court, a woman with whom Shakespeare became infatuated. Two purposes inspired Shakespeare to write poems. He wanted to be a poet, which to him was a noble occupation; he thought acting in and writing plays were merely jobs that brought income for his family. And he wrote sonnets to trade privately with other sonnet writers, who competed to create the most elaborate imagery and to express the most powerful suffering at the hands of a beautiful, proud mistress. In addition to the sonnets, Shakespeare wrote two long poems and a short one: *Venus and Adonis, The Rape of Lucrece,* and "The Phoenix and the Turtle."

By September 1592, Shakespeare had a reputation that elicited a comment in a journal left by Robert Greene, a popular Cambridge-educated playwright who died in 1592, by that time angry and jealous of the popularity of theater players. Greene, complaining that the professional actors had forsaken university men like him, specifically attacked Shakespeare:

> Yes trust them not: for there is an upstart Crow, beautified with our feathers, that with his *Tygers hart wrapt in a Players hyde,*[1] supposes he is as well able to bombast out a blanke verse as the

---

1. A parody on Shakespeare's line from *Henry VI*, which says, "O tiger's heart wrapt in a woman's hide!"

best of you: and beeing an absolute *Johannes fac totum*,[1] is in his owne conceit the onely Shake-scene in a countrey.

## THE TURNING POINT IN SHAKESPEARE'S CAREER

The year 1594 was a turning point in Shakespeare's career— he also turned thirty that April. With the end of the plague, the patronage of Southampton stopped, and Shakespeare stopped writing sonnets and reestablished himself with actors. By the summer of 1594, a group of actors formerly with other companies had obtained the patronage of Henry Lord Hunsdon, lord chamberlain to the queen, formed an acting company, and called themselves Lord Chamberlain's Men. They played at various theaters—the Theatre, the Curtain, the Swan— before the Globe was built. The company contained a permanent nucleus of men, among them Henry Condell, John Heminge, Shakespeare, Richard Burbage, William Sly, and Will Kempe. Burbage, the famous tragedian, and Kempe, the famous comedian, played leading roles in plays Shakespeare wrote specifically for their talents. From then on, Shakespeare was completely involved in the theater: He wrote for the company, acted in the plays, shared in the profits, and eventually became one of the owners of the Globe theater. While in London, he had no time for drinking, partying, or getting into trouble. He lived as a lodger in a quiet room where he could concentrate and think and imagine, uninterrupted. Stratford was still the center of his family and the place where he bought a house and invested his money.

In 1596 and 1597, Shakespeare was occupied with three different personal matters. First, in August 1596 Shakespeare's son, Hamnet, died. With the death of his eleven-year-old son, Shakespeare lost hope of perpetuating the family in his name. His wife, Anne, was forty and could not be expected to have another child. Shakespeare expressed his grief in the play he was writing at the time, *King John:*

> Grief fills the room up of my absent child,
> Lies in his bed, walks up and down with me,
> Puts on his pretty looks, repeats his words,
> Remembers me of all his gracious parts,
> Stuffs out his vacant garments with his form.    (act 3, scene 4)

Though he had no son to carry on the family name, Shakespeare set out next to obtain a coat of arms and the title of gentleman, an important status to him. So that he could be consid-

---

1. A "John Do-everything," a "jack of all trades".

ered born the son of a gentleman, Shakespeare applied for a grant in the name of his father and paid the cash for it. On October 20, 1596, Garter King of Arms William Dethick issued a coat of arms with a falcon and a silver spear and declared Shakespeare a gentleman by birth. Today, the coat of arms is displayed on the Shakespeare monument at Stratford. Then, in May 1597, Shakespeare purchased New Place, a large house in the center of Stratford with two barns and two orchards and gardens. Before he was thirty-five years old, Shakespeare had achieved the status of gentleman, property owner, and playwright.

The years between 1593 and 1598 marked the first phase of Shakespeare's success as a playwright. *The Taming of the Shrew* and *The Tragedy of Romeo and Juliet,* perhaps written earlier, exemplify the characteristics of his early plays: long explanatory speeches in stiff verse, plots that imitate Marlowe and the plays Shakespeare had studied earlier, elaborate imagery, and an abundance of puns and wordplay. *The Taming of the Shrew* is a farce with a double plot about the marriages of two sisters, Katherine and Bianca. Shakespeare's first great play, *The Tragedy of Romeo and Juliet,* has a finely crafted plot that recounts the love and destruction of young Romeo and Juliet, star-crossed lovers from the beginning. Critics have called several plays from this period Shakespeare's lyrical plays because they contain passages of beautiful description and lyrical feelings. Among these are *Love's Labour's Lost* and *A Midsummer Night's Dream,* a play celebrating Midsummer's Day and its merrymaking. This play, full of farce and fancy, includes lovers with mistaken identities, craftsmen, Bottom the Ass, and the king and queen of fairies. During this period, Shakespeare also wrote the history plays about England's past kings: *Richard II; Henry IV, Parts I* and *II; Henry V;* and *King John.* The plays about Henry IV and V were especially popular because the humorous character Falstaff appears in both. Also during this very productive period, Shakespeare wrote *The Two Gentlemen from Verona, Much Ado About Nothing,* and *The Merchant of Venice.*

## THE NEW GLOBE

In 1598, Lord Chamberlain's Men prepared to move to the new Globe theater, built with other theaters across the Thames River from the center of the City of London. Shakespeare had by then become prosperous enough to buy a one-eighth share in the Globe. The new theater held two thousand spectators and was equipped with a bigger stage, a cellerage for graves and ghosts, a curtained space for intimate and surprise scenes, and a balcony. The audience was closer to the players, and the players had more flexibility to move quickly from scene to scene. The production of *Henry V,* in which Shakespeare played the part of the chorus, anticipated the new Globe. In the prologue, he refers to the new theater:

> A kingdom for a stage, princes to act
> And monarchs to behold the swelling scene! . . .
>            Can this cockpit[1] hold
> The vasty fields of France? Or may we cram
> Within this wooden O[2] the very casques[3]
> That did affright the air at Agincourt[4]?

Besides referring humbly to the theater in the prologue, Shakespeare exemplifies in the epilogue his characteristic, gentlemanly humble attitude toward himself:

> Thus far, with rough and all-unable pen,
> Our bending[5] author hath pursued the story,
> In little room[6] confining mighty men,
> Mangling by starts[7]
> the full course of their glory.

Though he himself may not have believed the words, Shakespeare is self-deprecating throughout his works, humbly calling himself "a worthless boat," "inferior far" to Marlowe. This attitude proved charming and earned him a reputation for congeniality.

The opening of the Globe marked a new phase in Shakespeare's reputation and art. Shakespeare's fame had established him as the leading dramatist in London; no one could touch him, though Ben Jonson wished he could. Aubrey reports Jonson's envy of Shakespeare: "He[8] was wont to say that he[9] never blotted out a line in his life. Sayd Ben Johnson, I wish he had blotted out a thousand." Shakespeare's art was becoming more refined and subtle. Price says, "Art has replaced artifice. The style has become so fully expressive of the thought that audience and readers are unconscious of the poet's devices." Shakespeare, more interested in human character, objectively displayed the workings of his characters' minds. The soliloquies of Brutus, Hamlet, and Iago, for example, lay bare their intentions and their very souls.

After 1598, Shakespeare wrote speedily, as if with two hands—one for comedies and one for tragedies. He turned from English history to Roman history and used Greek

---

1. Playhouse. 2. The playhouse. 3. The actual helmets. 4. The French village where Henry V defeated a larger French army. 5. Bowing. 6. The theater. 7. Marring the story by telling it in fragments. 8. and 9. Shakespeare.

philosopher and biographer Plutarch's *Lives* as a source for plots. *The Tragedy of Julius Caesar,* dated 1599, explores Brutus's character and motives more thoroughly than those of other characters. Shakespeare uses Marc Antony's speech to expose the gullibility of the mob, but he does it with gentlemanly manners. Though he makes the masses look foolish, his audiences applauded him because he criticizes the mob with "friendly contempt," as Rowse calls it. Shakespeare wrote three comedies to suit Will Kempe's acting: *The Merry Wives of Windsor,* in which Shakespeare revived the character of Falstaff, *As You Like It,* and *Twelfth Night. As You Like It* portrays many kinds of love. An old servant shows his devotion, fathers and children reunite, and four couples marry. Aloof from the goings-on, cynical Jaques delivers his famous speech on the seven ages in the lives of human beings, beginning, "All the world's a stage / And all the men and women merely players." *Twelfth Night,* a popular romance regularly performed over centuries, is Shakespeare's most musical play; it has many songs and humor revolving around the characters Sir Toby Belch and the clown Feste.

After 1600, Shakespeare wrote his greatest tragedies, different from the earlier ones because the language is more subtle, the characters are more complex, and the themes more philosophical. *Hamlet* and *Othello* come first. Shakespearean scholar and critic G.B. Harrison says that "*Hamlet* is in every way the most interesting play ever written"; for nearly four hundred years, it has challenged actors and scholars to interpret Hamlet's character. In addition, the play tells about the Elizabethan theater wars, companies of boy actors, and Shakespeare's theory that drama should hold a mirror up to nature. *Othello,* a unified and focused play, portrays evil in the character of Iago as he exploits Othello's jealousy and Desdemona's innocence to destroy them and their love. Shakespeare structures the play without diversion into topics that interest him and tells the story with some of his most beautiful poetry.

Though Shakespeare continued to work, the period from 1598 to 1604 brought significant personal events. In September 1601, his father died in Stratford. The following May, Shakespeare bought 107 acres of farmland in Old Stratford for £320, and in September a cottage on Walkers Street. On March 24, 1603, Queen Elizabeth, who had actively supported Lord Chamberlain's Men, died. When James I became king, he took over the company, renamed it the King's Men, and supported the players even more avidly than the queen had. James made them an official part of the court, doubled their salaries, and increased their annual court appearances from three to thirteen. In addition, he gave them license to perform in any town or university. These changes required Shakespeare to write for the approval of two audiences, the court and the Globe. Shakespeare's increase in income allowed him to invest £440 in tithes in parishes in Stratford and surrounding towns, investments that brought additional income of £60 a year (churches and other institutions owning farmland leased portions by selling shares, or tithes, allowing the titheholder to earn money from crops grown on the land).

## THE KING'S MEN

From 1604 to 1608, as a member of the King's Men, Shakespeare's art changed again. He wrote two transitional comedies: *All's Well That Ends Well,* an uneven play seldom performed, about a young woman who tricks a man into becoming her husband, and *Measure for Measure,* called a problem play because the plot poorly fits the theme. The plot concerns a woman who gives up her chastity to save her brother's life. G.B. Harrison calls it "one of Shakespeare's unpleasant plays"; other critics have spoken of it more harshly.

After 1604, Shakespeare continued to write tragedies, but the two that followed *Hamlet* and *Othello* probe even deeper into the minds of their heroes. *The Tragedy of King Lear* was presented in King James's court during the Christmas holidays of 1606. Critics regard *Lear* as Shakespeare's greatest play, though not his most popular. The play has a double plot; Lear suffers at the hands of his daughters and Gloucester at the hands of his son. After Lear is turned out, he wanders and goes mad; after Gloucester is blinded, he too is turned out to wander. Both die, but each has one child who remains loyal. The play's greatness lies in the psychological depth of Lear's character and the stark reality of both human nature and nature's elements. G.B. Harrison explains:

> When he came to write *Lear,* Shakespeare was again experimenting with language. By this time his thoughts and feelings were coming too thick and powerful for balanced expression. . . . The thought became too intense for clear, logical expression; the idea in Shakespeare's mind did not always travel along the usual conductor of grammatical sentences, but leapt across in some mighty image which only laborious paraphrase can reduce to everyday speech. *Lear* and *Macbeth* are full of these passages, often packed with a complex imagery which suggests half a dozen different glints and meanings.

Shakespeare wrote *Macbeth* in 1606, as a tribute to James I when the king of Denmark visited England. The play is set in Scotland, James's home before he became king of England. The good character Banquo is a member of the Scottish Stuart family, an ancestor of James. Shakespeare also honored the king, who was interested in witchcraft, by incorporating three witches into the play. Though he did not find King James I an honorable man, Shakespeare fulfilled his duty to the king upon whose patronage he depended. Like *Lear*, *Macbeth* reaches below the rational level into the subconscious, where primitive experiences lie in recesses of the mind. Macbeth and Lady Macbeth plot the murder of King Duncan to put Macbeth on the throne. After the murder, their plan goes awry, and King Macbeth orders the killings of men, children, and a woman. Lady Macbeth, the more cold and cruel of the two, goes mad with guilt and tries to wash the blood, the "damned spot," from her hand. Macbeth knows the horror of his deeds. He acknowledges that his life signifies nothing as Macduff, a Scottish nobleman whose wife and children have been killed on Macbeth's orders, leads an army against him and beheads him, fulfilling the prophecy of the three witches.

Shakespeare returned to Plutarch's *Lives* as a source for three tragedies. *The Tragedy of Antony and Cleopatra* picks up the story of Roman history where *Julius Caesar* left off. *The Tragedy of Coriolanus* is a political play in which Shakespeare exposes the weakness of all manner of politicians and presents the crowd as a fickle mob reeking with stinking breath, a tone more bitter than his exposé of the crowd in *Julius Caesar*. *Timon of Athens*, an unfinished play, tells about an ancient Greek mentioned briefly in Plutarch's *Lives*.

During this period, when Shakespeare wrote one or more plays a year and managed a busy schedule of productions at court and at the Globe, little is known of his personal life. Only a few records exist. His daughter Susanna married a well-known medical doctor from Stratford named John Hall on June 5, 1607. In September 1608, his mother, Mary Arden Shakespeare died, and in October 1608, Shakespeare stood godfather to the son of Stratford alderman Henry Walker, whose son was named William in honor of Shakespeare.

## THE FINAL PERIOD

After the outpouring of tragedies, Shakespeare's art changed again, this time brought about because of changes in theater ownership and attendance. Blackfriars, a private theater owned by Richard Burbage, had been leased to a boys' company. Burbage, Shakespeare, and other actors bought back the lease and began performances there for upper-class audiences more like those at court. Blackfriars audiences liked new plays, while the public audiences at the Globe preferred old favorites. This situation suited Shakespeare, who could try new plays at Blackfriars, plays that were neither tragedies nor comedies. Some critics have called them romances, and others tragi-comedies. These plays express themes of reunion after long separation, reconciliation, and forgiveness. The plots tell about children lost and then found, divided parents brought together, and an innocent person threatened but rescued. Before a character finds a haven, he or she has been through storms and stress, encountered evil, or endured suffering. Rowse says of them: "For all their happy endings, these plays have an atmosphere full of suggestion and symbol, suffused with tears."

Shakespeare wrote four plays in this new form. *Pericles* is a transitional play, not totally written by Shakespeare. The first two acts are not in Shakespeare's style, but the last three are mostly his. After experimenting with *Pericles,* Shakespeare wrote *Cymbeline,* probably in 1610; it is a melodrama about an innocent girl who, after mistreatment, flees and encounters a host of crises before she is reunited with her repentant husband. The audience is entertained with disguises, sentimental characters, battles, and chase scenes. *The Winter's Tale,* written in 1610 or 1611, is a tale of wrongs committed by one generation and reconciled in the children. Leontes, extremely jealous, suspects his wife, Hermione, of unfaithfulness, accuses her, and has her tried. She dies, and Leontes discovers his error too late and repents. In the second part, Leontes' daughter, Perdita, falls in love with young Prince Florizel, who sacrifices his kingdom for his love. *The Winter's Tale* makes a moving production in the theater, but some critics think that Shakespeare was sloppy in establishing motives for Leontes' behavior.

*The Tempest,* a play written for the court of James I to celebrate a court wedding, is Shakespeare's farewell to the theater. The play, a fairy tale with a magician and a beautiful daughter, is about the reconciliation of two generations. G.B. Harrison praises *The Tempest,* saying:

> Shakespeare has finally achieved complete mastery over words in the blank-verse form. This power is shown throughout the play, but particularly in some of Prospero's great speeches, . . .

or in his farewell to his art. There is in these speeches a kind of organ note not hitherto heard. Shakespeare's thought was as deep as in his tragedies, but now he was able to express each thought with perfect meaning and its own proper harmony.

Shakespeare makes his farewell to the theater through the voice of Prospero, the magician. After recounting a catalog of scenes he had created over the years, from raging storms to corpses rising from the grave to dimming the sun, he announces "this rough magic / I here abjure. . . . I'll break my staff, / Bury it certain fathoms in the earth, / And . . . I'll drown my book."[1] His only writing after this farewell was *Henry VIII,* a play full of pageantry, music, and ceremony.

Shakespeare himself made no effort to publish his works, neither plays nor poems. His plays belonged to the members of the theater company, who sold individual plays for publication when readers requested them in the early 1600s. In 1609, a respected publisher, Thomas Thorpe, published Shakespeare's sonnets in a book entitled *Shakespeare's Sonnets: Never Before Imprinted.* In 1623, two actors from the King's Men, Henry Condell and John Heminge, collected Shakespeare's plays, published as the First Folio. Some skeptics have doubted that Shakespeare wrote the plays at all and speculated that Francis Bacon or someone else wrote them. Such doubts are put forth by the uninformed. As Price says: "No first-rate scholar has ever accepted the evidence offered by the Baconians or others who argue that Shakespeare did not write the dramas that his fellow-actors, Heminge and Condell, published as his."

Beginning in 1612, Shakespeare divided his time between Stratford and London, and once went to Parliament to lobby for better roads between the two cities. In 1612, his brother Gilbert died, and the following year, his brother Richard died. Shakespeare spent 1614 and 1615 in Stratford enjoying his retirement and his daughters, but information about his wife, Anne, seems to be nonexistent. The parish register of Holy Trinity shows that on February 10, 1616, Shakespeare's younger daughter, Judith, was married to Thomas Quiney, the son of Shakespeare's old friend Richard Quiney. On March 25, 1616, while he was in fine health, Shakespeare made a will. He left a dowry and additional money to Judith and all lands and houses to his older daughter, Susanna, and her heirs. He left his wife to the care of his daughters and willed her the next-best bed, reasoning that Susanna and her husband needed the

1. Of magic spells.

bigger, better one. To his sister, he left money for clothes and the home on Henley Street. He gave small amounts of money to friends and money for rings to fellow actors of the King's Men. And he left money for the poor in Stratford. A month later, after a trip to London, he suddenly became ill and died on April 23, 1616, at the age of fifty-two. As he lay dying, the chapel bell knelled for the passing of his soul, for the man for whom love was the center of the universe and the central subject of his many works.

# ABOUT THIS BOOK

The biography of William Shakespeare introducing this book provides students with factual information about Shakespeare's life as well as interpretations by scholars who have studied the plays and the commentary of Shakespeare's contemporaries. Readers will learn when and where Shakespeare lived, who his family was, how he was educated, how his acting and writing careers developed, and what influenced him. Because this literary companion focuses on the major tragedies, more attention has been given to the periods when he wrote them. Commentary about other plays is included to explain changes in the development of Shakespeare's art.

The essays selected for this literary companion provide teachers and students with a wide range of information and opinion about Shakespeare's major tragedies. Though Shakespeare wrote fourteen tragedies, the six chosen for this book are the ones students most often study first. Collectively, the essays address introductory literary criticism; they cover plot structure, character, theme, imagery, symbol, and author's viewpoint. Three essays generally define tragedy, explain Shakespeare's universal appeal, and discuss his treatment of women characters. The remainder discuss specific tragedies, each essay addressing one play and one element of literary criticism. Within the essays, authors assess Shakespeare's qualities as an author and evaluate particular plays. Students doing research for papers or oral presentations will find in this collection abundant material from which to generate topics. Though this companion provides an excellent starting point, students will want to extend their research, perhaps by consulting the bibliography at the back of this book.

A general plan governs the organization of the essays in this anthology. The general essays appear first. Following the first three are at least three essays devoted to each of the six tragedies. The plays are discussed in the order in which Shakespeare wrote them, except for the last two: Though Shakespeare wrote *King Lear* a few months before he wrote *Macbeth,* the order has been reversed. Concluding with *King Lear* seems the logical choice: It is Shakespeare's greatest tragedy; it is the most challenging to read and interpret; and students usually study it after they have studied *Macbeth.*

This volume brings together a wide range of scholars and critics. The oldest selection dates from 1811 and the most recent from the summer of 1995. With a selection that covers so broad a time span, students can see for themselves that critics have been analyzing Shakespeare's tragedies for at least the last two centuries, and they can see for themselves that Shakespeare's tragedies still hold scholars' interest. British writers Charles Lamb, Samuel Taylor Coleridge, and William Hazlitt represent historical criticism. In addition, this volume includes a range of the most respected Shakespearean critics of this century; A.C. Bradley, Northrop Frye, G.B. Harrison, and Caroline F.E. Spurgeon among them.

Several special features of this volume make research and literary criticism not necessarily easy, but, rather, accessible and understandable. Each essay has an introduction that clearly identifies its main points and summarizes the author's arguments. Within the essays, students will find subheads signaling points identified in the introduction. Also within the essays, students will find special inserts. Taken from a variety of sources, these present supporting or opposing viewpoints, offer background and related information, and add excerpts from the plays to illustrate concepts. Following the essays, a chronology lists in concise form the most significant events in Shakespeare's life and in England during his lifetime. A list of Shakespeare's works with dates follows the chronology. Scholars arrive at different dates depending on their interpretation of evidence; thus, dates may differ from those from another source. The dates for this list of works are based on the conclusions drawn by scholar and critic G.B. Harrison. Taken together, these aids for students make the task of research manageable and satisfying.

# Elements of Greek and Shakespearean Tragedy

Robert Di Yanni

In his *Poetics*, the Greek philosopher Aristotle, examining Greek dramas of the fifth century B.C., offered a set of working rules for the writing of tragedy. In the following essay, Robert Di Yanni applies Aristotle's criteria to a Shakespearean tragedy and finds a good fit. A tragedy is a serious play about the sorrows, failure, and death of a hero who occupies a highly respected, public position. In a unified drama, a tragedy tracks the hero's gradual downfall, usually brought about by his own misjudgment. The play progresses logically, showing the audience the step-by-step events that lead to destruction and death. At some pivotal point late in the play, an event, frequently a reversal of the hero's expectations, makes him recognize his dilemma and his own contribution to it. Despite the unhappy ending, a tragedy offers the audience an emotional release, or catharsis, rather than a depressing experience.

Some plays elicit laughter, others evoke tears. Some are comic, others tragic, still others a mixture of both. The two major dramatic modes, tragedy and comedy, have been represented traditionally by contrasting masks, one sorrowful, the other joyful. The two masks represent more than different types of plays: they also stand for contrasting ways of looking at the world, aptly summarized in [eighteenth-century British writer] Horace Walpole's remark that "the world is a comedy to those who think and a tragedy to those who feel."

The comic view celebrates life and affirms it; it is typically joyous and festive. The tragic view highlights life's sorrows; it is typically brooding and solemn. Tragic plays end unhappily, often with the death of the hero; comedies usually end happily, often with a celebration such as a marriage. Both comedy and tragedy contain changes of fortune, with the fortunes of comic characters turning from bad to good and those of tragic characters from good to bad.

In the *Poetics*, Aristotle described tragedy as "an imitation of an action that is serious, complete in itself, and of a certain magnitude." This definition suggests that tragedies are dignified plays concerned with consequential actions and further indicates that the action of a tragedy is complete—that it possesses a beginning, a middle, and an end. Elsewhere in the *Poetics*, Aristotle notes that the incidents of a tragedy must be causally connected. The events, that is, have to be logically related, one growing naturally out of another, each leading to the inevitable catastrophe, usually the downfall of the hero.

## A HERO'S FALL AND RECOGNITION

Some readers of tragedy have suggested that, according to Aristotle, the catastrophe results from a flaw in the character of the hero. Others have contended that the hero's tragic flaw results from fate or coincidence, from circumstances beyond the hero's control. A third view proposes that tragedy results from an error of judgment committed by the hero, one that may or may not have as its source a weakness in character. Typically, tragic protagonists make mistakes: they misjudge other characters, they misinterpret events, and they confuse appearance with reality. Shakespeare's Othello, for example, mistakes Iago for an honest, loving friend; and he mistakes his faithful wife, Desdemona, for an adultress. [Greek playwright] Sophocles' Oedipus mistakes his own identity and misconstrues his destiny. The misfortune and catastrophes of tragedy are frequently precipitated by errors of judgment; mistaken perceptions lead to misdirected actions that eventually result in catastrophe.

Tragic heroes such as Oedipus and Othello are grand, noble characters. They are men, as Aristotle says, "of high estate," who enjoy "great reputation and prosperity." Tragic heroes, in short, are privileged, exalted personages whose high repute and status have been earned by heroic exploit (Othello), by intelligence (Oedipus), or by their inherent nobility (Othello and Oedipus). Their tragedy resides in a fall from glory that crushes not only the tragic hero himself but other related characters as well. Othello's tragedy includes his wife and his faithful lieutenant, Cassio. Oedipus's tragedy extends to his entire family, including his wife-mother, his two sons, his daughters, and even his brother-in-law, Creon, and his family.

Greek tragedy, typically, involves the destruction and downfall of a house or family, reaching across generations. The catastrophe of Shakespearean tragedy is usually not as extensive.

## A DISTINGUISHING CHARACTERISTIC OF TRAGIC HEROES

*Noted Shakespearean critic A.C. Bradley explains that the tragic heroes described in Aristotle's* Poetics *manifest themselves as exceptional people in Shakespeare's tragedies.*

Ignoring the characteristics which distinguish [Shakespeare's] heroes from one another, let us ask whether they have any common qualities which appear to be essential to the tragic effect.

One they certainly have. They are exceptional beings. We have seen already that the hero, with Shakespeare, is a person of high degree or of public importance, and that his actions or sufferings are of an unusual kind. But this is not all. His nature also is exceptional, and generally raises him in some respect much above the average level of humanity. This does not mean that he is an eccentric or a paragon. Shakespeare never drew monstrosities of virtue; some of his heroes are far from being 'good'; and if he drew eccentrics he gave them a subordinate position in the plot. His tragic characters are made of the stuff we find within ourselves and within the persons who surround them. But, by an intensification of the life which they share with others, they are raised above them; and the greatest are raised so far that, if we fully realise all that is implied in their words and actions, we become conscious that in real life we have known scarcely any one resembling them. Some, like Hamlet and Cleopatra, have genius. Others, like Othello, Lear, Macbeth, Coriolanus, are built on the grand scale; and desire, passion, or will attains in them a terrible force. In almost all we observe a marked one-sidedness, a predisposition in some particular direction; a total incapacity, in certain circumstances, of resisting the force which draws in this direction; a fatal tendency to identify the whole being with one interest, object, passion, or habit of mind. This, it would seem, is, for Shakespeare, the fundamental tragic trait.

A.C. Bradley, *Shakespearean Tragedy: Hamlet, Othello, King Lear, Macbeth.* New York: World Publishing, 1904.

An essential element of the tragic hero's experience is a recognition of what has happened to him. Frequently this takes the form of the hero discovering something previously unknown or something he knew but misconstrued. According to Aristotle, the tragic hero's recognition (or discovery) is allied with a reversal of his expectations. Such an ironic reversal occurs in *Oedipus Rex* when the messenger's speech unsettles rather than reassures Oedipus about who he is and what he has done. Once the reversal and discovery occur, tragic plots move swiftly to their conclusions.

## THE AUDIENCE'S RELIEF

Another consideration raised by Aristotle in his discussion of tragedy is why, amidst such suffering and catastrophe, tragedies are not depressing. Perhaps, because as he himself suggested, the pity and fear aroused in the audience are purged or released so that the audience experiences a cleansing of those emotions and a sense of relief that the action is over. Or, because we recognize that tragedy represents the ultimate downfall we will all experience in death: we watch in fascination and awe a dramatic reminder of our own inevitable mortality. Or perhaps for still another reason: we are somehow exalted in witnessing the high human aspiration and the noble conception of human character embodied in tragic heroes like Oedipus and Othello.

# Shakespeare's Wisdom Is Relevant for All Times and Places

G.B. Harrison

G.B. Harrison contends that William Shakespeare is the greatest writer in the English language. Shakespeare, Harrison argues, understands a wider range of human experiences and re-creates them with greater wisdom than any other writer. Moreover, Shakespeare gives apt and powerful expression to feelings of highest joy and deepest despair. Though critics cannot always pinpoint the sources of Shakespeare's knowledge, they agree he understands many subjects; for example, the soldier's experience and the power of the sea. Through his work, one can discern his beliefs in the morality of marriage, in a divinity holding the universe in accord, and in the value of an orderly world. In *Hamlet*, Shakespeare says that a play should hold "the mirror up to nature." No writer, Harrison asserts, better holds a mirror up to nature and reflects its universal qualities.

No man can write a good book or play without revealing something of himself to the expert reader, and of all forms of writing drama is often the most revealing, because it is talk and thought. For even though the words of each character must naturally be appropriate, the author wrote the words; the sentiments have first occurred in his mind.

### SHAKESPEARE UNDERSTANDS PEOPLE'S EXPERIENCES

For [nearly four hundred] years Shakespeare has been regarded as the greatest writer in the English tongue, and since it is unusual for one generation to worship the gods of its fathers, it follows that he has been admired for very differ-

Excerpts from *Shakespeare: The Complete Works* by G.B. Harrison; copyright 1952 by Harcourt Brace & Company; renewed in 1980 by G.B. Harrison. Reprinted by permission of the publisher.

ent reasons, and that his plays possess an enduring vitality. This quality in art we call universality. When we try to analyze the universality of Shakespeare, we find that he is not particularly original as a thinker, nor is he the only great English writer. Others, in various ways, have written poetry as memorable. But he is the most universal of all, because he is the wisest; that is, he can understand and sympathize more than other men. He can see the whole picture of humanity and re-create it so that men of every kind, country, creed, and generation understand. Knowing humanity as no one else ever did, he is nevertheless neither a mocking nor a weeping philosopher. He views life with zest, and he is so great that he can refrain from moral judgments.

Accordingly, when we read Shakespeare's plays we are always meeting our own experiences and are constantly surprised by some phrase which expresses what we thought to be our own secret or our own discovery. It is for this reason that so often, consciously or unconsciously, we can find no words more apt than his to express ourselves in exultation or depression, in holiday mood, in love, or in the very pit of sorrow:

> Why should a dog, a horse, a rat have life
> And thou no breath at all? Thou'lt come no more,
> Never, never, never, never, never! [*King Lear*, act 5, scene 3]

Anyone who has suffered bereavement knows that experience, and has felt it almost in those words.

Shakespeare is thus continually reminding us of our own experiences and expressing them for us. Moreover, as we grow older and the range of our experience widens, so his range grows too. He is always giving us back our own, so that we understand his plays more and ourselves better. The reward of the study of literature is that we are constantly deepening our own experience and understanding, and of all English literature the study of Shakespeare is the most valuable. It gives us the power of detaching ourselves from ourselves and seeing our own lives as part of universal life, as players playing out our own seven acts on the universal stage, and at the same time enjoying the experience of the play as players on the stage and as critics in the audience. . . .

When we come to look closely into Shakespeare's plays, it is clear that he had an extraordinary knowledge of soldiers. Critics have not appreciated this in the past because one needs to have been a soldier to realize it. It is not only that Shakespeare can express the heroics of battle, as in Henry V's great speech before Harfleur:

Once more into the breach, dear friends, once more . . .

Any poet who has a proper flow of words can write heroics. It is rather that he knows how soldiers think and how they behave, as in the little scene in *Henry V* when the King wanders in disguise amongst his soldiers and hears some home truths from the company lawyer. This intimate knowledge is seen again and again in some casual image—"like a rich armor, worn in heat of day, that scalds with safety." Anyone who has served in a tank in a tropical climate knows the significance of that line. Or it may be a chance question, as in *Coriolanus*, to a messenger in battle: "How could'st thou in a mile confound an hour?" The first thing that a young recruit learns about messages is that he must always ascertain the time of origin. This is not the kind of fact that the heroic poet even dreams of, yet somehow Shakespeare came by such a knowledge of soldicring.

As notable is his use of the imagery of the sea, which recurs constantly throughout his plays. There are certain remarkable set pieces, such as Clarence's dream in *Richard III* or the shipwreck in *The Tempest.* These are not necessarily very significant. Any writer who wishes to create such effects can find his material. Far more important as reflections of Shakespeare's mind are the casual images of the sea used sometimes to illustrate something quite different:

Will all great Neptune's ocean wash this blood
Clean from my hand? No, this my hand will rather
The multitudinous seas incarnadine[1],
Making the green one red. [*Macbeth*, act 2, scene 2]

           Behold the threaden sails,
Borne with the invisible and creeping wind,
Draw the huge bottoms through the furrowed sea. . . .
[*Henry V*, act 3, prologue]

For do but stand upon the foaming shore,
The chidden billow seems to pelt the clouds,
The wind-shaked surge, with high and monstrous mane,
Seems to cast water on the burning Bear,
And quench the guards of the ever-fixèd Pole. . . .
[*Othello*, act 2, scene 1]

Surely Shakespeare's vision of the sea was something greater than can be picked up from an afternoon's cruise on a summer vacation. . . .

So in our analysis of Shakespeare's poetry we can say that there are traces of a considerable knowledge of soldiers and of the sea. Until some lucky researcher finds Shakespeare's

1. to make blood red

name in the records of a campaign or a voyage, we can go no further; but it follows that either he was—as [British playwright] George Bernard Shaw has drawn him in *The Dark Lady of the Sonnets*—a man with a notebook, jotting down everything he heard, or else he saw many more things with his own eyes than his biographers have hitherto recorded.

## SHAKESPEARE'S MORAL AND RELIGIOUS VIEWS

All this, however, is speculation. We are more firmly set when we try to recover Shakespeare's fundamental beliefs, his attitudes toward life. He had little use for those high-sounding proverbs of conduct or consolation which drip so readily from the lips of the professionally respectable, and he put into the mouth of Polonius a wonderful collection of such pearls of wisdom, which are often admiringly quoted by those ignorant of their context and of their irony.

Shakespeare himself had no rigid system of rules, of religion, of conduct, or of morality. He had no particular theories of any kind, but certain very marked instincts. While he never codified his thoughts into rules of right and wrong, he has certainly left us his prejudices and fundamental instincts, as shown, for instance, in his views on love and marriage.

Here he is normally sane, conventional almost, in his instincts, differing thereby from the smart dramatists of his own day, or of the Restoration, or of modern Broadway. He regards marriage as the natural end and fulfillment of love between man and woman. Love outside marriage is disastrous. None of the lovers whom Shakespeare likes—and surely we can see who they are—falls in love without the most honorable intentions. Even in *Romeo and Juliet*, his one great story of youth overwhelmed by elemental, irresistible, passionate love, hero and heroine marry before they mate. Shakespeare goes to great trouble to make the story entirely respectable. The disaster which comes to them is not their fault or of their making. It comes because of the stupidity of their parents; and in Shakespeare's plays most parents, especially fathers of daughters, are incredibly stupid. His other favorite lovers, Rosalind and Orlando, Benedick and Beatrice, march naturally forward to love in wedlock. And in his later plays—*The Winter's Tale* and *The Tempest*—Florizel and Perdita, Ferdinand and Miranda, pairs of lovers whom Shakespeare abundantly blesses, have the nicest regard for the sanctity of marriage. . . .

He has plenty of jokes about cuckold's horns, as have all

## THE CHAIN OF BEING

*Valuing order and fearing chaos, Elizabethans envisioned a
world ordered as a great chain, in which each angel, creature, plant, and object is a link. If a link breaks, disorder rip-
ples up and down, affecting the whole world, or chain. In*
The Elizabethan World Picture, *E.M.W. Tillyard quotes
fifteenth-century jurist Sir John Fortescue, from a collection of
his works published in 1869 by Lord Clermont. Here Fortescue describes the chain, and Tillyard comments on its merit.*

In this order angel is set over angel, rank upon rank in
the kingdom of heaven; man is set over man, beast over
beast, bird over bird, and fish over fish, on the earth in the
air and in the sea: so that there is no worm that crawls
upon the ground, no bird that flies on high, no fish that
swims in the depths, which the chain of this order does not
bind in most harmonious concord. Hell alone, inhabited by
none but sinners, asserts its claim to escape the embraces
of this order. . . . God created as many different kinds of
things as he did creatures, so that there is no creature
which does not differ in some respect from all other creatures and by which it is in some respect superior or inferi-
or to all the rest. So that from the highest angel down to the
lowest of his kind there is absolutely not found an angel
that has not a superior and inferior; nor from man down to
the meanest worm is there any creature which is not in
some respect superior to one creature and inferior to
another. So that there is nothing which the bond of order
does not embrace.

. . . A charming attribute of the chain of being is that it
allowed every class to excel in a single particular. The idea
is Pythagorean [in agreement with sixth-century B.C. Greek
philosopher Pythagoras] or Platonic [in agreement with
Greek philosopher Plato] and it finds noble expression in
the sixth chapter of the first book of [theologian Richard]
Hooker's *Laws of Ecclesiastical Polity.* Stones may be lowly
but they exceed the class above them, plants, in strength
and durability. Plants, though without sense, excel in the
faculty of assimilating nourishment. The beasts are
stronger than man in physical energy and desires. Man
excels the angels in his power of learning, for his very
imperfection calls forth that power, while the angels as perfect beings have already acquired all the knowledge they
are capable of holding. Only the angels, through their peculiar gift, the faculty of adoration, cannot claim to go beyond
the class of being above them.

E.M.W. Tillyard, *The Elizabethan World Picture.* New York: Random House, n.d.

Elizabethan dramatists, but he sees nothing comic in unfaithfulness or unchastity, which always bring disaster. In *Measure for Measure* all the troubles which descend so freely on the chief persons are first caused by Claudio's unchastity. Angelo, having wronged Mariana, is made to offer her the only possible restitution in marriage. In *Troilus and Cressida*, the fickle Cressida is presented not as amusing or even particularly attractive, but as essentially rotten to all decent men.

Infidelity brings disaster. Even a suspicion of infidelity brings disaster on Hero, Desdemona, Imogen, and Hermione. Shakespeare apparently condones the behavior of the wronged lovers; yet he has at the same time a horror of suspicion. He thus instinctively accepts normal morality not because it accords with any rigid code or sanction, but because his instinct tells him that moral customs are founded on that system of conduct which has been found to work best. . . .

Shakespeare's own religion is neither Catholic, Anglican, nor Puritan. He belongs to no sect. His characters from time to time utter the phrases of conventional piety, but he has little conception of God as a loving Father, nor does he regard Him as a revenging Jehovah. At its most optimistic his faith is that:

> There's a divinity that shapes our ends,
> Roughhew them how we will. [*Hamlet*, act 5, scene 2]

At its most pessimistic:

> As flies to wanton boys are we to the gods,
> They kill us for their sport. [Gloucester, *King Lear*, act 4,
>     scene 1]

His general belief seems to have been halfway between the extremes:

> There's special providence in the fall of a sparrow. If it be now,
> 'tis not to come; if it be not to come, it will be now; if it be not
> now, yet it will come. The readiness is all. Since no man has
> aught of what he leaves, what is't to leave betimes? [*Hamlet*, act
> 5, scene 2]

Like [poet Alfred Lord] Tennyson, he faintly trusts the larger hope.

His religion may be summed up as fulfillment. He seems not to have been greatly interested in the insoluble problems. He has none of [medieval French saint] Faustus's curiosity in the ultimate incomprehensibles, but he has an insatiable zest for all varieties of men and women. The universe is man's stage, but man holds the center and it is a sign that Hamlet has lost his balance in the depths of despair when he finds that he can no longer appreciate humanity:

> What a piece of work is a man! How noble in reason! How infinite in faculty! In form and moving how express and admirable! In action how like an angel! In apprehension how like a god! The beauty of the world! The paragon of animals! And yet, to me, what is this quintessence of dust? Man delights not me— no, nor woman neither.

Shakespeare had very little hope, or indeed interest, in any glorious or unending immortality. His one ghost who comes back to report on conditions hereafter gives a very gloomy picture of the next world. To Hamlet, death is a consummation devoutly to be wished so long as it means "to die, to sleep—no more." His fear is lest the sleep of death may be disturbed by those terrible dreams which make Claudio frantic when confronted by death. With Edgar in *Lear*, in dejection, the conclusion is that:

> Men must endure
> Their going hence, even as their coming hither.
> Ripeness is all.

Nevertheless, Shakespeare does not brood. . . .

In *The Tempest* Shakespeare, if ever, speaks directly and deliberately out of part through Prospero. He sees the universe ultimately dissolving, to leave not a rack behind:

> We are such stuff
> As dreams are made on, and our little life
> Is rounded with a sleep.

Life is a flicker of consciousness between two eternities of oblivion. The thought is not original; the expression is superbly his own.

As for Shakespeare's social beliefs and political instincts, they are from time to time clearly revealed. Certain instincts lie deep in the Englishman's character; one is a horror of civil disorder. . . .

It seemed for a while that anarchy would return, but . . . for some forty years peace at home had been symbolized in the person of Queen Elizabeth. Most sane men hoped that this state would continue and most feared that it would not. It is not, therefore, surprising that Shakespeare believed in the divinity of kings. Nevertheless, he saw that kings, if officially divine, were also in fact human—and seldom admirable; but yet they had a terrible responsibility and loneliness. Shakespeare was one of the very few Englishmen who saw that behind the pomp lay the intolerable burden:

> Upon the King! Let us our lives, our souls,
> Our debts, our careful wives,
> Our children, and our sins lay on the King!

> We must bear all. Oh, hard condition,
> Twin-born with greatness, subject to the breath
> Of every fool, whose sense no more can feel
> But his own wringing!

To Shakespeare, as to many of his contemporaries, the universe was an ordered system, a chain or pyramid. At the apex was God; on earth the Sovereign [the king or queen] was God's own immediate deputy; and below, ranged in degrees and orders down to the least, came lesser men. This fundamental belief he expressed in one of his finest philosophical utterances, Ulysses' great speech on degree or natural order in *Troilus and Cressida.* Everything, says Ulysses, from the planets and the sun and downward, observes degree [a place in the universe]. Once degree is broken, chaos follows. When Shakespeare wrote this speech, men's minds were troubled by threats at home of some vast revolution that was likely at any time to break down natural order. He wrote for the understanding of his contemporaries. Yet this speech is a fine instance of Shakespeare's universality; it means even more to our generation when degree and natural order and decency are still in the balance:

> Take but degree away, untune that string,
> And hark what discord follows!

When a man has so clearly indicated his political, religious, and social instincts, we can surely say we know something about him; and with a little patience in reading his plays we can discover for ourselves much more of the personality of the man Shakespeare. We may not always agree with what we find, as so often we disagree in our estimates of living acquaintances, but "the purpose of playing"—and of all creative literary art—"at the first and now was and is to hold as 'twere the mirror up to Nature," and it is the function of a mirror to give us back our own reflections. We look into Shakespeare's plays and find ourselves; it is for this reason that he is of all writers the most universal.

# Women in Shakespeare's Tragedies

Angela Pitt

Though Shakespeare gives no woman the status of such tragic heroes as Hamlet or Lear, Angela Pitt argues that he creates women with distinct personalities who serve important functions in the tragedies. In *Romeo and Juliet*, the heroine's role is as significant as the hero's. Women in other tragedies—Desdemona in *Othello*, Ophelia and Gertrude in *Hamlet*, Cordelia in *King Lear*, and Lady Macbeth in *Macbeth*—play supporting roles. These women are integral to the plots and, Pitt says, have Shakespeare's "stamp of individuality" on their personalities.

Shakespeare did not take sides in one of the hottest literary issues of his day, the 'dispute about women'. Many of his contemporaries either consistently idealised women in romantic tales and poems, or satirised them as harridans [scolding women], fools or whores, but Shakespeare scrupulously avoids such two-dimensional stereotyping. This is not to say that he accords them equal status with men, for that would have been too much at variance with their genuine social position to be credible. It was the way in which men and women influence each other and the whole complex sphere of human relationships that intrigued Shakespeare—perhaps above every other consideration. His plays are not vehicles for academic theories and so, although he tacitly accepts the conservative idea of a hierarchy in nature with man at the top and woman second, he does not preach it. This belief in man's unquestioned intrinsic superiority is implied in the plays nevertheless, and in *The Taming of the Shrew* is given voice by Katharina:

> Thy husband is thy lord, thy life, thy keper,
> Thy head, thy sovereign.
>
> (V.ii.)

Excerpted from *Shakespeare's Women* by Angela Pitt; ©1981 by Angela Pitt. Reprinted by permission of David & Charles, Ltd.

In the light of this underlying conviction about a woman's place, it is not surprising to find that Shakespeare's four great tragedies, *King Lear, Hamlet, Macbeth* and *Othello*, have a tragic hero as their central figure and not a tragic heroine. It is only where tragedy arises from mutual passionate love that the position of the heroine begins to approach the same significance as that of the hero, that is in *Antony and Cleopatra* and, to a lesser extent, in *Romeo and Juliet.* By its very nature, such love exerts a powerful force over the destinies of *both* parties, thus elevating the woman's position. . . .

Before considering the character of . . . Juliet in greater depth, it is essential to decide what is meant by 'tragic heroine'. Just because a character may die an unfortunate, unpleasant or distressing death does not of itself make her a heroine, or her death a tragic one. . . .

These . . . are the essential ingredients of the four great Shakespearian tragedies. A good man of high birth and considerable influence is confronted with a problem, mystery or challenge. Uncharacteristically he is unable to deal with the situation because it tests an area of himself that is deficient. While he cannot solve the problem, neither can he turn away from it—it exerts a fascination upon him that amounts to an obsession. The play chronicles his steady, unrelenting path to ruin and death, and shows how his misguided actions cause the downfall of others and the collapse of society. . . .

## JULIET

Neither Romeo nor Juliet is shown to suffer any deficiency of character, for as the Prologue makes clear, they are the victims of circumstances beyond their control:

> Two households, both alike in dignity. . .
> From ancient grudge, break to new mutiny. . .
> From forth the fatal loins of these two foes,
> A pair of star-crossed lovers, take their life:
> Whose misadventur'd piteous overthrows,
> Doth with their death bury their parents' strife.

Romeo and Juliet were predestined to fall in love and kill themselves; 'fatal loins' suggests that their fate had been decided from the moment of conception. They are 'star-cross'd', so their destiny does not rest with any decision they may or may not take. The influences on them are *external*, so there is no inherent fault in either of their characters to explain their path to death. In consequence there is no evolution of character necessary to reveal the cancerous effects of a fatal flaw. The

## WOMEN'S ROLES PLAYED BY MEN

*In Shakespeare's day, only men acted on the Elizabethan stage. Modern scholars have tried to investigate the quality of acting when men played women's roles. In "Elizabethan Actors: Men or Marionettes?" Marvin Rosenberg contends that many men played convincing women in Shakespeare's tragedies.*

Most of the modern believers in formalism [a rigid, impersonal method of acting] have concluded that Shakespeare could not hope to get naturalistic acting from the boys, and that therefore the acting of his time must have been either entirely or predominantly formal.

This is hardly fair to the actors who were good enough to play some of the tremendous women's roles of Shakespeare's day. First of all, they were not necessarily "boys." They were as likely to be young men, and are sometimes so referred to in legal documents of the time. Some were mature men. T.W. Baldwin mentions two actors playing women's parts in 1635 who must, from other figures he gives, have been between 24 and 28. . . . In the prologue spoken before the first appearance of an Englishwoman in *Othello* on the professional stage:

> For (to speak truth) men act, that are between
> Forty and fifty, Wenches of fifteen;
> With bone so large, and nerve so incomplyant,
> When you call *Desdemona*, enter Giant.

We know, too, that these adult male actors of women's parts were artists in their own right. We might guess this from the tremendous demands the playwrights made of them; but we have further assurance from observers. . . .

[Shakespeare] surely had equally skilled artists to play his great gallery of women. Consider this description of a performance of *Othello* by the King's Men at Oxford in 1610. It was contained in a Latin letter from one of the spectators; I will translate the significant part: "They also had tragedies, well and effectively acted. In these they drew tears, not only by their speech, but also by their action. Indeed Desdemona, killed by her husband, in her death moved us especially when, as she lay in her bed, her face alone implored the pity of the audience."

Here is a description of accomplished acting as we ourselves know it. The players added to the lines their own creative art of interpretive physical movement and speech; they made the sophisticated Oxford audience weep by their acting as well as by their words.

Marvin Rosenberg, in Gerald Eades Bentley, ed., *The Seventeenth-Century Stage.* Chicago: University of Chicago Press, 1968.

nobility and integrity of Romeo and Juliet remain unshaken throughout the course of the play. . . .

Juliet's stature can be measured only by comparing her with her lover, and what we need to establish is whether, given that they have no power over their own fates, Romeo and Juliet are of equal tragic significance in the play. . . . Romeo and Juliet have been sacrificed so that peace and order can be restored, but they triumph in another way. Their love is unswervingly described as true and pure, an idealisation that could not withstand the test of time. Death cuts their love off when it is at its height and so it remains unspoilt—Romeo and Juliet triumph over time. Throughout the course of their relationship, the lovers are described in parallel terms. The language they use is rapt, ecstatic and essentially chaste. . . .

Never for a moment is there a faltering or questioning of their love for each other. In this focus on an impossible ideal, their feelings are also shown to be identical. It is the first time that either of them has fallen in love (his affair with Rosaline is superficial, for all thought of her goes when he finds Juliet); they are utterly faithful, and they prefer death to the thought of living without each other. Juliet therefore has equal status with Romeo. But is the play really a tragedy? We have already seen that through death their love triumphs over time and brings their families together, so the tragedy cannot lie there. It exists on a much more human level: two young lives are wasted, an experience of great beauty vanishes, and brave hopes are dashed to the ground. As proved by its enduring popularity, the play appeals both to the human desire for perfection and the harsh realisation that ideals cannot last:

> Never was a story of more woe
> Than this of Juliet and her Romeo.
>                                             (V.iii.)

We are moved by Juliet's fate as we are by Romeo's; their tragedy affects us since it has a universal message. . . .

Although their dramatic realisation and function are so different, Cleopatra and Juliet are the only women in Shakespeare who hold the centre of the stage in tragedy. Others are there for a brief moment, or else play crucial supporting roles. . . .

## DESDEMONA

Handbooks of the period explain in some detail what is required of the ideal wife, and Desdemona seems to fulfil even the most conservative expectation. She is beautiful but also humble:

> A maiden never bold
> Of spirit so still and quiet that her motion
> Blushed at herself.
>
> (I.iii.)

Her concern for Cassio shows her generosity, for she will intercede for him with Othello. She is wise, and also a 'true and loving' wife—'the sweetest innocent that e'er did lift up eye'. However, there are other aspects of her behaviour that would have caused an Elizabethan audience to look slightly askance at her. . . .

Once married, she continues to commit slight offences against the correct code of conduct for the ideal wife. She is no sooner married than she leaves hearth and home (the traditional limits of the woman's realm) to be with Othello. She sees Cassio without her husband's permission and is far too concerned with Cassio's request. Her plan of how she will discuss the matter with Othello at every moment so that even 'his bed shall seem a school', shows far too much self-possession and strong will.

Desdemona has, therefore, some quite serious faults as a wife, including a will of her own, which was evident even before she was married. This does not mean that she merits the terrible accusations flung at her by Othello, nor does she in any way deserve her death, but she is partly responsible for the tragic action of the play. Othello's behaviour and mounting jealousy are made more comprehensible if we remember what Elizabethan husbands might expect of their wives. . . .

In spite of the moving simplicity of her loyalty, a modern audience tends to find this unswerving devotion to God and Othello implausible. Dramatically, the effect of Desdemona's death is greater if we allow that she is not *intended* to mirror reality. There is certainly no development of her character during the course of the play and perhaps it is easiest to make sense of her by seeing her as a symbol of purity, her white against the black contaminating evil of Iago that sweeps over Othello.

## OPHELIA

*Hamlet* is not in any sense a black-and-white play. . . . It is also exceptional amongst the tragedies in having two important female roles: Ophelia and Gertrude. Unlike Desdemona, Ophelia is not guilty of showing a dangerously strong mind of her own. Indeed, much of Ophelia's personal tragedy is that she has insufficient strength to sustain her after Hamlet's inexplicably harsh treatment and her father's murder. She is driven insane with grief, and Gertrude relates how she has fallen into a stream:

> Her clothes spread wide,
> And mermaid-like awhile they bore her up. . . .
> But long it could not be
> Till that her garments, heavy with their drink,
> Pulled the poor wretch from her melodious lay
> To muddy death.
>
> (IV.vii.)

The pathos of her drowning—still singing, she is drawn down under the water—is mirrored in the delicate harmonies of this speech. Gertrude's vision of her death presents her to us as a poor innocent, oblivious of danger to the last.

But another aspect of Ophelia is traced in her characterisation. Like Desdemona she has originally gone against social mores by seeing a young man unchaperoned and without her father's approval. . . .

Ophelia is initially shown as having a close, affectionate relationship with three men: her brother, her father and Hamlet. Laertes goes back to university in Paris early in the play and does not return to Denmark until too late to be of any assistance or counsel to Ophelia. Polonius, with the best of motives, interferes with Hamlet and Ophelia's relationship, but is killed before the tensions he has done much to help create have any chance of being resolved. Ophelia's only prop after Act III is thus Hamlet, the man whose behaviour she now finds incomprehensible, who insults and mocks her, and who, above all, has murdered her father. Then, even he is sent away, so effectively Ophelia is left alone to endure her grief. Sorrow overwhelms her and she is distracted with thinking obsessively of her dead father. . . .

Since her relationship with Hamlet is subsidiary to the main interest of the play, Ophelia's dramatic significance is frequently reduced to a structural one. It is true that she never challenges the wishes of father, brother or Hamlet and is borne along by the plot much as the cold stream takes her to her death, but it is also true that Shakespeare gives her briefly sketched personality sufficient dimension to make her psychologically credible. Her youthful chastity and anguished heart are implicitly contrasted with the venery and insensitivity of Hamlet's mother, Gertrude. . . .

## GERTRUDE

Gertrude evinces no such need to justify her actions and thereby does not betray any sense of guilt. She is concerned with her present good fortune, and neither lingers over the death of her first husband nor analyses her motives in taking another. Her unfeeling haste in marrying Claudius cuts Hamlet to the heart. . . . She seems a kindly, slow-witted, rather self-indulgent woman, in no way the emotional or intellectual equal of her son. . . .

Certainly she is fond of Hamlet. Not only is she prepared to listen to him when he storms at her, proof that he is sufficiently close to her to have a right to make comments on her personal life, but she is unfailingly concerned about him. . . . When she has drunk from the poisoned cup, almost her last words are: 'O my dear Hamlet!' The simple endearment is very poignant, reminding us that the bond between mother and son, and Hamlet's desperate jealousy of Claudius, account for as much of the tragic progress of the play as the need to avenge old Hamlet's death.

Desdemona, Ophelia and Gertrude all die because of direct association with the fate of a tragic hero, but none of their deaths approaches the wanton destruction of tender innocence witnessed in *King Lear*. . . .

## CORDELIA

Generations of readers have been vexed by the problem presented by Cordelia's reticence [reserve, privacy]. Although her integrity and genuine feeling are never questioned, no reason is advanced by herself or the other characters as to *why* she finds herself unable to take part in the game of declarations that Lear has masterminded. Ironically, the answer may lie in the words Goneril uses to describe her own affection:

> Sir, I love you more than word can wield the matter . . .
> A love that makes breath[1] poor, and speech unable.
>
> (I.i.)

For Cordelia this was only too painfully true. Her very silence is proof enough to the audience of her love, and contrasts with the outpourings of her sisters. She recognises her lack of 'that glib and oily art To speak and purpose not', and is glad not to have it even though it has cost her her father's favour.

Cordelia's sensitivity and high-minded resolution make such a powerful impression on us that it comes as a surprise to realise that she is absent from the play for long periods of time and speaks in all barely a hundred lines. Giving us such little sight of her on stage helps both to sustain her credibility

---

1. language

and add to her mystery. . . .

In terms of her function, Cordelia's relationship with Lear is central to the progress of the play. She also acts as a sounding-board by which the audience can assess the honesty or dishonesty of the other characters. The plain-spoken few (such as Kent, Edgar and the King of France) are allied with her, while the sly (notably Goneril, Regan and Edmund) are revealed by their hypocrisy and contrasted with her straightforwardness. It is possible to view her purely in symbolic terms, dramatising the notion that plainness is more honest and valuable than flattery or even eloquence. Her position is therefore both structurally and thematically crucial, although she plays a passive part in the actual development of the plot.

## LADY MACBETH

To turn to Lady Macbeth after Cordelia is to turn from the innocent lamb to the ravenous wolf. . . . The imagery of blood, violence, darkness and death reflects her true nature, for from the first she is set on an unrelenting course of destruction. This is not to say that her lust for power is a fatal flaw—we are given no hint that before the events of the play she was a good woman, now perverted. Neither does her character decline, for her final, fatal madness comes suddenly. . . .

The unfailing technique that Lady Macbeth uses to keep Macbeth to his purpose is to taunt him with suggestions of effeminacy and cowardice. As she herself possesses characteristics that are traditionally held to be possible only in the male— single-minded courage and cruelty—she can twit Macbeth for his failure to live up to the standard that she, a mere woman, has set. The combination of tender woman's body and savage man's mind is clearly shown when Lady Macbeth derides her husband for being unable to face the murder of Duncan, now that time and place are right. . . .

Her insanity and consequent death have no bearing on the course of the tragedy and she is in no sense a tragic heroine. Because her nature is of such unmitigated evil, neither are we able to feel sympathy for her on a personal level. Her crimes are so enormous that her only hope lies in God's forgiveness. As her doctor says, she is beyond help on this earth: 'more needs she the divine than the physician'. Any pathos that might be evoked by her sleep-walking scene is cancelled out by constant reminders of her horrendous brutality. She remains Shakespeare's most terrifying female figure. Lady Macbeth's claim to this dubious honour rests not only on the grim catalogue of her crimes, but also on the credibility of her character. We cannot be deeply disturbed by a creation that is patently unreal. . . .

Although none of the women in Shakespeare attains the tragic stature of the great heroes like Hamlet and Lear, they are far more than mere props for the main structure of the plays. Linked by their unmerited deaths, their personalities span a subtle but wide range. . . . Each of these characters is memorable because of her stamp of individuality, no matter how lightly Shakespeare may have imprinted it.

# Images of Light in *Romeo and Juliet*

Caroline F.E. Spurgeon

In an essay originally delivered as a lecture in 1930, Caroline F.E. Spurgeon contends that the repetition and variety of light images in Shakespeare's *Romeo and Juliet* give the play beauty and passion. She cites examples of lovers spoken of as different kinds of lights and of love as flashes of light. The vitality of the light images intensifies the power of the dark images, which, she notes, accompany parting and death. Together, the dark and light images contribute to the "sensation of swiftness and brilliance."

In *Romeo and Juliet* the beauty and ardour of young love is seen by Shakespeare as the irradiating glory of sunlight and starlight in a dark world. The dominating image is *light*, every form and manifestation of it; the sun, moon, stars, fire, lightning, the flash of gunpowder, and the reflected light of beauty and of love; while by contrast we have night, darkness, clouds, rain, mist, and smoke.

## LOVERS AS NATURE'S LIGHT

Each of the lovers thinks of the other as light; Romeo's overpowering impression when he first catches sight of Juliet on the fateful evening at the Capulets' ball is seen in his exclamation,

> O, she doth teach the torches to burn bright!

To Juliet, Romeo, is "day in night"; to Romeo, Juliet is the sun rising from the east, and when they soar to love's ecstasy, each alike pictures the other as stars in heaven, shedding such brightness as puts to shame the heavenly bodies themselves.

The intensity of feeling in both lovers purges even the most highly affected and euphuistic conceits of their artificiality [making even the most false and exaggerated comparisons

Excerpted from Caroline F.E. Spurgeon, "Leading Motives in the Imagery of Shakespeare's Tragedies," Shakespeare Association Lecture, 1930.

## THE UNCERTAIN LIGHT OF DAWN

*At the end of Romeo and Juliet's wedding night, when Romeo must leave for safety in Mantua, dawn has the uncertain light of neither day nor night. To the images of light and dark, Shakespeare adds the image of the nightingale, the bird of night, and the lark, the bird of morning, to heighten the tense moment when the lovers must part.*

[*Enter* ROMEO *and* JULIET, *above, at the window.*]
JUL. Wilt thou be gone? It is not yet near day.
It was the nightingale, and not the lark,
That pierced the fearful hollow of thine ear.
Nightly she sings on yond pomegranate tree.
Believe me, love, it was the nightingale.
ROM. It was the lark, the herald of the morn,
No nightingale. Look, love, what envious streaks
Do lace[1] the severing clouds in yonder east.
Night's candles are burnt out, and jocund day
Stands tiptoe on the misty mountaintops.
I must be gone and live, or stay and die.
JUL. Yond light is not daylight, I know it, I.
It is some meteor that the sun exhales,[2]
To be to thee this night a torchbearer
And light thee on thy way to Mantua.
Therefore stay yet–thou need'st not to be gone.
ROM. Let me be ta'en, let me be put to death,
I am content, so thou wilt have it so.
I'll say yon gray is not the morning's eye
'Tis but the pale reflex[3] of Cynthia's[4] brow;
Nor that is not the lark whose notes do beat
The vaulty heaven so high above our heads.
I have more care to stay than will to go.
Come, death, and welcome! Juliet wills it so
How is't, my soul? Let's talk. It is not day.
JUL. It is, it is. Hie hence, be gone, away!
It is the lark that sings so out of tune,
Straining harsh discords and unpleasing sharps.
Some say the lark makes sweet division.[5]
This doth not so, for she divideth us.
Some say the lark and loathèd toad change eyes.[6]
Oh, now I would they had changed voices too!
Since arm from arm that voice doth us affray,[7]
Hunting thee hence with hunt's-up to the day.
Oh, now be gone, more light and light it grows.
ROM. More light and light. More dark and dark our woes!

G.B. Harrison, ed., *Romeo and Juliet*, act 3, scene 5, in *Shakespeare: The Complete Works*. New York: Harcourt, Brace and Company, 1952.

1. cover with stripes. 2. draws out. 3. reflection. 4. the moon's. 5. melody. 6. The toad has bright eyes and a harsh croak, the lark dull eyes but a lovely voice. 7. frighten.

sound natural], and transforms them into the exquisite and passionate expression of love's rhapsody.

Thus Romeo plays with the old conceit that two of the fairest stars in heaven, having some business on earth, have entreated Juliet's eyes to take their place till they return, and he conjectures,

> What if her eyes were there, they in her head?

If so,

> The brightness of her cheek would shame those stars,
> As day-light doth a lamp:

and then comes the rush of feeling, the overpowering realization and immortal expression of the transforming glory of love,

> her eyes in heaven
> Would through the airy region stream so bright
> That birds would sing and think it were not night.

And Juliet, in her invocation to night, using an even more extravagant conceit such as [seventeenth-century British writer Abraham] Cowley or [seventeenth-century British poet John] Cleveland at his wildest never exceeded, transmutes it into the perfect and natural expression of a girl whose lover to her not only radiates light but is, indeed, very light itself:

> Give me my Romeo; and, when he shall die,
> Take him and cut him out in little stars,
> And he will make the face of heaven so fine,
> That all the world will be in love with night,
> And pay no worship to the garish sun.

Love is described by Romeo, before he knows what it really is, as

> a smoke raised with the fume of sighs;
> Being purged, a fire sparkling in lovers' eyes;

and the messengers of love are seen by Juliet, when she is chafing under the nurse's delay, as one of the most exquisite effects in nature, especially on the English hills in spring, of the swift, magical, transforming power of light; "love's heralds," she cries, "should be thoughts,

> Which ten times faster glide than the sun's beams,
> Driving back shadows over louring hills."

The irradiating quality of the beauty of love is noticed by both lovers; by Juliet in her first ecstasy, when she declares that lovers' "own beauties" are sufficient light for them to see by, and at the end by Romeo, when, thinking her dead, he gazes on her and cries

> her beauty makes
> This vault a feasting presence full of light.

There can be no question, I think, that Shakespeare saw the story, in its swift and tragic beauty, as an almost blinding flash of light, suddenly ignited and as swiftly quenched. He quite deliberately compresses the action from over nine months to the almost incredibly short period of five days; so that the lovers meet on Sunday, are wedded on Monday, part at dawn on Tuesday, and are reunited in death on the night of Thursday. The sensation of swiftness and brilliance, accompanied by danger and destruction, is accentuated again and again; by Juliet when she avows their bethrothal

> is too rash, too unadvised, too sudden,
> Too like the lightning, which doth cease to be
> Ere one can say 'It lightens';

and by Romeo and the Friar, who instinctively make repeated use of the image of the quick destructive flash of gunpowder (III.iii.; V.i.). Indeed the Friar, in his well-known answer to Romeo's prayer for instant marriage, succinctly, in the last nine words, sums up the whole movement of the play,

> These violent delights have violent ends,
> And in their triumph die; like fire and powder
> Which as they kiss consume.

Even old Capulet, whom one does not think of as a poetical person, though he uses many images—some of great beauty—carries on the idea of light to represent love and youth and beauty, and of the clouding of the sun for grief and sorrow. He promises Paris that on the evening of the ball he shall see at his house

> Earth-treading stars that make dark heaven light,

and when he encounters Juliet weeping, as he thinks for her cousin Tybalt's death, he clothes his comment in similar nature-imagery of light quenched in darkness,

> When the sun sets, the air doth drizzle dew;
> But for the sunset of my brother's son
> It rains downright.

## PARTING LIGHT AND COMING DARK

... [When she waits for Romeo,] Juliet so ardently desires [the sunset] to be swift "and bring in cloudy night immediately." The exquisite play of quivering light [surrounds the lovers] from darkness through dawn, till

> jocund day
> Stands tip-toe on the misty mountain tops,

which forms the theme of the lovers' parting song. And at the last, Romeo's anguished reply to Juliet, pointing the contrast between the coming day and their own great sorrow, [suggests]

More light and light: more dark and dark our woes!

And then at the end we see the darkness of the churchyard, lit by the glittering torch of Paris, quickly quenched; Romeo's arrival with his torch, the swift fight and death, the dark vault, which is not a grave but a lantern irradiated by Juliet's beauty, Romeo's grim jest on the "lightning before death," followed immediately by the self-slaughter of the "star-crossed" lovers, the gathering together of the stricken mourners as the day breaks, and the "glooming" peace of the overcast morning when

The sun for sorrow will not show his head.

# *Romeo and Juliet:* More Than Conventions of Love

Northrop Frye

Many poets in William Shakespeare's time followed the same artistic conventions, or methods, when they wrote about love. Northrop Frye identifies the conventions—love as a religion; the proud, cruel mistress; the poet in despair; and comparisons to famous beauties— and explains their uses in *Romeo and Juliet.* According to Frye, the play is, however, more than a skillful display of an artistic form. *Romeo and Juliet* is a tragedy, and Shakespeare evokes the sadness of pure love destroyed and the anguish of feuding fathers' allowing it to happen. *Romeo and Juliet* is well known and well loved, Frye thinks, because Shakespeare tells a very old story in a new, and magical, way.

*Romeo and Juliet* is a love story, but in Shakespeare's day love included many complex rituals. Early in the Middle Ages a cult had developed called Courtly Love, which focussed on a curious etiquette that became a kind of parody [a ridiculous imitation] of Christian experience. Someone might be going about his business, congratulating himself on not being caught in the trap of a love affair, when suddenly the God of Love, Eros or Cupid, angry at being left out of things, forces him to fall in love with a woman. The falling in love is involuntary and instantaneous, no more "romantic," in the usual sense, than getting shot with a bullet. It's never gradual: "Who ever loved that loved not at first sight?" says [Christopher] Marlowe, in a line that Shakespeare quotes in *As You Like It.* From that time on, the lover is a slave of the God of Love, whose will is embodied in his mistress, and he is bound to do whatever she wants.

Reprinted with permission from *Northrop Frye on Shakespeare*, edited by Robert Sandler. Copyright 1986 by Northrop Frye. (New Haven, CT: Yale University Press; Markham, ON: Fitzhenry & Whiteside).

This cult of love was not originally linked to marriage. Marriage was a relationship in which the man had all the effective authority, even if his wife was (as she usually was) his social equal. The conventional role of the Courtly Love mistress was to be proud, disdainful and "cruel," repelling all advances from her lover. The frustration this caused drove the lover into poetry, and the theme of the poetry was the cruelty of the mistress and the despair and supplications of the lover. . . .

It was [Italian poet] Petrarch who popularized the convention [an accepted literary style or subject] in sixteenth-century England. In the 1590s, when the vogue was at its height, enormous piles of sonnets more or less imitating Petrarch were being written. By Shakespeare's time the convention had become more middle-class, was much more frequently linked to eventual marriage, and the more overtly sexual aspects of such relationships were more fully explored. So "love" in *Romeo and Juliet* covers three different forms of a convention. First, the orthodox Petrarchan convention in Romeo's professed love for Rosaline at the beginning of the play. Second, the less sublimated love for which the only honourable resolution was marriage, represented by the main theme of the play. Third, the more cynical and ribald [humorously vulgar and coarse] perspective that we get in Mercutio's comments, and perhaps those of the Nurse as well.

On the principle that life imitates art, Romeo has thrown himself, before the play begins, into a love affair with someone called Rosaline, whom we never see (except that she was at Capulet's party, where she must have wondered painfully what had happened to Romeo), and who tried to live up to the proud and disdainful role that the convention required. So Romeo made the conventional responses: he went around with his clothes untidy, hardly heard what was said to him, wrote poetry, talked endlessly about the cruelty of his mistress, wept and kept "adding to clouds more clouds with his deep sighs." In short, he was afflicted with love melancholy, and we remember that melancholy in Shakespeare's time was a physical as well as an emotional disturbance. More simply, he was something of a mooning bore. . . .

I said that the Courtly Love convention used an elaborate and detailed parody, or counterpart, of the language of religion. The mistress was a "saint"; the "god" supplicated with so many prayers and tears was Eros or Cupid, the God of Love; "atheists" were people who didn't believe in the convention; and "heretics" were those who didn't keep to the rules. Benvolio suggests that Romeo might get Rosaline into better perspective if he'd compare her with a few other young women. . . .

This is close to another requirement of the convention, that the lover had to compare his mistress to the greatest heroines of history and literature (heroines from the point of view of love, that is), always to their disadvantage. These included Helen of Troy, Dido in the *Aeneid* [of Virgil], Cleopatra, heroines of Classical stories like Hero and Thisbe, and, of course, Laura [the conventional mistress in Petrarch's sonnets]. Mercutio, who knows all about the convention even though he assumes that Romeo has taken a different approach to it, says:

> Now is he for the numbers that Petrarch flowed in. Laura, to his lady, was a kitchen wench . . . Dido a dowdy, Cleopatra a gypsy, Helen and Hero hildings and harlots, Thisbe a grey eye or so, but not to the purpose. (II.iv.)

However, Romeo takes Benvolio's advice, goes to the Capulet party, sees Juliet, and the "real thing" hits him. Of course, the "real thing" is as much a convention, at least within the framework of the play, as its predecessor, but its effects on both Romeo and Juliet are very different. . . .

## LOVE CHANGES ROMEO'S AND JULIET'S LANGUAGE

The most dramatic change is in their command of language. Before she sees Romeo we hear Juliet making proper-young-lady noises like, "It is an honour that I dream not of" ("it" being her marriage to Paris). After she sees Romeo, she's talking like this:

> Gallop apace, you fiery-footed steeds,
> Towards Phoebus' lodging! Such a wagoner
> As Phaëton would whip you to the west
> And bring in cloudy night immediately. (III.ii.)

It appears that Juliet, for all her tender years and sheltered life, has had a considerably better education than simply a technical training to be a wife and mother. The point is that it would never have occurred to her to make use of her education in her speech in the way she does here without the stimulus of her love.

As for Romeo, when we first meet him he's at the stage where he hardly knows what he's saying until he hears himself saying it. We don't hear any of the poetry he wrote about Rosaline, . . . and something tells us that we could do without most of it. But after he meets Juliet he turns out, to Mercutio's astonishment and delight, to be full of wit and repartee. "Now art thou what thou art, by art as well as by nature," Mercutio says, and even Mercutio knows nothing of the miraculous duets with Juliet in the great "balcony scene" and its successor. When he visits Friar Laurence, the Friar sees him approaching and feels rather apprehensive, thinking, "Oh no, not Rosaline again," and is considerably startled to hear Romeo saying, in effect, "Who's Rosaline?" More important, especially after Juliet also visits him, he realizes that two young people he has previously thought of as rather nice children have suddenly turned into adults, and are speaking with adult authority. He is bound to respect this, and besides, he sees an excellent chance of ending the feud by marrying them and presenting their furious parents with a *fait accompli* [an accomplished fact]. . . .

It is through the language, and the imagery the language uses, that we understand how the *Liebestod* [literally, "love-death"] of Romeo and Juliet, their great love and their tragic death, are bound up together as two aspects of the same thing. I spoke of the servants' jokes in the opening scene associating sexuality with weapons, love and death in the context of parody. Soon after Romeo comes in, we hear him talking like this:

> Here's much to do with hate, but more with love.
> Why then, O brawling love! O loving hate!
> O anything, of nothing first create!                          (I.i.)

The figure he is using is the oxymoron or paradoxical union of opposites: obviously the right kind of figure for this play, though Romeo is still in his Rosaline trance and is not being very cogent. From there we go on to Friar Laurence's wonderfully concentrated image of

> fire and powder
> Which, as they kiss, consume,                          (II.vi.)

with its half-concealed pun on "consummation," and to Juliet's

> Too like the lightning, which doth cease to be
> Ere one can say it lightens.                          (II.ii.)

suggesting that their first glimpse of one another determined their deaths as well as their love.

The love-death identity of contrasts expands into the imagery of day and night. The great love scenes begin with Juliet hanging upon the cheek of night and end with the macabre horrors of the Capulet tomb, where we reluctantly can't believe Romeo when he says:

> For here lies Juliet, and her beauty makes
> This vault a feasting presence full of light.                          (V.iii.)

The character who makes the most impressive entrances in the play is a character we never see, the sun. The sun is greeted by Friar Laurence as the sober light that does away with the

## PYRAMUS AND THISBE

*Romeo and Juliet's story is an old story: Young lovers, forbidden by parents to marry, die for their love. Eminent classical scholar Edith Hamilton retells the Greek story of young Pyramus and Thisbe, who also die for their love. The story was originally told by the Roman poet Ovid in* Metamorphoses, *written near the beginning of the first century.*

Pyramus and Thisbe, he the most beautiful youth and she the loveliest maiden of all the East, lived in Babylon, the city of Queen Semiramis, in houses so close together that one wall was common to both. Growing up thus side by side they learned to love each other. They longed to marry, but their parents forbade. . . .

In the wall both houses shared there was a little chink. No one before had noticed it, but there is nothing a lover does not notice. Our two young people discovered it and through it they were able to whisper sweetly back and forth. Thisbe on one side, Pyramus on the other. . . .

Finally a day came when they could endure no longer. They decided that that very night they would try to slip away and steal out through the city into the open country where at last they could be together in freedom. They agreed to meet at a well-known place, the Tomb of Ninus. . . .

In the darkness Thisbe crept out and made her way in all secrecy to the tomb. Pyramus had not come; still she waited for him, her love making her bold. But of a sudden she saw by the light of the moon a lioness. The fierce beast had made a kill; her jaws were bloody and she was coming to slake her thirst in the spring. She was still far enough away for Thisbe to escape, but as she fled she dropped her cloak. The lioness came upon it on her way back to her lair and she mouthed it and tore it before disappearing into the woods. That is what Pyramus saw when he appeared a few minutes later. Before him lay the bloodstained shreds of the cloak and clear in the dust were the tracks of the lioness. The conclusion was inevitable. He never doubted that he knew all. Thisbe was dead. . . . He drew his sword and plunged it into his side. The blood spurted up over the [white] berries and dyed them a dark red. . . .

Peering through the shadows, [Thisbe] saw what was there. It was Pyramus, bathed in blood and dying. She flew to him and threw her arms around him. She kissed his cold lips and begged him to look at her, to speak to her. "It is I, your Thisbe, your dearest," she cried to him. At the sound of her name he opened his heavy eyes for one look. Then death closed them. . . .

"Only death would have had the power to separate us. It shall not have that power now." She plunged into her heart the sword that was still wet with his life's blood.

Edith Hamilton, *Mythology.* New York: New American Library, 1942.

drunken darkness, but the Friar is speaking out of his own temperament, and there are many other aspects of the light and dark contrast. In the dialogue of Romeo and Juliet, the bird of darkness, the nightingale, symbolizes the desire of the lovers to remain with each other, and the bird of dawn, the lark, the need to preserve their safety. When the sun rises, "The day is hot, the Capulets abroad," and the energy of youth and love wears itself out in scrambling over the blockades of reality.

The light and dark imagery comes into powerful focus with Mercutio's speech on Queen Mab. Queen Mab, Mercutio tells us, is the instigator of dreams, and Mercutio takes what we would call a very Freudian approach to dreams: they are primarily wish-fulfilment fantasies.

> And in this state she gallops night by night
> Through lovers' brains, and then they dream of love.    (I.iv.)

## THE MYSTERY OF THE PLAY'S POPULARITY

. . . Who or what is responsible for a tragedy that kills half a dozen people, at least four of them young and very attractive people? The feud, of course, but in this play there doesn't seem to be the clearly marked villain that we find in so many tragedies. We can point to Iago in *Othello* and say that if it hadn't been for that awful man there'd have been no tragedy at all. But the harried and conscientious Prince, the kindly and pious Friar Laurence, the quite likable old buffer Capulet: these are a long way from being villainous. Tybalt comes closest, but Tybalt is a villain only by virtue of his position in the plot. According to his own code—admittedly a code open to criticism—he is a man of honour, and there is no reason to suppose him capable of the kind of malice or treachery that we find in Iago or in Edmund in *King Lear.* He may not even be inherently more quarrelsome or spoiling for a fight than Mercutio. Juliet seems to like him, if not as devoted to his memory as her parents think. Setting Tybalt aside, there is still some mystery about the fact that so bloody a mess comes out of the actions of what seem to be, taken one by one, a fairly decent lot of human beings. . . .

The question of the source of the tragic action is bound up with another question: why is the story of the tragic love and death of Romeo and Juliet one of the world's best-loved stories? Mainly, we think, because of Shakespeare's word magic. But, while it was always a popular play, what the stage presented as *Romeo and Juliet,* down to about 1850, was mostly a series of travesties of what Shakespeare wrote. There's something about the story itself that can take any amount of mistreatment from stupid producing and bad casting. I've seen a performance with a middle-aged and corseted Juliet who could have thrown Romeo over her shoulder and walked to Mantua with him, and yet the audience was in tears at the end. The original writer is not the writer who thinks up a new story—there aren't any new stories, really—but the writer who tells one of the world's great stories in a new way. To understand why *Romeo and Juliet* is one of those stories we have to distinguish the specific story of the feuding Montague-Capulet families from an archetypal [a recurring and symbolic] story of youth, love and death that is probably older than written literature itself. . . .

## TRAGEDY'S BIGGER MEANING

In this play we often hear about a kind of fatality at work in the action, usually linked with the stars. As early as the Prologue we hear about "star-crossed lovers," and Romeo speaks, not of the feud, but of "some consequence still hanging in the stars" when he feels a portent of disaster. Astrology, as I've said, was taken quite seriously then, but here it seems only part of a network of unlucky timing that's working against the lovers. Romeo gets to see Juliet because of the sheer chance that the Capulet servant sent out to deliver the invitations to the party can't read, and comes to him for help. There's the letter from Friar Laurence in Verona to Friar John in Mantua, which by accident doesn't get to him, and another hitch in timing destroys Friar Laurence's elaborate plan that starts with Juliet's sleeping potion. If we feel that Friar Laurence is being meddlesome in interfering in the action as he does, that's partly because he's in a tragedy and his schemes are bound to fail. In *Much Ado About Nothing* there's also a friar with a very similar scheme for the heroine of that play, but his scheme is successful because the play he's in is a comedy.

But when we have a quite reasonable explanation for the tragedy, the feud between the families, why do we need to bring in the stars and such? The Prologue, even before the play starts, suggests that the feud demands lives to feed on, and sooner or later will get them:

> And the continuance of their parents' rage,
> Which, but their children's end, nought could remove.

The answer, or part of the answer, begins with the fact that we shouldn't assume that tragedy is something needing an explanation. Tragedy represents something bigger in the total scheme of things than all possible explanations combined. All we can say—and it's a good deal—is that there'd have been no tragedy without the feud.

This, I think, is the clue to one of those puzzling episodes in Shakespeare that we may not understand at first hearing or reading. At the very end of the play, Montague proposes to erect a gold statue of Juliet at his own expense, and Capulet promises to do the same for Romeo. Big deal: nothing like a couple of gold statues to bring two dead lovers back to life. But by that time Montague and Capulet are two miserable, defeated old men who have lost everything that meant anything in their lives, and they simply cannot look their own responsibility for what they have done straight in the face. There's a parallel with Othello's last speech, which ends with his suicide, when he recalls occasions in the past when he has served the Venetian state well. [Twentieth-century poet and critic] T.S. Eliot says that Othello in this speech is "cheering himself up," turning a moral issue into an aesthetic one. I'd put it differently: I'd say it was a reflex of blinking and turning away from the intolerably blazing light of judgment. And so with Montague and Capulet, when they propose to set up these statues as a way of persuading themselves that they're still alive, and still capable of taking some kind of positive action. The gesture is futile and pitiful, but very, very human.

So far as there's any cheering up in the picture, it affects the audience rather than the characters. Tragedy always has an ironic side, and that means that the audience usually knows more about what's happening or going to happen than the characters do. But tragedy also has a heroic side, and again the audience usually sees that more clearly than the characters. Juliet's parents don't really know who Juliet is: we're the ones who have a rather better idea. Notice Capulet's phrase, "Poor sacrifices of our enmity!" Romeo and Juliet are sacrificial victims, and the ancient rule about sacrifice was that the victim had to be perfect and without blemish. The core of reality in this was the sense that nothing perfect or without blemish can stay that way in this world, and should be offered up to another world before it deteriorates. That principle belongs to a still larger one: nothing that breaks through the barriers of ordinary experience can remain in the world of ordinary experience. One of the first things Romeo says of Juliet is: "Beauty too rich for use, for earth too dear!" But more than beauty is involved: their kind of passion would soon burn up the world of heavy fathers and snarling Tybalts and gabby Nurses if it stayed there. Our perception of this helps us to accept the play as a whole, instead of feeling only that a great love went wrong. It didn't go wrong: it went only where it could, out. It always was, as we say, out of this world.

That's why the tragedy is not exhausted by pointing to its obvious cause in the feud. We need suggestions of greater mysteries in things: we need the yoke of inauspicious stars and the vision of Queen Mab and her midget team riding across the earth like the apocalyptic [prophetic] horsemen. These things don't explain anything, but they help to light up the heroic vision in tragedy, which we see so briefly before it goes. It takes the greatest rhetoric of the greatest poets to bring us a vision of the tragic heroic, and such rhetoric doesn't make us miserable but exhilarated, not crushed but enlarged in spirit.

# Complexity as a Theme in *Romeo and Juliet*

Lawrence Edward Bowling

Many critics call William Shakespeare's *Romeo and Juliet* an immature play because he uses excessive imagery and lacks a significant theme for tragedy. Lawrence Edward Bowling, however, argues that the play has a central unifying theme and that the action and language support it. According to Bowling, Shakespeare illustrates the reality that people are a blend of saint *and* villain; they are not saints *or* villains. Romeo's confidant Friar Laurence understands this reality from the outset. Romeo learns it through two experiences: the rejection of his first false love, Rosaline, for his purer love, Juliet, and his slaying of Tybalt and Paris. And Juliet learns that Romeo is neither the villainous member of an enemy family, the Montagues, nor a saintly lover. She learns to accept Romeo as both husband and Tybalt's killer.

In its broadest terms, *Romeo and Juliet* deals with the wholeness and complexity of things, in contrast with a partial and simple view. This theme is functional on various levels in almost every speech and action in the play. . . .

The most important embodiment of the general theme deals with the discovery on the part of Romeo and Juliet and members of their families that individual human beings are not composed of abstract good or evil—that humanity is composed not of villains and saints but of human beings more or less alike. This central phase of the theme, which embraces the greater part of the paradoxical elements [those that seem contradictory but true], comes clearly to the surface. . . .

## SHAKESPEARE STATES THE THEME

In the prologue Shakespeare addresses the audience most directly in his own person and outlines not only the main action

Excerpted from Lawrence Edward Bowling, "The Thematic Framework of *Romeo and Juliet*," *PMLA*, vol. 64, (1949), pp. 208–20.

of the play but also the philosophy which this action demonstrates. Here, as throughout the play, he insists that the conflict is not between villains and saints but between two ordinarily good families "both *alike* in dignity." Paradoxically, the evil consequences are caused not by evil blood and evil hands but by blood and hands ordinarily considered civil; a thing so good as pure love is responsible for many persons' deaths, and a thing so bad as death accomplishes the good effect of removing the parents' hatred and bringing them together in sympathetic understanding—a result which, according to the prologue, could not have been accomplished in any other way by any "good" means.

The clearest statement of this philosophy from the point of view of a character within the play is Friar Laurence's soliloquy on good and evil. . . .

> The earth that's nature's mother is her tomb;
> What is her burying grave, that is her womb,
> And from her womb children of divers kind
> We sucking on her natural bosom find,
> Many for many virtues excellent,
> None but for some, and yet all different.
> O, mickle is the powerful grace that lies
> In plants, herbs, stones, and their true qualities:
> For nought so vile that on the earth doth live
> But to the earth some special good doth give,
> Nor aught so good but strain'd from that fair use
> Revolts from true birth, stumbling on abuse:
> Virtue itself turns vice, being misapplied,
> And vice sometimes by action dignified.
> Within the infant rind of this weak flower
> Poison hath residence and medicine, power . . .
> Two such opposed kings encamp them still
> In man as well as herbs, grace and rude will.
> And where the worser is predominant,
> Full soon the canker death eats up that plant.

Contrary to the conventional way of viewing matters, a particular thing or action may be either good or bad, depending upon the relative situation and its outcome; good and evil (like birth and death, medicine and poison) come together in the same place, and every human being has both grace and rude will.

The whole impasse between the Montagues and the Capulets is due to the fact that each acts as if he is completely good and his enemy completely bad. . . . The Friar is the only character who knows from the start that this way of viewing humanity is false; the others have to find it out by experience, and their process of becoming educated constitutes their tragedy.

The term *villain* is of unique significance in *Romeo and*

*Juliet*, where it appears more frequently than in any other of Shakespeare's plays in which there is not a villain. Every time the term *villain* occurs in *Romeo and Juliet*, it reveals more about the person who uses it than it does about the one to whom it is being applied. If a character avoids using the term, this is indicative of a high degree of maturity. Friar Laurence never once uses it, for such a concept is inconsistent with his mature way of viewing things in their diverse aspects. The simple-minded Tybalt, the predominance of whose "rude will" is well illustrated by his frequent use of *villain*, is soon eaten up by "the canker death.". . . Romeo uses the term only once, and then indirectly when he challenges Tybalt; it indirectly seals his fate. Juliet uses the word many times, up to and including her great maturing scene in the third act; but after this point she never again uses it.

In tracing the progress of enlightenment of various characters in the play, it is best to begin with Romeo since, except for the Friar, Romeo is always one step ahead of the others in development. Romeo's major experiences come in pairs: he loves twice, kills twice, and clearly expresses his philosophical discoveries twice; and, in each pair, the second shows a marked degree of depth and maturity over the first.

## ROMEO LEARNS FROM THE WOMEN HE LOVES

The starting point of Romeo's education is his love affair with Rosaline. Like other members of the two households, he seems previously to have viewed the conflict and the enemy in single-minded terms. Recently, however, he has discovered admirable qualities in a Capulet and fallen in love with her. Although it is sufficiently puzzling to him to find goodness in a "villain," Romeo is further disturbed by a second discovery: in the love affair with Rosaline, he finds that love is not always lovely but may have much discord and misery mixed up in it. Whereas he had previously expected to find in life only such phenomena as "brawling hate" and "loving love," he now finds himself loving where he should be hating and quarreling where he should be loving, and consequently discovers that one often needs to think in terms of "loving hate" and "brawling love." In order to express his bewilderment at such paradoxes, as he stands at the scene of the recent outbreak between his family and Rosaline's, Romeo resorts (quite appropriately) to the violent antitheses of the following passage:

> Here's much to do with hate, but more with love:
> Why then, O brawling love! O loving hate!

> O any thing! of nothing first create.
> O heavy lightness! serious vanity!
> Mis-shapen chaos of well-seeming forms!
> Feather of lead, bright smoke, cold fire, sick health!
> Still-waking sleep, that is not what it is!

But the next time we hear Romeo making observations upon the contradictions of life, he is a wiser man, no longer surprised at such paradoxes. Here is his second expression, in his famous relativity speech to the apothecary on the subject of gold and poison:

> There is thy gold, worse poison to men's souls,
> Doing more murders in this loathsome world
> Than these poor compounds that thou mayst not sell:
> I sell thee poison, thou hast sold me none . . .
> Come, cordial and not poison, go with me
> To Juliet's grave, for there must I use thee.

As a child, one thinks of poison as always poisonous and gold as always golden; but as one grows up and experiences life, he is likely to discover as Romeo does, and as the Friar had pointed out, that gold is often more poisonous than poison and poison may be more golden than gold.

Romeo's love affair with Rosaline prepares for his later, more mature love of Juliet. Having discovered in his first experience that the enemy is not completely bad, Romeo is not surprised later to discover that he can love Juliet. . . .

## ROMEO LEARNS FROM THE MEN HE KILLS

His growth in maturity can be further illustrated by contrasting his fight with Paris in the tomb and his earlier duel with Tybalt. Although all the elements of the later experience are not identical with those of the first, the two situations are about as much alike as they could be without becoming merely repetitive. At the time of the fight with Tybalt, Romeo has got well along in his development, but has not yet arrived at a really high degree of understanding. When in complete control of himself, he knows what he should do; but he is not yet able, under extreme emotional strain, to do what he knows he should. When Tybalt kills Mercutio, this violent action upsets Romeo's better judgment and throws him back upon his emotional reactions, so that for the first and only time in the play he calls an enemy a villain; but the fact that even here he does not apply the term directly indicates that he does not revert completely to family prejudice. However, he does willfully enter into the duel with Tybalt without being physically attacked, and he does this despite the fact that there are two good reasons why he should have taken every possible means to avoid this encounter: the Prince had forbidden such fighting in the streets, and Romeo was now married to Tybalt's cousin.

In the encounter with Paris in the tomb, although Romeo has neither of these reasons nor any other particular reason for not fighting, he does not willfully allow himself to become involved in physical conflict until after he is first directly attacked—and this despite the fact that Paris, after the manner of Tybalt, challenges Romeo with such terms as "vile Montague" and "condemned villain" and despite the fact also that Romeo is now suffering under an emotional strain even greater than that in the previous incident (he describes himself in this scene as "a mad man"). Furthermore, although Romeo has not yet recognized Paris and therefore has no specific evidence that the boy has good intentions, he still insists upon addressing him by such terms as "good gentle youth" and pleads with him to go away before he becomes involved in serious conflict. After he is finally attacked and has to kill Paris, Romeo does not in any way blame the boy or call him vile names; on the contrary, he complies with Paris's last requests, clasps his hand sympathetically, and accepts him on equal terms with himself, as "one writ with me in sour misfortune's book." After the duel with Tybalt, Romeo had expressed no such sympathy for his victim; but now he turns to Tybalt's corpse in the tomb and expresses his sincere regret and begs forgiveness:

> Tybalt, liest thou there in thy bloody sheet?
> O! what more favour can I do thee,
> Than with that hand that cut thy youth in twain
> To sunder his that was thine enemy?
> Forgive me, cousin!

## JULIET LEARNS STEP BY STEP ABOUT COMPLEXITY

... Juliet's development during the play may appear less dramatic and less important than Romeo's, since she loves only once and is never the direct instrument of any person's death, as Romeo is on two occasions. Although it is true that Juliet is in these respects less active than Romeo, her development is no less marked than his and is really presented more completely and more dramatically. ... Although she always arrives at a clear decision ultimately, her mind is first revealed in the preliminary stages of stumbling back and forth. It is this blow-by-blow account of the whole process as it is taking place in present time which makes Juliet's discoveries more dramatic than Romeo's and sets them more completely and vividly before the audience.

Juliet's later development can best be seen by first considering the kind of person she is at the beginning of the play. In her very first speech to her mother, Juliet reveals that she does not question either the wisdom or the authority of her parents, when she says: "Madam, I am here. What is your will?" And as soon as she discovers that her mother's will is for her to love Paris, she immediately and unquestioningly consents to "look to like" Paris but to go no further than her mother gives "consent." To Juliet at this point, love is, like hate, a duty to be performed at the decree of one's parents. As implied by the Nurse's remark that Romeo is "the only son of your great enemy," Juliet has always hated the Montagues without asking why.

Her views on both love and hate, however, are to change radically before the evening is over. On the former, they change even before the masquerade is over, for Juliet discovers that love is something which strikes like lightning, whether it is willed or not; but her views on hate do not undergo revision until she discovers that the person she now loves is one she is supposed to hate. Perplexed at this paradox, she expresses her bewilderment in paradoxical terms:

> My only love sprung from my only hate!
> Too early seen unknown and known too late!
> Prodigious birth of love it is to me,
> That I must love a loathed enemy.

Juliet's dilemma is the result of a conflict between her new attitude toward love and her old attitude toward hate.... Her solution to this problem is both interesting in itself and central to the theme of the play. Puzzling over the problem in her balcony soliloquy, she first concludes that it is only Romeo's "name that is my enemy," whereas Romeo himself she is willing to accept as "dear perfection." After Romeo speaks up from below her window and urges his suit, she comes by degrees to accept and love even his name. First, she calls him "gentle Romeo," but later in the same scene he becomes "fair Montague," "sweet Montague," and "the god of my idolatry." Before Romeo leaves her, she loves even his name so well that she wants to chant it over and over and "tear the cave where Echo lies . . . with repetition of my Romeo's name."

This unqualified acceptance of Romeo continues increasingly up to the second scene of the third act, where it reaches its climax in

> here comes my nurse,
> And she brings news; and every tongue that speaks
> But Romeo's name speaks heavenly eloquence.

Ironically, Juliet is on the brink of discovering that the tongue which speaks Romeo's name *may* speak hellish dissonance, for she is now to learn that Romeo's "dear perfection" is sufficiently imperfect to kill her cousin Tybalt. At first, she refuses to believe that "Romeo's hand" could possibly "shed Tybalt's blood." If the two had fought a few days earlier, such a conflict would then have conformed to Juliet's pattern of thinking, for at that time she considered every Montague a villain. Now that she has accepted Romeo as perfect goodness like the Capulets, she cannot conceive the possibility of a conflict between good and good. This sudden and strange news throws Juliet at first into a dilemma. It is therefore both appropriate that she should, and significant that she does, express her bewilderment in the following paradoxical terms:

> O serpent heart, hid with a flowering face!
> Did ever dragon keep so fair a cave?
> Beautiful tyrant! fiend angelical!
> Dove-feather'd raven! wolvish-ravening lamb!
> Despised substance of divinest show!
> Just opposite to what thou justly seem'st;
> A damned saint, an honourable villain!
> O, nature! what hadst thou to do in hell
> When thou didst bower the spirit of a fiend
> In mortal paradise of such sweet flesh!
> Was ever book containing such vile matter
> So fairly bound? O! that deceit should dwell
> In such a gorgeous palace.

This speech is almost identical in phrasing and meaning with Romeo's love-hate speech in the first scene of the play and is properly understood in relation to that speech. In each instance, the speaker has suddenly discovered that the old grudge has flared up anew between his family and the family of the lover, and is puzzled to find love and hate so contradictorily mixed up in the same affair. In each case, the speaker expresses his surprise and bewilderment in the same type of antithesis [with contrasting words and ideas]. With Juliet's "beautiful tyrant, fiend angelical," "dove-feather'd raven," "damned saint," "honourable villain" may be compared Romeo's "brawling love," "loving hate," "feather of lead, bright smoke, cold fire, sick health." The two speeches are so nearly alike that both the meaning and the expression of Juliet's passage may be well summarized in Romeo's generalized statement, "mis-shapen chaos of well-seeming forms . . . that is not what it is," which is the same as Juliet's "just opposite to what thou justly seem'st."

Recovering some of her intellectual balance, Juliet begins to realize that Romeo cannot possibly be at heart the villain that she has been calling him. She now attempts to make sense of what has happened. The following passage reveals how she moves by degrees to a correct appraisal of both Romeo and Tybalt:

> *Nurse:* Shame come to Romeo!
> *Juliet:*                         Blister'd be thy tongue
> For such a wish! he was not born to shame:
> Upon his brow shame is ashamed to sit;
> For it is a throne where honour may be crown'd
> Sole monarch of the universal earth.
>     *Nurse:* Will you speak well of him that kill'd your cousin?
>     *Juliet:* Shall I speak ill of him that is my husband?
> Ah! poor my lord, what tongue shall smooth thy name,
> When I, thy three-hours wife, have mangled it?
> But, wherefore, villain, didst thou kill my cousin?
> That villain cousin would have kill'd my husband:
> Back, foolish tears, back to your native spring;
> Your tributary drops belong to woe,
> Which you, mistaken, offer up to joy.
> My husband lives, that Tybalt would have slain;
> And Tybalt's dead, that would have slain my husband.

Juliet first reverts to her conventional family reaction of condemning the non-Capulet as a villain, but finding that this contradicts her recent conviction that Romeo is good, she swings to the other extreme and condemns her cousin Tybalt as the villain. Finding this position also untenable, she finally reaches in the last two lines the correct comprehensive evaluation of both persons. The one is no longer righteous Tybalt or "villain cousin" but merely Tybalt, and the other is no longer "villain husband" or "dear perfection" but "my husband." After this point, Juliet never ceases to see each in his entirety. Later she can say of Romeo:

> God pardon him! I do with all my heart;
> And yet no man like he doth grieve my heart.

And this is not mere double talk.

It may seem strange that Juliet should now have so much difficulty solving the present problem, since she had faced a similar situation before, when upon falling in love with Romeo she discovered that he was not really "a loathed enemy." In that experience, however, she had not really solved the problem but had merely side-stepped it by plucking him out of one extreme classification and placing him in the other. Her real discovery is, therefore, postponed until the problem comes up the second time in a more complex form and demands a complex solution. Only then does she realize that both "grace and rude will" exist simultaneously in the same person. . . .

But later, when she is about to take her life in the tomb, Juliet is not surprised to discover contradictory qualities existing in the same thing. Finding that Romeo has killed himself by drinking poison, she regrets that he has left "no friendly drop" for her, and remarks:

> I will kiss thy lips;
> Haply, some poison yet doth hang on them
> To make me die with a restorative.

Juliet's realization that poison may be thought of as a "friendly drop" and "a restorative" echoes Romeo's reference to poison as cordial and Friar Laurence's observation that medicine and poison have residence in the same flower. The theme that things, people, and actions are not always abstract and single in their qualities but may vary according to the relative situation is evidenced in almost every element of the play.

# Timeless Politicians in *Julius Caesar*

Gareth Lloyd Evans

Gareth Lloyd Evans contends that although *Julius Caesar* fails to reach the highest sense of tragedy, it engages audiences with portrayals of politicians who appear in all ages. According to Evans, the play's Roman political figures exhibit opposing qualities. For example, Caesar displays arrogant public power, but private pettiness. Brutus is honest and thoughtful, but lacks the single-minded practicality to lead effectively. Antony lures the mob away from Brutus's influence, but does it with ruthless manipulation. Evans shows that each character's public morality is incompatible with his private morality, and the actions that result cause disorder in Roman society.

In the theatre *Julius Caesar* does not engage us as a tragedy in the highest sense, though it has its own magnetism which has its source and power in the play's ability to seem (and, indeed, often to be) 'contemporary'. The play has, in successive decades, not only provided its readers with points of reference for contemporary political events, but has seemed particularly amenable to being presented in contemporary dress.... More than this it gives the kind of insight into the political world demanded by our curiosity and imagination. We are shown the inside workings as well as the outside configurations of that world; our view is double-focused. We are, for example, given glimpses of the reasons why Caesar held such sway, but these singularities are shown in parallel with other elements in him which are common to lesser and weaker men. Some qualities he shares with modern dictators, his courage, his bravura, his ability to command, his expectation of immediate obedience, his peremptory assumption of absolute authority, yet we are also shown the pettiness of mind,

Excerpted from *The Upstart Crow* by Lloyd Gareth Evans (London: J.M. Dent, 1982). Reprinted with permission of the publisher.

the fears, the almost absurdly ordinary emotional response of the man. The contrast between public and private, between great singularity and petty plurality—titillations of our curiosity about political men—is vividly encapsuled in a play of remarkable political and human insight. . . .

*Julius Caesar* demonstrates that Shakespeare's prevailing detestation of disorder, his celebration of order, his loathing of irrationality in thought and action, had not abated. The Boar's Head, the Courts of Richard of Gloucester, of Harry of Monmouth, of Bolingbroke, Richard II, Henry VI and, indeed, the Forest of Arden [settings from other plays by Shakespeare], are now joined by Rome as emblems of Shakespeare's view of what makes for good and bad societies. But what gives *Julius Caesar* such a sharpness of outline is the number of different ways in which the perils of disorder are displayed and manipulated. Each one of the characters—Caesar, Brutus, Cassius, Antony and Octavius Caesar as well as the mob—is a distinct example of the incompatibility of political and private moralities, particularly where the element of power dominates. The play shows the corrosive effect of power on these men, ranging from Octavius Caesar's cold embrace of it to Brutus's self-torturing attempts to allay its destructive force.

## CAESAR'S DOMINATION AND PETTINESS

Julius Caesar we see after power has completed its work of raising the public man high at the expense of ruining the private man. It is on Caesar that Shakespeare exerts the fullest rigour of his bifocal view, showing us relentlessly his effortless, conceited, assumed public domination and, at the same time, his pettiness. For most onlookers the public man is respected, not for his humanity, but for his power:

> Who else would soar above the view of men,
> And keep us all in servile fearfulness.                  [I.1.]

. . . In virtually the same breath Cassius refers both to Caesar's 'feeble temper' and to his bestriding the world 'like a Colossus'. As a result the Caesar presented in this play is both strong and weak—he has both a good and a bad profile, is shown from different angles so that we receive a constantly changing impression of the reality of the man.

Caesar's ability to assess those around him is peremptory but superbly accurate:

> Yond Cassius has a lean and hungry look;
> He thinks too much. Such men are dangerous.              [I.2.]

His stoicism seems natural, not assumed, yet there is a self-pride in it:

> It seems to be most strange that men should fear,
> Seeing that death, a necessary end
> Will come when it will come.                    [II.2.]

His authoritarianism has a petulance [bad temper] about it:

> The cause is in my will; I will not come.
> That is enough to satisfy the Senate.             [II.2.]

Even egocentric authority—a most obviously typical characteristic—is made to appear a form of self-indulgence—his vulnerability to believing what he wants to believe. He is taken in by Decius's speciously flattering interpretation of a dream which his own wife regards as ominous and his self-conscious assumption of the mantle of Caesardom is both dignified and slightly absurd:

> But I am constant as the northern star,
> Of whose true-fix'd and resting quality,
> There is no fellow in the firmament.               [III.1.]

. . . When this Caesar dies our emotions are mixed. On the evidence presented by the play his death seems unnecessary, and while we are not over-sorry for him—his death may seem a relief—neither are we completely glad. The likes of him fascinate our curiosities, turning awry our judgements and our power to be sure of what we feel and think, which is why they are so dangerous yet so attractive.

## BRUTUS: TOO HONEST, NAIVE, AND HUMANE TO LEAD

Brutus could never become a Caesar because he is too honest a man and incapable of play-acting. Yet we as listeners and observers lack confidence in him. His courage, his fidelity to a cause, his intellectual and emotional honesty—none of these are in doubt; yet we constantly wonder if his heart is indeed capable of being, committed to the pursuance of those actions which will be necessary once he has thrown in his lot with the conspirators. He is unequipped for the harsh political word; the private, the human and the personal are at odds with the public, the political, the expedient, and his purpose is blunted. We observe him at various stages of the journey that starts with Caesar's death and which ends at Philippi. It might have ended back in Rome with laurel wreaths about his head, but in our hearts we know all along that Philippi will be the end. The fight between political necessity and personal sensibility atrophies his well-meant intentions. He is a man to whom introspection is natural, who is happiest when least in company, when:

I turn the trouble of my countenance
Merely upon myself.                                    [I.2.]

He gives the impression that he is not a natural leader of
active opposition, least of all of the kind which will lead to

---

## A STUDY IN CHARACTER

*Shakespeare created characters in* Julius Caesar *with such vitality that his interpretation of them has fixed their personalities. According to Louis B. Wright and Virginia LaMar in their introduction to* Julius Caesar, *though Caesar, Brutus, Cassius, and Antony are historical figures, readers and actors envision them as they appear in Shakespeare's play, instead of as historical people.*

He [Shakespeare] wrote in *Julius Caesar* a play that possessed elements of enduring interest. The dramatist found himself concerned with a study in character and he brought the major figures in the play to life with such vividness that the qualities that he attributed to them have become invincibly fixed in the consciousness of later ages. . . . If the average American of our time thinks of Caesar, Brutus, Cassius, or Mark Antony, he visualizes him in Shakespeare's characterization.

Brutus is the noble patriot, filled with memories of a great patriot-ancestor whom he must emulate. If to us he seems stuffy and self-consciously virtuous, the audience who first listened to his lines probably approved of his sententious utterances, so like axioms they had often heard. He represents the contemplative type and, ironically, his decisions, reached with so much show of justice and wisdom, usually turn out to be the wrong ones. Cassius, on the other hand, is more Machiavellian [more concerned with the end or goal than the method of getting there]; he is the "lean and hungry" type of introspective thinker who instinctively knows what ruthless measures are necessary but allows himself to be talked out of them by Brutus's show of virtuous wisdom. Mark Antony in this play is presented as the master politician, possessed of both shrewdness and eloquence. That he is a lover of pleasure, gaiety, and luxury is made clear. . . .

The interplay of these personalities clearly fascinated Shakespeare as it has fascinated actors and readers of *Julius Caesar* ever since. In this play an actor's ambition is satisfied with something besides the title role; other parts are as good or better. Any actor can rejoice at success in the roles of Brutus, Cassius, or Antony.

Louis B. Wright and Virginia LaMar, Introduction to *The Tragedy of Julius Caesar* by William Shakespeare. New York: Simon & Schuster, 1959.

assassination. His observation of Caesar causes him to reflect pessimistically to fear the direction which Caesar's rule is taking, but he has to be cajoled into taking action. Although he says to Cassius, 'What you would work me to, I have some aim', we cannot really believe that he would have contemplated assassination except as an abstract solution. It has gone unremarked by most commentators that Brutus is finally pushed to commit himself to the conspiracy by a cheap trick. The letters that Cassius throws through his window are forged:

> I will this night,
> In several hands, in at his windows throw,
> As if they came from several citizens,
> Writings, all tending to the great opinion
> That Rome holds of his name;                [I.2.]

Brutus's decision is founded upon a deception:

> Am I entreated
> To speak and strike? O Rome, I make thee promise,
> If the redress will follow, thou receivest
> Thy full petition at the hand of Brutus.        [II.1.]

The effect of our knowing that the letters are forgeries is, or should be, twofold. First, that Brutus should be thus so easily deceived increases our sense of his vulnerability in the harsh political world; second, that he should so quickly respond to them initiates a conviction that he is politically naive. From the moment of the delivery of the letters Brutus's vulnerability and political insufficiency are frequently emphasized by Shakespeare. Cassius's calculating practicality is in stark contrast to Brutus's impracticality. Cassius says, 'Let Antony and Caesar fall together' and Brutus replies, 'Let's be Sacrificers, but not Butchers Caius'. Cassius is right but Brutus is the more human. Later, after the assassination, Brutus says of Antony, 'I know that we shall have him well to Friend', and Cassius, right again, replies:

> my misgiving still
> Falls shrewdly to the purpose.              [III.1.]

Brutus commits simple, fundamental errors of political tactics. The first is to invite Antony to speak at all at Caesar's funeral, then, having done so, to allow him to have last voice. The emergence of Antony as a leading character in the play serves, among other things, to underline Brutus's *naïveté*. Antony is a natural politician. The difference between his and Brutus's handling of the funeral speeches is immense. Brutus, idealist and theorist, indulges in rhetoric—we feel that speech-making (certainly to a mob) is not his forte—idealism is:

Romans, Country-men, and lovers! hear me for my
cause, and be silent, that you may hear. Believe me for
mine honour, and have respect to mine honour, that you may
believe.                                                    [III.2.]

Antony manipulates his audience as if they were puppets,
making most of his points succinctly but never failing to
labour the one theme he knows will appeal to the acquisitive
appetites of his listeners—the contents of Caesar's will. He is
completely aware of what he does:

Mischief thou art afoot,
Take thou what course thou wilt.                            [III.2.]

## THE FOREBODING END

... No other play of Shakespeare's has such a valedictory [ex-
pressing farewell] atmosphere as has *Julius Caesar* in its final
act. Foreboding, resignation and death are in the air. The discovered love between the once entirely political man and Brutus makes the very enterprise on which they are embarked
seem irrelevant. Victory or defeat seems less important than
that Brutus and Cassius have found love and respect for each
other. Portia's death is of greater moment to Cassius than dis-
cussions about tactics and strategy and it seems more to the
point that Cassius and Brutus should part well and lovingly
than that Brutus 'gave the word too early' and ensured defeat
for his army. . . .

Yet, up to this last act, *Julius Caesar* is less concerned with
individual tragedy than with a vividly naturalistic evocation of
historical events. Shakespeare's ability to give a present-tense
actuality to those events is proven in several scenes—in Act I.1,
where Flavius and Marullus berate the common citizenry, in
Act II.1, where Brutus greets and talks to the conspirators, and
the following scene, where we see Caesar in his domestic
habitat before departing for the Capitol. One scene is remarkable also for other reasons. In Act III.3, the poet Cinna is mas-
sacred by the Roman mob. It is not difficult, with Cinna's
opening words in our minds, to imagine the fiery glow of
burning property with, perhaps, a context of sultry thunder
and vivid lightning:

I dreamt to-night that I did feast with Caesar,
And things unluckily charge my fantasy:                     [III.3.]

The brutality of the scene, achieved with such economy, attaches itself inexorably to the imagination. It is, in a sense, just
one painful minor event in a day full of important and unimportant happenings, and is often cut by theatre directors who

claim that we already know that this Roman mob is dangerous and brutal and that the death of an obscure, frightened poet is of little dramatic consequence. Such argument ignores the fact that the scene is a clear example of Shakespeare's superb sense of thematic and theatrical values. Shakespeare realized what, so often, his modern directors fail to grasp—that the brutal reality of mindless killing is best conveyed to an audience not when groups confront other groups with physical violence but when a single individual is menaced by a group. The death of Hector in *Troilus and Cressida,* of York in *Henry VI* and of Cinna in this play, are ample testimony. The doomed individual takes on a terrible vulnerability becoming representative of all threatened men, and his loneliness in the face of calculated death makes cruelty all the more vicious.

In the particular instance of Cinna the poet, another sensitivity of Shakespeare's is revealed. One of the first victims of social anarchy is a society's culture—modern history bears ample testimony to this—for what unreason fears most is the reason, order, and imaginative and intellectual freedom represented by art and culture. This Roman mob which, in any case, probably cannot read, is prepared to 'tear' Cinna for 'his bad verses'. Ironically, it is even more poignant evidence of the rule of anarchy when even minor poets are killed. . . .

We are reminded of the most obvious quality, then, of *Julius Caesar*—its innate ability to be always 'contemporary'. Shakespeare's sense of politics, of man in society, of the tension between personal sensibility and public necessity, is so accurate that this play remains an eternal reflection of the ironies, cruelties, and pains which the individual suffers in a politically organized society in trying to reconcile the (probably) irreconcilable—private and public morality, wisdom, and sensibility.

# Caesar Pitted Against Fate

Edith Sitwell

Edith Sitwell acknowledges the title character of Shakespeare's *Julius Caesar* as a great and powerful ruler, but, she explains, he is destined to lose a battle with fate. Because Caesar is proud and powerful, he refuses to heed warnings to stay home on the Ides of March, warnings given to him by the soothsayer and suggested by the elements. By defying both, he gives the conspirators an opportunity to kill him. For this great theme—a powerful man pitted against fate— Sitwell believes Shakespeare wrote some of his most beautiful poetry. Sitwell, a poet herself, wrote verse in the 1920s that exploited the musical quality of language. She was made a D.B.E. in 1954.

In this play, the great Caesar, bright as the Prince of the Powers of the Air, the fallen Angel whose sin was pride, says, almost at the moment of his death:

> I could be well mov'd if I were as you;
> If I could pray to moove,
> Prayers would moove me;
> But I am constant as the Northerne Starre,
> Of whose true fixt and resting quality
> There is no fellow in the Firmament.
> The skyes are painted with unnumber'd Sparkes,
> They are all Fire and every one doth shine:
> But there's but one in all doth hold his place:
> So in the World. 'Tis furnished well with Men,
> And Men are Flesh and Blood, and apprehensive.
> Yet in the number I do know but One
> That unassayleable holds on to his Ranke,
> Unshak'd of Motion: and that I am he (III, 1).

But, in the end, the unshakeable star proved to be Fate,—a disastrous planet hidden behind the gross mists of the breath of crowds,—'the stinking breath' of the crowd that 'had almost

Excerpted from *A Notebook on William Shakespeare* by Edith Sitwell (London: Macmillan, 1948).

choaked Caesar: for hee swoonded and fell downe at it' (I, 2).

The voice of Fate sounds not only through the lips of the Soothsayer [one who can foretell events] who said but five words: 'Beware the Ides of March' [March 15], or amid the strange dream-like mutterings of the Conspirators in the market-place—one of whom had seen the swoon of Caesar:

BRUTUS

'Tis very like: he hath the Falling sicknesse.

CASSIUS

No, Caesar hath it not; but you, and I,
And honest Casca, we have the Falling sicknesse.

CASCA

I know not what you meane by that; but I am sure Caesar fell downe. If the tag-ragge people did not clap him, and hisse him, according as he pleas'd and displeas'd them, as they use to doe the Players in the theatre, I am no true man (I, 2).

---

## UPSETTING THE ELEMENTS

*Shakespeare's audience believed in fate—the notion that natural external powers affected human events. According to E.M.W. Tillyard in* The Elizabethan World Picture, *when nature's order was disrupted, it was not God's doing; a man's wrongdoing brought the trouble both to himself and to the physical world.*

The Elizabethan believed in the pervasive operation of an external fate in the world. The twelve signs of the zodiac had their own active properties. The planets were busy the whole time; and their fluctuating conjunctions produced a seemingly chaotic succession of conditions, theoretically predictable but in practice almost wholly beyond the wit of man. Their functions differed, with the moon the great promoter of change. Though there were sceptics like Edmund in *Lear* and though the quack astrologer was hated and satirised, the general trend was of belief.

It must not be thought that the evident havoc in nature's order wrought by the stars at all upset the evidence of God's Providence. The havoc was all within the scheme. The answer to the question why God allowed the havoc was almost self-evident. It was not primarily God who allowed it but man who inflicted it on both himself and the physical universe. In their own natures the stars are beneficent, and when they were first created they worked together to do good.

E.M.W. Tillyard, *The Elizabethan World Picture.* New York: Random House, n.d.

Not these alone, but the Elements, speak of danger:

CASSIUS

> ... for now, this fearfull Night,
> There is no stirre, or walking in the streets;
> And the Complexion of the Element
> In Favor's like the Worke we have in hand,
> Most bloudie, fierie, and most terrible (I, 3).

> ... Never till now,

says Casca,

> Did I goe through a tempest dropping fire.

> A common slave—you know him well by sight—
> Held up his left hand, which did flame and burne
> Like twentie torches joyn'd; and yet his Hand,
> Not sensible of fire, remain'd unscorch'd.
> Besides,—I have not since put up my sword,—
> Against the Capitoll I met a Lyon,
> Who glar'd upon me, and went surly by (I, 3).

Calpurnia says to Caesar:

> A lioness hath whelped in the streets (II, 2);

—and this seems like the birth of Disaster, or of some terrible new-fallen Angel—half lion, half spirit, fallen before his birth. But Caesar does not heed the complexion of the elements. He remains deaf to the dream of his wife, as to the voice of the Soothsayer:

CAESAR

> What say the augurers[1]?

SERVANT

> They would not have you to stirre forth to-day.
> Plucking the intrailes[2] of an offering forth,
> They could not finde a heart within the beast.

CAESAR

> The Gods do this in shame of Cowardice:
> Caesar should be a Beast without a heart
> If he should stay at home to-day for feare.
> No, Caesar shall not; Danger knowes full well
> That Caesar is more dangerous than he:
> We are two Lyons litter'd in one day,
> And I the elder and more terrible (II, 2).

Even [French philosopher and writer] Voltaire, in the midst of his cavilling [quibbling], was moved to exclaim that this is of

1. seers or prophets.
2. In ancient times the study of animal entrails, especially the liver, was thought to give divine answers to perplexing questions.

an inconceivable elevation.

The play is amongst the most *pure* poetry written by Shakespeare. The theme is the greatness of Man pitted against the power of Fate. The poetry itself has the complexion of the elements. It moves with an incredible grandeur, as it tells of the bright Angel Caesar—the Angel, perhaps, of Death, who must fall from his place as Lucifer fell, because of pride, or because of the pride that his killers believed existed in him.

BRUTUS

It must be by his death: and, for my part,
I know no personall cause to spurne at him,
But for the generall. He would be crowned:
How that might change his nature, there's the question:
It is the bright day that brings forth the adder;
And that craves warie walking. Crowne him?—that!
And then, I graunt, we put a Sting in him.
That at his will he may doe danger with.
The abuse of Greatnesse is, when it dis-joynes
Remorse from Power (II, 1).

There is a strange beauty in this scene, when Brutus, returning from his orchard to the closet, says:

The exhalations whizzing in the Ayre
Give so much light that I may reade by them (II, 1).

A few moments later, comes the knock on the door. It is the knock of Fate.

# Marc Antony: A Man of Skill and Honor

T.S. Dorsch

T.S. Dorsch argues that Shakespeare's Marc Antony is a skilled and honorable man, a view that differs from the views of many critics. Antony acted to restore Caesar's reputation and avenge his death, a cause Dorsch says is more moral than the conspirators' cause of killing Caesar to save Rome from tyranny. Though Antony accomplishes his cause by manipulation, he is not self-serving. Moreover, Antony, who moves the Roman crowd on Caesar's behalf, deserves admiration for his skill in oratory and, in the last part of the play, for the generosity he shows toward his enemies.

The development of Antony's character belongs largely to the last three acts [of William Shakespeare's play *Julius Cæsar*]. In the first two he is an unimportant figure, and appears little more than "a limb of Cæsar". By the end of the play he has, by the talents he has displayed as orator, statesman, and soldier, made himself the avenger of Cæsar and a "triple pillar of the world". He has shown that he possesses, as [critic R.G.] Moulton puts it [in *Shakespeare as a Dramatic Artist*], "all the powers that belong both to the intellectual and practical life". I cannot, however, agree with Moulton when he says, as other critics also say, that Antony "has concentrated his whole nature in one aim, . . . unmitigated self-seeking".

His first appearance is as one of the Lupercalian [festival in honor of god Lupercus] runners, anxious to please and serve Cæsar. Cæsar reminds him to touch Calphurnia [Cæsar's wife] in the holy chase, and he replies,

> I shall remember:
> When Cæsar says, "Do this," it is perform'd.

He speaks only three more lines before the assassination of Cæsar. In two of them he gives an estimate as mistaken as

Excerpted from T.S. Dorsch, Introduction to *Julius Caesar*, in the Arden Edition of the Works of William Shakespeare (London: Methuen, 1955). Reprinted by permission of Routledge publishers.

Cæsar's is correct of the character of Cassius, whom he describes as "well given" and not at all dangerous. But this is the last error of judgement he is to make. . . .

## THE ORATOR AND THE MAN

*Harley Granville-Barker comments on Antony's effective oration to the mob. With his words, Antony moves the gathered Romans to switch their allegiance from Brutus to Caesar. While moving the mob, Antony also reveals himself.*

Shakespeare shows us his mind at its swift work, its purposes shaping.

> Passion, I see, is catching, for mine eyes,
> Seeing those beads of sorrow stand in thine,
> Began to water.

—from which it follows that if the sight of Cæsar's body can so move the man and the man's tears so move him, why, his own passion may move his hearers in the market place presently to some purpose! His imagination, once it takes fire, flashes its way along, not by reason's slow process though in reason's terms.

To what he is to move his hearers we know: and it will be worth while later to analyze the famous speech, that triumph of histrionics [a performance calculated to have an effect]. For though the actor of Antony must move us with it also—and he can scarcely fail to—Shakespeare has set him the further, harder and far more important task of showing us an Antony the mob never see, of making him clear to us, moreover, even while we are stirred by his eloquence, of making clear to us just by what it is we are stirred. It would, after all, be pretty poor playwriting and acting which could achieve no more than a plain piece of mob oratory, however gorgeous; a pretty poor compliment to an audience to ask of it no subtler response than the mob's. But to show us, and never for a moment to let slip from our sight, the complete and complex Antony, impulsive and calculating, warm-hearted and callous, aristocrat, sportsman and demagogue, that will be for the actor an achievement indeed; and the playwright has given him all the material for it.

Harley Granville-Barker, in Leonard F. Dean, *Twentieth-Century Interpretations of Julius Caesar: A Collection of Critical Essays.* Englewood Cliffs, NJ: Prentice-Hall, 1968.

In the first two acts the only hints we have of his potential greatness are the fact that Cæsar has singled him out for his special regard, and the opinion of Cassius that he is a "shrewd contriver" who, with the means at his command, may well prove a danger if he is allowed to outlive Cæsar.

## ANTONY'S RESPONSE TO CÆSAR'S DEATH

When Cæsar is struck down, Antony flies to his house in stupefaction. But before the assassins have left the scene of their crime he has sent his servant with a tactfully worded request for an interview. His first object is to win the confidence of Brutus. Backed by the countenance of Brutus, he may be able to set in motion some plan of vengeance for Cæsar. In his message he makes no attempt to conceal his love and reverence for Cæsar; these emotions are genuine, but he is also aware that Brutus will respect him all the more for his loyalty to his dead friend. He plays upon the vanity of Brutus, and upon the magnanimity that he knows such a man will display towards one who comes to him as a suppliant; and he ends with an ambiguously worded promise that he will throw in his lot with Brutus if he can be satisfied that Cæsar deserved to die. Brutus is completely taken in. In the assurance that Antony will prove a good friend he promises him safe conduct, and as Cassius is voicing misgivings, Antony himself appears.

Though surrounded by men whose arms are red to the elbows with Cæsar's blood, Antony for the first few moments has eyes for nothing but the body at their feet. Then he turns to the murderers, and in words that are charged with irony expresses his readiness, if it so please them, to die by Cæsar's side, at the hands of "the choice and master spirits of this age". Brutus hastens to declare that they have nothing but "kind love, good thoughts, and reverence" for him; and Cassius too reassures him, though, being more worldly-wise, he appeals to his ambition and offers him an equal share with the conspirators "in the disposing of new dignities".

Antony has made a good start. . . . But Cassius is a realist. He asks what compact Antony is prepared to make with them. Antony is ready with his answer, and if it is a rather evasive answer, at least it satisfies the conspirators:

> Therefore I took your hands, but was indeed
> Sway'd from the point by looking down on Cæsar.
> Friends am I with you all, and love you all,
> Upon this hope, that you shall give me reasons
> Why, and wherein, Cæsar was dangerous.

Brutus promises to satisfy him, and Antony at last feels it safe to come to the real point of the interview he has sought.

He asks permission to take Cæsar's body to the market-place

and to speak a funeral oration, as becomes a friend. Brutus at once consents, and brushes aside the objections that Cassius raises. Antony desires no more; he has won the first round.

Left alone with Cæsar's body, he shows his true feelings:

> O, pardon me, thou bleeding piece of earth,
> That I am meek and gentle with these butchers.
> Thou art the ruins of the noblest man
> That ever lived in the tide of times.
> Woe to the hand that shed this costly blood!

And he prophesies a period of fierce civil strife, blood, and destruction that shall end only when a terrible vengeance for the foul murder has been exacted. There is no dissembling in this speech of Antony. It is impossible to doubt here the depth and sincerity of his love and grief for Cæsar, or the fury and tenacity with which he will hound the murderers to their doom. . . .

## ANTONY'S HONESTY AND MORALITY QUESTIONED

Shakespeare's Antony has been frequently censured as unstable, immoral, and dishonest. . . . Other critics who see nothing but nobility in Brutus have come close to making Antony the villain of the piece.

We may grant that he is unscrupulous in his methods; but is he any more so than the men with whom he is dealing? Does he do more than turn the methods of the conspirators upon themselves? These blood-guilty men have secretly plotted the murder of the greatest man of the age, have butchered the man whom of all men he most deeply loved and admired, and he takes upon himself the sacred duty of vengeance. The *virtuous* Brutus and his confederates hid the monstrous visage of conspiracy in smiles and affability; Antony's dissimulation is certainly no worse than theirs. Cassius whets Brutus against Cæsar; Antony will whet the Roman people against Cassius and Brutus. Apart from Brutus, the conspirators "did that they did in envy of great Cæsar"; envy and malice are not nobler motives for the taking of life than the desire and duty to avenge a murdered friend and national leader. Antony is no less straightforward in his speech or honourable in his tactics than the men to whom he truthfully says:

> You show'd your teeth like apes, and fawn'd like hounds,
> And bow'd like bondmen, kissing Cæsar's feet;
> Whilst damned Casca, like a cur, behind
> Struck Cæsar on the neck.

He is no whit less stable and steadfast than Cassius; no man could be more single-hearted than he shows himself in planning and carrying through his vengeance on the assassins. I can see no signs whatever that he is seeking honour and power for himself in pursuing this aim; amongst other things, he ignores Cassius's offer to let him share the honour and power that the conspirators anticipate for themselves. Nor does he keep his emotions less securely under lock and key than Cassius in the second and third scenes of the play, or, for that matter, than Brutus when he is quarrelling with Cassius. In the earlier acts we are told that he is something of a voluptuary [a person who indulges in luxury and pleasure], which is not the same thing as saying that he is dissolute [lacking moral restraint]; we must suppose that with Cæsar's death he renounced the lighter pleasures of former days, for we hear no more of them except in a sneering remark of Cassius. Cæsar's death brings out all the strength and greatness of Antony, and his conduct rapidly effaces any impression we may have formed earlier that he is a trifler or a mere limb of Cæsar. . . .

We have it on the authority of Brutus that Cassius, who belongs to the "honourable" party, is much condemned for selling and marting his offices for gold to undeservers. Are we to believe that Shakespeare intends us to regard Antony as a man of baser motives and principles than Cassius and Casca? He is much cleverer at their own game than they are, and more amiable, and he has better justification for almost all his actions than they have. . . . In the circumstances in which he is placed by Cæsar's murder he reveals what can only be called genius in exploiting every turn in a situation to the advantage of the cause to which he has dedicated himself.

## Antony's Genius as an Orator

If we admire Antony's resource and daring when he faces the conspirators in their moment of triumph—or rather what should be triumph, but utterly fails to be—how are we to name the qualities he displays in the Forum [Roman marketplace] on the following day? If ever Shakespeare wished to show genius at work, surely it was in Antony's oration. By a magnanimous and calmly reasonable appeal to their Roman sense of independence, Brutus has convinced an initially uneasy crowd that Cæsar was an ambitious tyrant who had to be slain for the good of Rome, and they are ready to shower every honour on him as their deliverer. Antony is there on sufferance; he is to speak by the kind permission of the hero of the hour, and the crowd he faces is actively hostile to Cæsar and likely to tear to pieces any one who exalts Cæsar at the expense of Brutus. As on the previous day, he must tread very warily; and he must pick his words even more carefully than then, for the crowd, already wrought to a state of high feeling, will be infinitely more suggestible and inflammable than a small band of nobles. A mistake may cost him his life; the exploitation of a single favourable current may carry him to where Brutus now stands.

Antony begins circumspectly by disclaiming any intention of praising Cæsar. There is a touch of his characteristic irony in what he adds to the disclaimer: let Cæsar, he says, suffer the common fate of being remembered solely for his bad qualities. He passes on to the question of Cæsar's ambition, the grievous fault for which he was slain, according to Brutus; and whenever he mentions Brutus he is careful to couple expressions of respect with his name. He does not try to prove that Cæsar was not ambitious. He merely speaks of actions of Cæsar which were not ambitious; he can count on mob-logic to do the rest. With the instinct of the natural orator he keeps his line of thought simple, and uses catch-phrases to hammer home his points. "Cæsar was ambitious"; "Brutus is an honourable man": these are the phrases of which he makes his refrain.

> But Brutus says he was ambitious,
> And Brutus is an honourable man.

With each increasingly striking instance of Cæsar's lack of ambition the irony of this refrain becomes increasingly apparent, and when Antony sees that it is beginning to penetrate the consciousness of the crowd, he manufactures a pause:

> Bear with me.
> My heart is in the coffin there with Cæsar,
> And I must pause till it come back to me.

This is a telling stroke. The crowd are given time to put their heads together and carry the argument to the illogical conclusion that Cæsar was not ambitious, and that he has had great wrong; and they are also able to see Antony with a manly effort pull himself together to resume his speech.

Two minutes earlier Antony's hearers had been suspicious of him and hostile to Cæsar. Now he has won their sympathy both for himself and for Cæsar, and he can afford to remind them of Cæsar's might and renown, and of their own fickleness in forgetting them now he is dead:

> But yesterday the word of Cæsar might
> Have stood against the world; now lies he there,
> And none so poor to do him reverence.

But he has another important task to accomplish. Insidiously, under the pretext of deprecating violence, he sows in their minds the seeds of mutiny and rage against the honourable men who have killed Cæsar, and whom he can now begin to lash more openly. Better, he says, that Cæsar, and he, and his countrymen in general, should suffer wrong than such honourable men as Brutus. But he does not want the hint to be taken yet, not until he has stirred up such an implacable fury as can only be assuaged by blood. He produces another card. Here is Cæsar's will, he says; no, no, you must not hear it, for if you did, what a saint you would make of Cæsar. No, I must not read it.

> It is not meet you know how Cæsar lov'd you.
> ... It will inflame you, it will make you mad.
> 'Tis good you know not that you are his heirs;
> For if you should, O, what would come of it?

Naturally the crowd clamours to hear the will. But not yet.

> Will you be patient? Will you stay awhile?
> I have o'ershot myself to tell you of it.
> I fear I wrong the honourable men
> Whose daggers have stabb'd Cæsar; I do fear it.

One might expect Antony to be satisfied with the reception given this time to the catch-phrase, and to read the will at last. Even now he holds it back. Let his good friends but look on Cæsar's mantle, the mantle he first put on the day he won that glorious victory over the Nervii [a battle in the Gallic Wars, in which Cæsar fought bravely]; let them see the rents made by the swords of his trusted friends, especially the well-beloved Brutus; let them see his body, hacked by traitors; then they will know what bloody treason has flourished over them.

## ANTONY ROUSES THE MOB TO MUTINY

Tears of pity fill the eyes of the beholders, succeeded by blind rage and lust for blood. Remorselessly Antony holds them back. The wise and honourable men who slew Cæsar, he says, no doubt had good private reasons for their deed; no doubt they will make fine speeches and justify it. For himself, he is no orator, has no glib powers of persuasion; he can only speak what is in his heart. Of course, an orator like Brutus would know how to ruffle up their spirits and rouse them to mutiny. With a roar the crowd take up the word "mutiny", and Antony can only just prevent them from rushing off to rend the traitors limb from limb by raising his voice above the clamour to gain silence for the will. And at last they hear that Cæsar has left a sum of money to every Roman citizen, and his private gardens to them all in common as pleasure-grounds.

Here was a royal Cæsar indeed! Nothing could hold them after this, and exultantly Antony watches them stream away, to burn the body in "the holy place", and to fire the traitors' houses with the brands.

Now let it work. Mischief, thou art afoot,
Take thou what course thou wilt!

Where the triumph of Cæsar's assassins fizzled out in vapouring speeches and irresolution, Antony's triumph is complete. It is a twofold triumph. Antony has roused mighty powers of mischief to vengeance for Cæsar; in a few minutes he hears with grim calmness that "Brutus and Cassius are rid like madmen through the gates of Rome". Just as important to him, he has vindicated Cæsar's good name, has indeed added new lustre to it. Insistently, throughout his oration, he has dinned Cæsar's name into the ears of his auditors, and, with increasing emphasis, Cæsar's greatness. When he began his speech, Cæsar was a lifeless clod, deservedly slain—so Brutus had persuaded the citizens—because he was an ambitious tyrant and a danger to the state. When he ended, Cæsar was a godlike conqueror and a royally munificent benefactor, the greatest of all Romans. There is nothing in the speech to suggest that Antony is seeking anything for himself; everything has been directed towards two ends, the extinction of Cæsar's murderers, and the re-establishment of Cæsar's name and fame. For himself he has gained only a long period of warfare and peril. . . .

## A DECENT MAN

Antony's last two appearances [in the play] are calculated to leave an entirely favourable impression. He shows a thorough appreciation of the devotion and loyalty of Lucilius [a friend to Brutus and Cassius], who has been captured while masquerading as Brutus, and who, in words which might well be his last, courageously asserts the nobility of Brutus. "Keep this man safe", says Antony; "give him all kindness. I had rather have such men my friends than enemies". And in the penultimate speech of the play, Shakespeare brings out in Antony a full understanding of the essential integrity of Brutus, and in the epitaph he speaks over the body of his fallen enemy shows him capable of the highest magnanimity.

No more than any other of the major persons in the play has Antony a wholly attractive and sympathetic personality; but for what he does and what he stands for, he is intended, I think, to gain a generous measure of sympathy and admiration.

# Place and Time in *Hamlet*

Harley Granville-Barker

Harley Granville-Barker analyzes the way William
Shakespeare structures place and time in *Hamlet*.
Though characters make journeys outside the castle,
the entire play is set in Elsinore, from which characters report on action in other places. By keeping the
play's events in one place, Granville-Barker says,
Shakespeare heightens the tension of Hamlet's inability to act. Likewise, Shakespeare heightens awareness
of Hamlet's inaction by associating time with Hamlet's
moods. Shakespeare alternately ignores and remarks
on references to time when Hamlet deliberates or
waits. When he acts, Shakespeare gives events an
hour or day or month. This use of place and time
brings Hamlet's hesitation into sharper focus,
Granville-Barker contends.

There is both a place-structure and a time-structure in *Hamlet*. The place-structure depends upon no exact localization of
scenes. The time-structure answers to no scheme of act-
division. But each has its dramatic import.

The action of *Hamlet* is concentrated at Elsinore; and this
though there is much external interest, and the story abounds
in journeys. As a rule in such a case, unless they are mere
messengers, we travel with the travelers. But we do not see
Laertes in Paris, nor, more surprisingly, Hamlet among the pi-
rates; and the Norwegian affair is dealt with by hearsay till the
play is two-thirds over. This is not done to economize time, or
to leave space for more capital [important] events. Scenes in
Norway or Paris or aboard ship need be no longer than the
talk of them, and Hamlet's discovery of the King's plot against
him is a capital event. Shakespeare is deliberately concentrat-
ing his action at Elsinore. When he does at last introduce Fort-

Excerpted from *Prefaces to Shakespeare* by Harley Granville-Barker, vol. 1 (Princeton,
NJ: Princeton University Press, 1946).

inbras he stretches probability to bring him and his army seemingly to its very suburbs; and, sooner than that Hamlet should carry the action abroad with him, Horatio is left behind there to keep him in our minds. On the other hand he still, by allusion, makes the most of this movement abroad which he does not represent; he even adds to our sense of it by such seemingly superfluous touches as tell us that Horatio has journeyed from Wittenberg, that Rosencrantz and Guildenstern have been "sent for"—and even the Players are traveling.

The double dramatic purpose is plain. Here is a tragedy of inaction; the center of it is Hamlet, who is physically inactive too, has "foregone all custom of exercises," will not "walk out of the air," but only, book in hand, for "four hours together, here in the lobby." The concentration at Elsinore of all that happens enhances the impression of this inactivity, which is enhanced again by the sense also given us of the constant coming and going around Hamlet of the busier world without. The place itself, moreover, thus acquires a personality, and even develops a sort of sinister power; so that when at last Hamlet does depart from it (his duty still unfulfilled) and we are left with the conscience-sick Gertrude and the guilty King, the mad Ophelia, a Laertes set on his own revenge, among a

>                          people muddied,
> Thick and unwholesome in their thoughts and whispers . . .

we almost seem to feel it, and the unpurged sin of it, summoning him back to his duty and his doom. Shakespeare has, in fact, here adopted something very like unity of place; upon no principle, but to gain a specific dramatic end.

He turns time to dramatic use also, ignores or remarks its passing, and uses clock or calendar or falsifies or neglects them just as it suits him.

## THE BEGINNING FRAMED BY NIGHTS

The play opens upon the stroke of midnight, an ominous and "dramatic" hour. The first scene is measured out to dawn and gains importance by that. In the second Hamlet's "not two months dead" and "within a month . . ." give past events convincing definition, and his "tonight . . . tonight . . . upon the platform 'twixt eleven and twelve" a specific imminence to what is to come. The second scene upon the platform is also definitely measured out from midnight to near dawn. This framing of the exordium [introduction] to the tragedy within a precise two nights and a day gives a convincing lifelikeness to the action, and sets its pulse beating rhythmically and arrestingly.

## SLOWING THE PACE BY IGNORING TIME

But now the conduct of the action changes, and with this the treatment of time. Hamlet's resolution—we shall soon gather—has paled, his purpose has slackened. He passes hour upon hour pacing the lobbies, reading or lost in thought, oblivious apparently to time's passing, lapsed—he himself supplies the phrase later—"lapsed in time." So Shakespeare also for a while tacitly ignores the calendar. When Polonius dispatches Reynaldo we are not told whether Laertes has already reached Paris. Presumably he has, but the point is left vague. The Ambassadors return from their mission to Norway. They must, one would suppose, have been absent for some weeks; but again, we are not told. Why not insist at once that Hamlet has let a solid two months pass and made no move, instead of letting us learn it quite incidentally later? There is more than one reason for not doing so. If the fact is explicitly stated that two months separate this scene from the last, that breaks our sense of a continuity in the action; a thing not to be done if it can be avoided, for this sense of continuity helps to sustain illusion, and so to hold us attentive. An alternative would be to insert a scene or more dealing with occurrences during these two months, and thus bridge the gap in time. But a surplusage of incidental matter is also and always to be avoided. Polonius' talk to Reynaldo, Shakespeare feels, is relaxation and distraction enough; for with that scene only halfway through he returns to his main theme.

He could, however, circumvent such difficulties if he would. His capital reason for ignoring time hereabouts is that Hamlet is ignoring it, and he wants to attune the whole action—and us—to Hamlet's mood. He takes advantage of this passivity; we learn to know our man, as it were, at leisure. Facet after facet of him is turned to us. Polonius and Rosencrantz and Guildenstern are mirrors surrounding and reflecting him. His silence as he sits listening to the Players—and we, as we listen, watch him—admits us to closer touch with him. And when, lest the tension of the action slacken too much in this atmosphere of timelessness, the clock must be restarted, a simple, incidental, phrase or two is made to serve.

It is not until later that Shakespeare, by a cunning little stroke, puts himself right—so to speak—with the past. *The Murder of Gonzago* is about to begin when Hamlet says to Ophelia:

> look you, how cheerfully my mother looks, and my father died within's two hours.

—to be answered

> Nay, 'tis twice two months, my lord.

There is the calendar reestablished; unostentatiously, and therefore with no forfeiting of illusion. Yet at that moment we are expectantly attentive, so every word will tell. And it is a stroke of character too. For here is Hamlet, himself so lately roused from his obliviousness, gibing at his mother for hers.

## TIME CORRESPONDS TO ACTION

But the use of time for current effect has begun again, and very appropriately, with Hamlet's fresh impulse to action, and his decision, reached while he listens abstractedly to the Player's speech, to test the King's guilt:

> we'll hear a play to-morrow. Dost thou hear me, old friend; can you play the Murder of Gonzago? . . . We'll ha't to-morrow night.

We do not yet know what is in his mind. But from this moment the pressure and pace of the play's action are to increase; and the brisk "tomorrow" and "tomorrow night" help give the initial impulse. The increase is progressive. In the next scene the play is no longer to be "tomorrow" but "tonight." The King, a little later, adds to the pressure. When he has overheard Hamlet with Ophelia:

> I have in quick determination
> Thus set it down; he shall with speed to England. . . .

And this—still progressively—becomes, after the play-scene and the killing of Polonius:

> The sun no sooner shall the mountains touch
> But we will ship him hence. . . .

After the spell of timelessness, then, we have an exciting stretch of the action carried through in a demonstrated day and a night. But the time-measure is not in itself the important thing. It is only used to validate the dramatic speed, even as was timelessness to help slow the action down.

## OPHELIA'S MADNESS HAS NO TIME

After this comes more ignoring of the calendar, though the dramatic purpose in doing so is somewhat different. The scene which follows Hamlet's departure opens with the news of Ophelia's madness. We are not told how much time has elapsed. For the moment the incidental signs are against any pronounced gap. Polonius has already been buried, but "in hugger-mugger"; and Ophelia, whom we last saw smiling and suffering under Hamlet's torture, might well have lost her wits at the very news that her father had been killed, and that the man she loved had killed him. But suddenly Laertes appears in full-blown rebellion. With this it is clear why the calendar has been ignored. Shakespeare has had to face the same sort

### THE ARTIST: INSPIRED OR DELIBERATE

*Critics write about poets' use of methods and techniques and devices, as if they deliberately chose to write with these in mind. Other readers envision the inspired artist whose work arrives full blown on paper when the spirit is moved. In a chapter entitled "Construction in Shakespeare's Tragedies," A.C. Bradley concludes that Shakespeare was both inspired and deliberate.*

In speaking, for convenience, of devices and expedients, I did not intend to imply that Shakespeare always deliberately aimed at the effects which he produced. But *no* artist always does this, and I see no reason to doubt that Shakespeare often did it, or to suppose that his method of constructing and composing differed, except in degree, from that of the most 'conscious' of artists. The antithesis of art and inspiration, though not meaningless, is often most misleading. Inspiration is surely not incompatible with considerate workmanship. The two may be severed, but they need not be so, and where a genuinely poetic result is being produced they cannot be so. The glow of a first conception must in some measure survive or re-kindle itself in the work of planning and executing. . . . It is probable that Shakespeare often wrote fluently, for [man of letters Ben] Jonson (a better authority than [John] Heminge and [Henry] Condell [fellow actors of Shakespeare who published the first folio in 1623]) says so; and for anything we can tell he may also have constructed with unusual readiness. But we know that he revised and re-wrote (for instance in *Love's Labour's Lost* and *Romeo and Juliet* and *Hamlet*); it is almost impossible that he can have worked out the plots of his best plays without much reflection and many experiments; and it appears to me scarcely more possible to mistake the signs of deliberate care in some of his famous speeches. If a 'conscious artist' means one who holds his work away from him, scrutinises and judges it, and, if need be, alters it and alters it till it comes as near satisfying him as he can make it, I am sure that Shakespeare frequently employed such conscious art. If it means, again, an artist who consciously aims at the effects he produces, what ground have we for doubting that he frequently employed such art, though probably less frequently than a good many other poets?

A.C. Bradley, *Shakespearean Tragedy: Hamlet, Othello, King Lear, Macbeth.* New York: World Publishing, 1961.

of difficulty as before. Let him admit a definite gap in time, realistically required for the return of Laertes and the raising of the rebellion, and he must either break the seeming continuity of the action, or build a bridge of superfluous matter and slacken a tension already sufficiently slackened by the passing of the Fortinbras army and Hamlet's "How all occasions . . ." soliloquy. So he takes a similar way out, ignoring incongruities, merely putting in the King's mouth the passing excuse that Laertes

> is *in secret* come from France . . .
> And wants not buzzers to infect his ear
> With pestilent speeches of his father's death . . .

—an excuse which would hardly bear consideration if we were allowed to consider it; but it is at this very instant that the tumult begins. And once again the technical maneuvering is turned to dramatic account. The surprise of Laertes' appearance, the very inadequacy and confusion of its explanation, and his prompt success, are in pertinent contrast to Hamlet's elaborate preparations—and his failure.

## TIME RETURNS WHEN HAMLET RETURNS

Only with news of Hamlet do we revert to the calendar, and then with good reason. By setting a certain time for his return, the tension of the action is automatically increased. First, in the letter to Horatio, the past is built up:

> Ere we were *two days* old at sea, a pirate of very warlike appointment gave us chase.

Then, in a letter to the King:

> *To-morrow* shall I beg leave to see your kingly eyes. . . .

—the resumption of the war between them is made imminent. The scene in the graveyard thus takes place on the morrow; and this is verified for us as it ends, by the King's whisper to Laertes:

> Strengthen your patience in our *last night's* speech. . . .

The general effect produced—not, and it need not be, a very marked one—is of events moving steadily now, unhurriedly, according to plan; the deliberation of Hamlet's returning talk to the Gravediggers suggests this, and it accords with the King's cold-blooded plot and Laertes' resolution.

The calendar must again be ignored after the angry parting of Hamlet and Laertes over Ophelia's grave. If it were not, Shakespeare would either have to bring in superfluous matter and most probably slacken tension (which he will certainly not want to do so near the end of his play) or explain and excuse an indecently swift passing from a funeral to a fencing match. He inserts instead a solid wedge of the history of the King's treachery and the trick played on the wretched Rosencrantz and Guildenstern. This sufficiently absorbs our attention, and dramatically separates the two incongruous events. It incidentally builds up the past still more solidly; and there is again a falsifying hint of time elapsed in Horatio's comment that

> It must be shortly known to him [Claudius] from England
> What is the issue of the business there.

—which is to be justified when all is over by the actual arrival of the English ambassadors to announce that the

> commandment is fulfilled,
> That Rosencrantz and Guildenstern are dead.

But this will simply be to give a sense of completeness to the action. Nothing is said or done to check its steady progress from the graveyard scene to the end; for that is the capital consideration involved.

## SHAKESPEARE'S CONCERN WITH TEMPO, NOT TIME

It comes to this, I think. Shakespeare's true concern is with *tempo*, not time. He uses time as an auxiliary, and makes free with it, and with the calendar to make his use of it convincing.

When he came to playwriting, time, it is true enough to say, was commonly being put to no dramatic use at all. A few passing references to "tonight," "tomorrow" or "the other day" there might be; for the rest, a play's end would leave a vague impression that so many events must have asked a fair amount of time for their enacting. This was not freedom—though it might seem to be—but anarchy; and he soon saw that some scheme of time would strengthen a play's action and add to the illusion. For the unlikeliest story can be made more convincing by supplying it with a date or so.

An accurately realistic time-scheme, with the clock of the action going tick by tick with the watches in our pockets—that the theater can hardly be brought to accommodate. Few good stories can be made to pass in the two or three hours allowed for the acting of a play, still fewer if they must include striking and varied events. There are three main ways of dealing with the matter. Each belongs to a different sort of theater and a different type of drama. There is the so-called "classic" way. This may involve rather the ignoring than any plain falsifying of time. The drama accommodating it is apt to concentrate upon one capital event, the approaches to it elaborately prepared;

and—with a master dramatist at work—motive after motive, trait after trait of character, will be unfolded like petals, till the heart of the matter is disclosed and the inevitable conclusion reached. There is the normal modern method of a suggested realism in "time," appropriate to a scenic theater's realism of place. This commonly goes with a selecting of various events to be presented, one (or it may be more) to an act, the gaps in time between them accounted for by the act-divisions, the rest of the story relegated to hearsay and a sort of no man's land between the acts. Each act then becomes something of a play in itself as well as a part of one, the resulting whole a solid multiple structure, the economy of its technique akin to that of sound building, as thrifty and precise.

## SHAKESPEARE'S FREEDOM IN TIME AND IN SPACE

Lastly there is Shakespeare's freedom in time, which is the natural product of his stage's freedom in space, and which— coupled with this—permits him a panoramic display of his entire story if need be, and uninterrupted action. And, having brought time out of anarchy, he is not concerned to regulate his use of it very strictly. He adds it to his other freedoms. Moreover he may take the greater liberties with it, because, for his audience, in their own actual world, the sense of time is so uncertain.

In nothing are we more open to illusion and suggestion than in our sense of time. We live imaginative lives of our own to quite another measure than the calendar's; a year ago might be yesterday; tomorrow will be days in coming, and gone in an hour. The Elizabethan convention of freedom in space, which depended upon the planning of the theater, shrank with each restrictive change in this and at last disappeared; but the dramatist may still exercise—in the most realistic surroundings—a discreet freedom in time. We readily welcome that fiction.

Study of Shakespeare's stagecraft has shown us how we wrong it by depriving the plays when we present them of their freedom in space, by obstructing those swift, frictionless passages from here to there, or by defining whereabouts when he knew better than to define it. This freedom in time is also a part of his imaginative privilege. He makes his play a thing of movement, even as music is, and obedient to much the same laws; and the clock and the calendar are merely among the means by which this movement is made expressive.

# Hamlet's Melancholy

A.C. Bradley

For nearly four centuries, scholars and critics have speculated about the qualities in Hamlet's character that make him unable to act on behalf of his murdered father. A.C. Bradley argues that melancholy, as the Elizabethans thought of it, best explains Hamlet's inaction. Bradley also argues that Hamlet's nature—his morality, optimism, idealism, and intelligence—incline him to melancholy, and his situation, losing a father and seeing his mother remarry his uncle, intensifies the inclination. Of all the theories, melancholy is the most logical because it accounts for the largest number of words and actions in the play, according to Bradley.

Trying to reconstruct from the Hamlet of the play, one would not judge that his temperament was melancholy in the present sense of the word; there seems nothing to show that; but one would judge that by temperament he was inclined to nervous instability, to rapid and perhaps extreme changes of feeling and mood, and that he was disposed to be, for the time, absorbed in the feeling or mood that possessed him, whether it were joyous or depressed. This temperament the Elizabethans would have called a melancholic; and Hamlet seems to be an example of it. . . . [Shakespeare] gives to Hamlet a temperament which would not develop into melancholy unless under some exceptional strain, but which still involved a danger. In the play we see the danger realised, and find a melancholy quite unlike any that Shakespeare had as yet depicted, because the temperament of Hamlet is quite different.

## HAMLET'S NATURAL TEMPERAMENT: MORAL, OPTIMISTIC, IDEALISTIC, AND INTELLECTUAL

Next, we cannot be mistaken in attributing to the Hamlet of earlier days an exquisite sensibility, to which we may give the name 'moral.'. . . He had the soul of the youthful poet as

From *Shakespearean Tragedy: Hamlet, Othello, King Lear, Macbeth* by A.C. Bradley, 1st edition (New York: Macmillan, 1904).

[British poets Percy Bysshe] Shelley and [Alfred, Lord] Tennyson have described it, an unbounded delight and faith in everything good and beautiful. We know this from himself. The world for him was *herrlich wie am ersten Tag*—[splendid as on the first day] 'this goodly frame the earth, this most excellent canopy the air, this brave o'er hanging firmament, this majestical roof fretted with golden fire.' And not nature only: 'What a piece of work is a man! how noble in reason! how infinite in faculty! in form and moving how express and admirable! in action how like an angel! in apprehension how like a god!' This is no commonplace to Hamlet; it is the language of a heart thrilled with wonder and swelling into ecstasy. . . .

To the very end, his soul, however sick and tortured it may be, answers instantaneously when good and evil are presented

## HAMLET THINKS TOO MUCH

*Nineteenth-century British Romantic poet and critic Samuel Taylor Coleridge read in Shakespeare a belief that successful functioning requires a person's imagination balanced with reality acquired through the senses. Here Coleridge professes that Hamlet is unable to act because the equilibrium between his imagination and his sense reality of the world is disrupted. Hamlet broods and reflects excessively and loses his will and power to act.*

In Hamlet [Shakespeare] seems to have wished to exemplify the moral necessity of a due balance between our attention to the objects of our senses, and our meditation on the workings of our minds—an *equilibrium* between the real and the imaginary worlds. In Hamlet this balance is disturbed. . . .

The effect of this overbalanced of the imaginative power is beautifully illustrated in the everlasting broodings and superfluous activities of Hamlet's mind, which, unseated from its healthy relation, is constantly occupied with the world within, and abstracted from the world without—giving substance to shadows, and throwing a mist over all commonplace actualities. It is the nature of thought to be indefinite—definiteness belongs to external imagery alone. . . .

Hamlet's character is the prevalence of the abstracting and generalizing habit over the practical. He does not want [lack] courage, skill, will, or opportunity; but every incident sets him thinking; and it is curious, and, at the same time strictly natural, that Hamlet, who all the play seems reason itself, should be impelled, at last, by mere accident to effect his object.

Samuel Taylor Coleridge, *Shakespearean Criticism*. Edited by T.M. Raysor. 2 vols. Boston: Harvard University Press, 1930.

to it, loving the one and hating the other. He is called a sceptic who has no firm belief in anything, but he is never sceptical about *them.*

And the negative side of his idealism, the aversion to evil, is perhaps even more developed in the hero of the tragedy than in the Hamlet of earlier days. It is intensely characteristic. Nothing, I believe, is to be found elsewhere in Shakespeare (unless in the rage of the disillusioned idealist Timon) of quite the same kind as Hamlet's disgust at his uncle's drunkenness, his loathing of his mother's sensuality, his astonishment and horror at her shallowness, his contempt for everything pretentious or false, his indifference to everything merely external. This last characteristic appears in his choice of the friend of his heart, and in a certain impatience of distinctions of rank or wealth. When Horatio calls his father 'a goodly king,' he answers, surely with an emphasis on 'man,'

> He was a man, take him for all in all,
> I shall not look upon his like again.

. . . With this temperament and this sensibility we find, lastly, in the Hamlet of earlier days, as of later, intellectual genius. It is chiefly this that makes him so different from all those about him, good and bad alike, and hardly less different from most of Shakespeare's other heroes. And this, though on the whole the most important trait in his nature, is also so obvious and so famous that I need not dwell on it at length. But against one prevalent misconception I must say a word of warning. Hamlet's intellectual power is not a specific gift, like a genius for music or mathematics or philosophy. It shows itself, fitfully, in the affairs of life as unusual quickness of perception, great agility in shifting the mental attitude, a striking rapidity and fertility in resource; so that, when his natural belief in others does not make him unwary, Hamlet sees through them and masters them, and no one can be much less like the typical helpless dreamer. It shows itself in conversation chiefly in the form of wit or humour; and, alike in conversation and in soliloquy, it shows itself in the form of imagination quite as much as in that of thought in the stricter sense. . . .

## HAMLET: A WELL-ROUNDED, THINKING INDIVIDUAL

There was a necessity in his soul driving him to penetrate below the surface and to question what others took for granted. That fixed habitual look which the world wears for most men did not exist for him. He was for ever unmaking his world and rebuilding it in thought, dissolving what to others were solid facts, and discovering what to others were old truths. . . . It has appeared that Hamlet did *not* live the life of a mere student, much less of a mere dreamer, and that his nature was by no means simply or even one-sidedly intellectual, but was healthily active. Hence, granted the ordinary chances of life, there would seem to be no great danger in his intellectual tendency and his habit of speculation; and I would go further and say that there was nothing in them, taken alone, to unfit him even for the extraordinary call that was made upon him. . . .

## MELANCHOLY MAKES REFLECTIVENESS AND GENIUS DANGEROUS

On the other hand, under conditions of a peculiar kind, Hamlet's reflectiveness certainly might prove dangerous to him, and his genius might even (to exaggerate a little) become his doom. Suppose that violent shock to his moral being of which I spoke; and suppose that under this shock, any possible action being denied to him, he began to sink into melancholy; then, no doubt, his imaginative and generalising habit of mind might extend the effects of this shock through his whole being and mental world. And if, the state of melancholy being thus deepened and fixed, a sudden demand for difficult and decisive action in a matter connected with the melancholy arose, this state might well have for one of its symptoms an endless and futile mental dissection of the required deed. And, finally, the futility of this process, and the shame of his delay, would further weaken him and enslave him to his melancholy still more. Thus the speculative habit would be *one* indirect cause of the morbid state which hindered action; and it would also reappear in a degenerate form as one of the *symptoms* of this morbid state.

Now this is what actually happens in the play. Turn to the first words Hamlet utters when he is alone; turn, that is to say, to the place where the author is likely to indicate his meaning most plainly. What do you hear?

> O, that this too too solid flesh would melt,
> Thaw and resolve itself into a dew!
> Or that the Everlasting had not fix'd
> His canon 'gainst self-slaughter! O God! God!
> How weary, stale, flat and unprofitable,
> Seem to me all the uses of this world!
> Fie on't! ah fie! 'tis an unweeded garden,
> That grows to seed; things rank and gross in nature
> Possess it merely.

Here are a sickness of life, and even a longing for death, so intense that nothing stands between Hamlet and suicide except religious awe. And what has caused them? The rest of the soliloquy so thrusts the answer upon us that it might seem impossible to miss it. It was not his father's death; that doubtless brought deep grief, but mere grief for some one loved and lost does not make a noble spirit loathe the world as a place full only of things rank and gross. It was not the vague suspicion that we know Hamlet felt. Still less was it the loss of the crown; for though the subserviency of the electors might well disgust him, there is not a reference to the subject in the soliloquy, nor any sign elsewhere that it greatly occupied his mind. It was the moral shock of the sudden ghastly disclosure of his mother's true nature, falling on him when his heart was aching with love, and his body doubtless was weakened by sorrow. And it is essential, however disagreeable, to realise the nature of this shock. It matters little here whether Hamlet's age was twenty or thirty: in either case his mother was a matron of mature years. All his life he had believed in her, we may be sure, as such a son would. He had seen her not merely devoted to his father, but hanging on him like a newly-wedded bride, hanging on him

As if increase of appetite had grown
By what it fed on.

He had seen her following his body 'like Niobe, all tears.' And then within a month—'O God! A beast would have mourned longer'—she married again, and married Hamlet's uncle, a man utterly contemptible and loathsome in his eyes; married him in what to Hamlet was incestuous wedlock; married him not for any reason of state, nor even out of old family affection, but in such a way that her son was forced to see in her action not only an astounding shallowness of feeling but an eruption of coarse sensuality, 'rank and gross,' speeding post-haste to its horrible delight. Is it possible to conceive an experience more desolating to a man such as we have seen Hamlet to be; and is its result anything but perfectly natural? It brings bewildered horror, then loathing, than despair of human nature. His whole mind is poisoned. He can never see Ophelia in the same light again: she is a woman, and his mother is a woman: if she mentions the word 'brief' to him, the answer drops from his lips like venom, 'as woman's love.' The last words of the soliloquy, which is *wholly* concerned with this subject, are,

But break, my heart, for I must hold my tongue!

He can do nothing. He must lock in his heart, not any suspicion of his uncle that moves obscurely there, but that horror and loathing; and if his heart ever found relief, it was when those feelings, mingled with the love that never died out in him, poured themselves forth in a flood as he stood in his mother's chamber beside his father's marriage-bed.

If we still wonder, and ask why the effect of this shock should be so tremendous, let us observe that *now* the conditions have arisen under which Hamlet's highest endowments, his moral sensibility and his genius, become his enemies. A nature morally blunter would have felt even so dreadful a revelation less keenly. A slower and more limited and positive mind might not have extended so widely through its world the disgust and disbelief that have entered it. But Hamlet has the imagination which, for evil as well as good, feels and sees all things in one. Thought is the element of his life, and his thought is infected. He cannot prevent himself from probing and lacerating the wound in his soul. One idea, full of peril, holds him fast, and he cries out in agony at it, but is impotent to free himself ('Must I remember?' 'Let me not think on't'). And when, with the fading of his passion, the vividness of this idea abates, it does so only to leave behind a boundless weariness and a sick longing for death.

### FATE STRIKES IN HAMLET'S HOUR OF WEAKNESS

And this is the time which his fate chooses. In this hour of uttermost weakness, this sinking of his whole being towards annihilation, there comes on him, bursting the bounds of the natural world with a shock of astonishment and terror, the revelation of his mother's adultery and his father's murder, and, with this, the demand on him, in the name of everything dearest and most sacred, to arise and act. And for a moment, though his brain reels and totters, his soul leaps up in passion to answer this demand. But it comes too late. It does not strike home the last rivet in the melancholy which holds him bound.

> The time is out of joint! O cursed spite
> That ever I was born to set it right,—

so he mutters within an hour of the moment when he vowed to give his life to the duty of revenge; and the rest of the story exhibits his vain efforts to fulfil this duty, his unconscious self-excuses and unavailing self-reproaches, and the tragic results of his delay. . . .

### RESULTS OF MELANCHOLY

Let me try to show now, briefly, how much this melancholy accounts for.

It accounts for the main fact, Hamlet's inaction. For the *immediate* cause of that is simply that his habitual feeling is one of disgust at life and everything in it, himself included,—a disgust which varies in intensity, rising at times into a longing for death, sinking often into weary apathy, but is never dispelled for more than brief intervals. Such a state of feeling is inevitably adverse to *any* kind of decided action; the body is inert, the mind indifferent or worse; its response is, 'it does not matter,' 'it is not worth while,' 'it is no good.' And the action required of Hamlet is very exceptional. It is violent, dangerous, difficult to accomplish perfectly, on one side repulsive to a man of honour and sensitive feeling, on another side involved in a certain mystery (here come in thus, in their subordinate place, various causes of inaction assigned by various theories [other critics have theories to explain Hamlet's inaction, all of which Bradley refutes]. These obstacles would not suffice to prevent Hamlet from acting, if his state were normal; and against them there operate, even in his morbid state, healthy and positive feelings, love of his father, loathing of his uncle, desire of revenge, desire to do duty. But the retarding motives acquire an unnatural strength because they have an ally in something far stronger than themselves, the melancholic disgust and apathy; while the healthy motives, emerging with difficulty form the central mass of diseased feeling, rapidly sink back into it and 'lose the name of action.'. . .

Again, this state accounts for Hamlet's energy as well as for his lassitude [diminished energy], those quick decided actions of his being the outcome of a nature normally far from passive, now suddenly stimulated, and producing healthy impulses which work themselves out before they have time to subside. It accounts for the evidently keen satisfaction which some of these actions give to him. He arranges the play-scene with lively interest, and exults in its success, not really because it brings him nearer to his goal, but partly because it has hurt his enemy and partly because it has demonstrated his own skill. . . .

It accounts no less for the painful features of his character as seen in the play, his almost savage irritability on the one hand, and on the other his self-absorption, his callousness, his insensibility to the fates of those whom he despises, and to the feelings even of those whom he loves. These are frequent symptoms of such melancholy, and they sometimes alternate, as they do in Hamlet, with bursts of transitory, almost hysterical, and quite fruitless emotion. It is to these last (of which a

part of the soliloquy, 'O what a rogue,' gives a good example)
that Hamlet alludes when to the Ghost, he speaks of himself as
'lapsed in *passion*,' and it is doubtless partly his conscious
weakness in regard to them that inspires his praise of Horatio
as a man who is not 'passion's slave.'

Finally, Hamlet's melancholy accounts for two things which
seem to be explained by nothing else. The first of these is his
apathy or 'lethargy.' We are bound to consider the evidence
which the text supplies of this, though it is usual to ignore it.
When Hamlet mentions, as one possible cause of his inaction,
his 'thinking too precisely on the event,' he mentions another,
'bestial oblivion'; and the thing against which he inveighs in
the greater part of that soliloquy is not the excess or the mis-
use of reason (which for him here and always is god-like), but
this *bestial* oblivion or '*dullness*,' this 'letting all *sleep*,' this allowing of heaven-sent reason to 'fust unused':

> What is a man,
> If his chief good and market of his time
> Be but to sleep and feed? a beast, no more.

... The second trait which is fully explained only by Hamlet's melancholy is his own inability to understand why he delays. This emerges in a marked degree when an occasion like
the player's emotion or the sight of Fortinbras's army stings
Hamlet into shame at his inaction. '*Why*,' he asks himself in
genuine bewilderment, 'do I linger? Can the cause be cowardice? Can it be sloth? Can it be thinking too precisely of the
event? And does *that* again mean cowardice? What is it that
makes me sit idle when I feel it is shameful to do so, and when
I have *cause, and will, and strength, and means*, to act?' A man
irresolute merely because he was considering a proposed action too minutely would not feel this bewilderment. A man
might feel it whose conscience secretly condemned the act
which his explicit consciousness approved; but we have seen
that there is no sufficient evidence to justify us in conceiving
Hamlet thus. These are the questions of a man stimulated for
the moment to shake off the weight of his melancholy, and because for the moment he is free from it, unable to understand
the paralysing pressure which it exerts at other times.

I have dwelt thus at length on Hamlet's melancholy because, from the psychological point of view, it is the centre of
the tragedy, and to omit it from consideration or to underrate
its intensity is to make Shakespeare's story unintelligible. But
the psychological point of view is not equivalent to the tragic;
and, having once given its due weight to the fact of Hamlet's

melancholy, we may freely admit, or rather may be anxious to insist, that this pathological condition would excite but little, if any, tragic interest if it were not the condition of a nature distinguished by that speculative genius on which the [German Romantic writer August Wilhelm von] Schlegel-Coleridge type of theory lays stress [both Schlegel and Coleridge thought Hamlet failed to act because of his reflective mind]. Such theories misinterpret the connection between that genius and Hamlet's failure, but still it is this connection which gives to his story its peculiar fascination and makes it appear (if the phrase may be allowed) as the symbol of a tragic mystery inherent in human nature. Wherever this mystery touches us, wherever we are forced to feel the wonder and awe of man's godlike 'apprehension' and his 'thoughts that wander through eternity,' and at the same time are forced to see him powerless in his petty sphere of action, and powerless (it would appear) from the very divinity of his thought, we remember Hamlet. And this is the reason why, in the great ideal movement which began towards the close of the eighteenth century, this tragedy acquired a position unique among Shakespeare's dramas, and shared only by [German writer Johann Wolfgang von] Goethe's *Faust*. It was not that *Hamlet* is Shakespeare's greatest tragedy or most perfect work of art; it was that *Hamlet* most brings home to us at once the sense of the soul's infinity, and the sense of the doom which not only circumscribes that infinity but appears to be its offspring.

# Imagery in *Hamlet* Reveals Character and Theme

W.H. Clemen

W.H. Clemen analyzes a new form of imagery William Shakespeare created in *Hamlet*. In the earlier plays, his imagery is more formal, more literary, but Hamlet speaks naturally in everyday, precise images. He ably and quickly shifts the kind of images to fit the person he speaks to or to fit the person who overhears him. Clemen argues that Hamlet's imagery reveals his education and intellectual insight, serves as a relief for inner tension, and helps him feign madness. In particular, the Ghost's leprous skin disease and the image of weeds introduced early in the play symbolize a major theme of the play.

It is Hamlet who creates the most significant images, images marking the atmosphere and theme of the play, which are paler and less pregnant in the speech of the other characters. Hamlet's way of employing images is unique in Shakespeare's drama. When he begins to speak, the images fairly stream to him without the slightest effort—not as similes or conscious paraphrases, but as immediate and spontaneous visions. Hamlet's imagery shows us that whenever he thinks and speaks, he is at the same time a visionary, a seer, for whom the living things of the world about him embody and symbolize thought. His first monologue may show this; the short space of time which lies between his father's death and his mother's remarriage is to him a series of pictures taken from real life:

> A little month, or ere those shoes were old
> With which she follow'd my poor father's body
> Like Niobe, all tears: (I. ii.)

From W.H. Clemen, "Hamlet," in *The Development of Shakespeare's Imagery* (London: Methuen, 1951). Reprinted by permission of Routledge publishers.

> Ere yet the salt of most unrighteous tears
> Had left the flushing in her galled eyes,                    (I. ii.)

or a little later, addressed to Horatio:

> the funeral baked meats
> Did coldly furnish forth the marriage tables.                (I. ii.)

These are no poetic similes, but keen observations of reality. Hamlet does not translate the general thought into an image paraphrasing it; on the contrary, he uses the opposite method: he refers the generalization to the events and objects of the reality underlying the thought. This sense of reality finds expression in all the images Hamlet employs. Peculiar to them all is that closeness to reality which is often carried to the point of an unsparing poignancy. They are mostly very concrete and precise, simple and, as to their subject matter, easy to understand; common and ordinary things, things familiar to the man in the street dominate, rather than lofty, strange or rare objects. Illuminating in this connection is the absence of hyperbole, of great dimensions in his imagery. In contrast to Othello or Lear, for example, who awaken heaven and the elements in their imagery and who lend expression to their mighty passions in images of soaring magnificence, Hamlet prefers to keep his language within the scope of reality, indeed, within the everyday world. It is not spacious scenery and nature which dominate in Hamlet's imagery, but rather trades and callings, objects of daily use, popular games and technical terms; his images are not beautiful, poetic, magnificent, but they always hit their mark, the matter in question, with surprisingly unerring sureness. They do not waft the things of reality into a dream-world of the imagination; on the contrary, they make them truly *real*, they reveal their inmost, naked being. All this, the wealth of realistic observation, of real objects, of associations taken from everyday life, is enough to prove that Hamlet is no abstract thinker and dreamer. As his imagery betrays to us, he is rather a man gifted with greater powers of observation than the others. He is capable of scanning reality with a keener eye and of penetrating the veil of semblance even to the very core of things. "I know not seems."

## HAMLET'S IMAGERY REVEALS THE MAN

At the same time, Hamlet's imagery reveals the hero's wide educational background, his many-sidedness and the extraordinary range of his experience. That metaphors taken from natural sciences are specially frequent in Hamlet's language again emphasizes his power of observation, his critical objective way

of looking at things. But Hamlet is also at home in classical an-
tiquity or Greek mythology, in the terminology of law, he is not
only familiar with the theatre and with acting—as everyone
knows—but also with the fine arts, with falconry and hunting,
with the soldier's trade and strategy, with the courtier's way of
life. All these spheres disclosing Hamlet's personality as that of
a "courtier, soldier and scholar," (in Ophelia's words, III. i.) are
evoked by the imagery which, however, turns them to living
account by a fit application to situations, persons and moods.
Hamlet commands so many levels of expression that he can attune his diction as well as his imagery to the situation and to
the person to whom he is speaking. This adaptability and ver-
satility is another feature in Hamlet's use of language which
can also be traced in his imagery.

At the same time, this wide range of imagery can, in certain
passages, serve to give relief to his conflicting moods, to his
being torn between extremes and to the abruptness of his
changes of mood. This characteristic which has been particularly emphasized and partly attributed to "melancholy" by L.L.
Schücking [in *The Meaning of Hamlet*] and John Dover Wilson
[in *What Happens in Hamlet*], also expresses itself in the sudden change of language and in the juxtaposition [placement
side by side] of passages which are sharply contrasted in their
diction [word choice]. With no other character in Shakespeare
do we find this sharp contrast between images marked by a
pensive mood and those which unsparingly use vulgar words
and display a frivolous and sarcastic disgust for the world.

Let us consider further how Hamlet's use of imagery reflects his ability to penetrate to the real nature of men and
things and his relentless breaking down of the barriers raised
by hypocrisy. Many of his images seem in fact designed to un-
mask men; they are meant to strip them of their fine appearances and to show them up in their true nature. Thus, by
means of the simile of fortune's pipe, Hamlet shows Rosencrantz and Guildenstern that he has seen through their intent,
and thus he unmasks Rosencrantz when he calls him a
"sponge," "that soaks up the king's countenance" (IV. ii.). He
splits his mother's heart "in twain," because he tells her the
truth from which she shrinks and which she conceals from
herself. And again it is by means of images that he seeks to
lead her to a recognition of the truth. He renews the memory
of his father in her by means of that forceful description of his
outward appearance which could be compared with Hyperi-
on, Mars and Mercury. On the other hand, another series of

comparisons seeks to bring home to his mother the real nature of Claudius:

> a mildew'd ear,
> Blasting his wholesome brother.                               (III. iv.)

> a vice of kings;
> A cutpurse of the empire and the rule,
> That from a shelf the precious diadem stole,
> And put it in his pocket!...
> A king of shreds and patches...                              (III. iv.)

---

### MIXING STYLES IN HAMLET

*Shakespeare gives Hamlet a full range of language—from vul-
gar and everyday imagery to lyrical and courtly language—
sometimes within the same speech. At times Hamlet speaks a
mixture of prose and poetry, according to Paul A. Cantor in*
Shakespeare: Hamlet.

This mixture of style can even be found in some of Hamlet's
sustained passages in prose, for example, this speech to
Rosencrantz and Guildenstern:

> I will tell you why, so shall my anticipation prevent your dis-
> covery, and your secrecy to the King and Queen moult no feath-
> er. I have of late—but wherefore I know not—lost all my mirth,
> forgone all custom of exercises; and indeed it goes so heavily
> with my disposition, that this goodly frame, the earth, seems to
> me a sterile promontory; this most excellent canopy, the air,
> look you, this brave o'erhanging firmament, this majestical roof
> fretted with golden fire, why, it appeareth nothing to me but a
> foul and pestilent congregation of vapors. What a piece of work
> is a man, how noble in reason, how infinite in faculties, in form
> and moving, how express and admirable in action, how like an
> angel in apprehension, how like a god! the beauty of the world;
> the paragon of animals; and yet to me what is this quintessence
> of dust? Man delights not me—nor women neither, though by
> your smiling you seem to say so.                              (II. ii.)

This speech arises naturally out of Hamlet's dialogue with
Rosencrantz and Guildenstern as he discovers that they have
appeared in Elsinore at the request of the king and queen. The
quaint, almost barnyard imagery of his opening sentence
('moult no feather') seems to promise a colloquial [informal]
speech, and the way Hamlet begins to open up his heart to his
old friends further suggests that the speech will remain on the
conversational level. But Hamlet's speech quickly modulates
into something higher, as his agile mind begins to move outward from his immediate situation to adopt a worldwide and
then a cosmic perspective. Though the speech remains in
prose, it soons develops something like the rhythms of poetry.

Paul A. Cantor, *Shakespeare: Hamlet.* New York: Cambridge University Press, 1989.

So Hamlet sees through men and things. He perceives what is false, visualizing his recognition through imagery.

Hamlet's imagery, which thus calls things by their right names, acquires a peculiar freedom from his feigned madness. Hamlet needs images for his "antic disposition." He would betray himself if he used open direct language. Hence he must speak ambiguously and cloak his real meaning under quibbles [irrelevant objections] and puns, images and parables. The other characters do not understand him and continue to think he is mad, but the audience can gain an insight into the true situation. Under the protection of that mask of "antic disposition," Hamlet says more shrewd things than all the rest of the courtiers together. So we find the images here in an entirely new role, unique in Shakespeare's drama. Only the images of the fool in *King Lear* have a similar function.

Hamlet suffers an injustice when he is accused of merely theoretical and abstract speculation which would lead him away from reality. His thoughts carry further than those of others, because he sees more and deeper than they, not because he would leave reality unheeded. It is true that his is a nature more prone to thought than to action; but that signifies by no means, as the Hamlet critics would often have us believe, that he is a philosopher and dreamer and no man of the world. When, in the graveyard scene, he holds Yorick's skull in his hand, he sees *more* in it than the others, for whom the skull is merely a lifeless object. And precisely because he is more deeply moved by the reality and significance of these earthly remains, his fantasy is able to follow the "noble dust of Alexander" through all its metamorphoses [transformations]. The comparisons which spring from this faculty of thinking a thing to the end, as it were, derive in fact from a more intense experience of reality. . . .

## THE GHOST'S LEPROUS DISEASE TRANSFORMED INTO IMAGERY

It is characteristic of Hamlet, to express even those things which would have permitted of a generalizing formulation, in a language which bears the stamp of a unique and personal experience. Hamlet sees this problem under the aspect of a process of the human organism. The original bright colouring of the skin is concealed by an ailment. Thus the relation between thought and action appears not as an opposition between two abstract principles between which a free choice is possible, but as an unavoidable condition of human nature. The image of the leprous ailment emphasizes the malignant, disabling, slowly disintegrating nature of the process. It is by no mere chance that Hamlet employs just this image. Perusing the description which the ghost of Hamlet's father gives of his poisoning by Claudius (I. v.) one cannot help being struck by the vividness with which the process of poisoning, the malicious spreading of the disease, is portrayed:

> And in the porches of mine ears did pour
> The leperous distilment; whose effect
> Holds such an enmity with blood of man
> That swift as quicksilver it courses through
> The natural gates and alleys of the body,
> And with a sudden vigour it doth posset
> And curd, like eager droppings into milk,
> The thin and wholesome blood: so did it mine;
> And a most instant tetter bark'd about,
> Most lazar-like, with vile and loathsome crust,
> All my smooth body.                                    (I. v.)

A real event described at the beginning of the drama has exercised a profound influence upon the whole imagery of the play. What is later metaphor, is here still reality. The picture of the leprous skin disease, which is here—in the first act—described by Hamlet's father, has buried itself deep in Hamlet's imagination and continues to lead its subterranean existence, as it were, until it reappears in metaphorical form.

As [Caroline F.E.] Spurgeon has shown [in *Shakespeare's Imagery*], the idea of an ulcer dominates the imagery, infecting and fatally eating away the whole body; on every occasion repulsive images of sickness make their appearance. It is certain that this imagery is derived from that one real event. Hamlet's father describes in that passage how the poison invades the body during sleep and how the healthy organism is destroyed from within, not having a chance to defend itself against attack. But this now becomes the *leitmotif* [a dominant and recurring theme] of the imagery: the individual occurrence is expanded into a symbol for the central problem of the play. The corruption of land and people throughout Denmark is understood as an imperceptible and irresistible process of poisoning. And, furthermore, this poisoning reappears as a *leitmotif* in the action as well—as a poisoning in the "dumb-show," and finally, as the poisoning of all the major characters in the last act. Thus imagery and action continually play into each other's hands and we see how the term "dramatic imagery" gains a new significance....

## THE WORLD AS AN UNWEEDED GARDEN

In the first part of the play the atmosphere of corruption and decay is spread in a more indirect and general way. Hamlet declares in the first and second acts how the world appears to him:

> ... Ah fie! 'tis an unweeded garden,
> That grows to seed; things rank and gross in nature
> Possess it merely.                                    (I. ii.)

> ... and indeed it goes so heavily with my disposition that this
> goodly frame, the earth, seems to me a sterile promontory, this
> most excellent canopy, the air, look you, this brave o'erhanging
> firmament, this majestical roof fretted with golden fire, why, it
> appears no other thing to me than a foul and pestilent congre-
> gation of vapours.                                    (II. ii.)

The image of weeds, touched upon in the word "unweeded," is related to the imagery of sickness in Shakespeare's work. It appears three times in *Hamlet.* The ghost says to Hamlet:

> And duller shouldst thou be than the fat weed
> That roots itself in ease on Lethe wharf,            (I. v.)

In the dialogue with his mother, this image immediately follows upon the image of the ulcer:

> And do not spread the compost on the weeds,
> To make them ranker,                                  (III. iv.)

Images of rot, decay and corruption are especially numerous in the long second scene of the second act. There are, for example, Hamlet's remarks on the maggots which the sun breeds in a dead dog (II. ii.), on the deep dungeons in the prison Denmark (II. ii.), on the strumpet [prostitute] Fortune (II. ii.), who reappears in the speech of the first Player (II. ii.), his comparison of himself with a whore, a drab [a prostitute] and a scullion [a kitchen maid] (II. ii.).

Seen individually, such images do not seem to be very important. But in their totality they contribute considerably to the tone of the play.

# The World of *Hamlet*

Maynard Mack

After explaining that the world of a play is a well-planned microcosm of people, places, and events, Maynard Mack describes the world of William Shakespeare's *Hamlet*. Questions and riddles, Mack says, compose Hamlet's mysterious world, a world Shakespeare intentionally created that way. Throughout the play, Hamlet struggles in this world, but in the end, Mack says, Hamlet accepts his world as it is, though it has cost everything.

My subject is the world of *Hamlet*. I do not of course mean Denmark, except as Denmark is given a body by the play; and I do not mean Elizabethan England, though this is necessarily close behind the scenes. I mean simply the imaginative environment that the play asks us to enter when we read it or go to see it.

Great plays, as we know, do present us with something that can be called a world, a microcosm—a world like our own in being made of people, actions, situations, thoughts, feelings and much more, but unlike our own in being perfectly, or almost perfectly, significant and coherent. In a play's world, each part implies the other parts, and each lives, each means, with the life and meaning of the rest. . . .

## A WORLD OF QUESTIONS AND RIDDLES

Hamlet's world is preëminently in the interrogative mood. It reverberates with questions, anguished, meditative, alarmed. There are questions that in this play, to an extent I think unparalleled in any other, mark the phases and even the nuances of the action, helping to establish its peculiar baffled tone. There are other questions whose interrogations, innocent at first glance, are subsequently seen to have reached beyond their contexts and to point towards some pervasive inscrutability in Hamlet's world as a whole. Such is that tense

Excerpted from Maynard Mack, "The World of *Hamlet*," *Yale Review*, vol. 41 (1952), pp. 502–23. Reprinted by permission of the author.

series of challenges with which the tragedy begins: Bernardo's of Francisco, "Who's there?" Francisco's of Horatio and Marcellus, "Who is there?" Horatio's of the ghost, "What art thou . . . ?" And then there are the famous questions. In them the interrogations seem to point not only beyond the context but beyond the play, out of Hamlet's predicaments into everyone's: "What a piece of work is a man! . . . And yet to me what is this quintessence of dust?" "To be, or not to be, that is the question." "Get thee to a nunnery. Why wouldst thou be a breeder of sinners?" "I am very proud, revengeful, ambitious, with more offences at my beck than I have thoughts to put them in, imagination to give them shape, or time to act them in. What should such fellows as I do crawling between earth and heaven?" "Dost thou think Alexander look'd o' this fashion i' th' earth?. . . And smelt so?"

Further, Hamlet's world is a world of riddles. The hero's own language is often riddling, as the critics have pointed out. When he puns, his puns have receding depths in them, like the one which constitutes his first speech: "A little more than kin, and less than kind." His utterances in madness, even if wild and whirling, are simultaneously, as Polonius discovers, pregnant: "Do you know me, my lord?" "Excellent well. You are a fishmonger." Even the madness itself is riddling: How much is real? How much is feigned? What does it mean? Sane or mad, Hamlet's mind plays restlessly about his world, turning up one riddle upon another. The riddle of character, for example, and how it is that in a man whose virtues else are "pure as grace," some vicious mole of nature, some "dram of eale," can "all the noble substance oft adulter." Or the riddle of the player's art, and how a man can so project himself into a fiction, a dream of passion, that he can weep for Hecuba. Or the riddle of action: how we may think too little—"What to ourselves in passion we propose," says the player-king, "The passion ending, doth the purpose lose"; and again, how we may think too much: "Thus conscience does make cowards of us all, And thus the native hue of resolution/Is sicklied o'er with the pale cast of thought."

There are also more immediate riddles. His mother—how could she "on this fair mountain leave to feed, And batten on this moor?" The ghost—which may be a devil, for "the de'il hath power/T' assume a pleasing shape." Ophelia—what does her behavior to him mean? Surprising her in her closet [bedroom or sitting room], he falls to such perusal of her face as he would draw it. Even the king at his prayers is a riddle. Will a revenge that takes him in the purging of his soul be vengeance, or hire and salary? As for himself, Hamlet realizes, he is the greatest riddle of all—a mystery, he warns Rosencrantz and Guildenstern, from which he will not have the heart plucked out. He cannot tell why he has of late lost all his mirth, forgone all custom of exercises. Still less can he tell why he delays: "I do not know/Why yet I live to say, 'This thing's to do,'/Sith I have cause and will and strength and means To do't."

## HAMLET BECOMES DISCOURAGED WITH THE WORLD

*In act 2, scene 2, Hamlet tells Rosencrantz and Guildenstern that he has of late become melancholy, a condition that has affected his view of the world and the humans who populate it. What was magnificent and beautiful has become a collection of vapors and an essence of dust.*

I have of late—but wherefore I know not—lost all my mirth, forgone all custom of exercises; and indeed it goes so heavily with my disposition that this goodly frame, the earth, seems to me a sterile promontory; this most excellent canopy, the air, look you, this brave o'erhanging firmament, this majestical roof fretted with golden fire, why, it appears no other thing to me than a foul and pestilent congregation of vapors. What a piece of work is a man! how noble in reason! how infinite in faculty! in form and moving how express and admirable! in action how like an angel! in apprehension how like a god! the beauty of the world! the paragon of animals! And yet, to me, what is this quintessence of dust? man delights not me; no, nor woman neither.

Shakespeare, *Hamlet.*

Thus the mysteriousness of Hamlet's world is of a piece. It is not simply a matter of missing motivations, to be expunged [eliminated] if only we could find the perfect clue. It is built in. It is evidently an important part of what the play wishes to say to us. And it is certainly an element that the play thrusts upon us from the opening word. Everyone, I think, recalls the mysteriousness of that first scene. The cold middle of the night on the castle platform, the muffled sentries, the uneasy atmosphere of apprehension, the challenges leaping out of the dark, the questions that follow the challenges, feeling out the darkness, searching for identities, for relations, for assurance. "Bernardo?" "Have you had quiet guard?" "Who hath reliev'd you?" "What, is Horatio there?" "What, has this thing appear'd again tonight?" "Looks 'a not like the king?" "How now, Horatio! . . . Is

not this something more than fantasy? What think you on 't?"
"Is it not like the king?" "Why this same strict and most obser-
vant watch . . . ?" "Shall I strike at it with my partisan?" "Do you
consent we shall acquaint [young Hamlet] with it?"

We need not be surprised that critics and playgoers alike
have been tempted to see in this an evocation not simply of
Hamlet's world but of their own. Man in his aspect of baffle-
ment, moving in darkness on a rampart between two worlds,
unable to reject, or quite accept, the one that, when he faces it,
"to-shakes" his disposition with thoughts beyond the reaches
of his soul—comforting himself with hints and guesses. We
hear these hints and guesses whispering through the darkness
as the several watchers speak. "At least, the whisper goes so,"
says one. "I think it be no other but e'en so," says another. "I
have heard" that on the crowing of the cock "Th' extravagant
and erring spirit hies/To his confine," says a third. "Some say"
at Christmas time "this bird of dawning" sings all night, "And
then, they say, no spirit dare stir abroad." "So have I heard,"
says the first, "and do in part believe it." However we choose to
take the scene, it is clear that it creates a world where uncer-
tainties are of the essence. . . .

The mysteriousness of Hamlet's world, while it pervades
the tragedy, finds its point of greatest dramatic concentration
in the first act, and its symbol in the first scene. The problems
of appearance and reality also pervade the play as a whole, but
come to a climax in Acts II and III, and possibly their best
symbol is the play within the play. Our third attribute, though
again it is one that crops out everywhere, reaches its full development in Acts IV and V. It is not easy to find an appropriate name for this attribute, but perhaps "mortality" will serve,
if we remember to mean by mortality the heartache and the
thousand natural shocks that flesh is heir to, not simply
death. . . .

## HAMLET ACCEPTS HIS WORLD

In the last act of the play (or so it seems to me, for I know there
can be differences on this point), Hamlet accepts his world
and we discover a different man. Shakespeare does not outline
for us the process of acceptance any more than he had done
with Romeo or was to do with Othello. But he leads us strong-
ly to expect an altered Hamlet, and then, in my opinion, provides him. We must recall that at this point Hamlet has been
absent from the stage during several scenes, and that such ab-
sences in Shakespearean tragedy usually warn us to be on the

watch for a new phase in the development of the character. . . .

After the graveyard and what it indicates has come to pass in him, we know that Hamlet is ready for the final contest of mighty opposites. He accepts the world as it is, the world as a duel, in which, whether we know it or not, evil holds the poisoned rapier and the poisoned chalice waits; and in which, if we win at all, it costs not less than everything. I think we understand by the close of Shakespeare's *Hamlet* why it is that unlike the other tragic heroes he is given a soldier's rites upon the stage. For as [Irish poet] William Butler Yeats once said, "Why should we honor those who die on the field of battle? A man may show as reckless a courage in entering into the abyss of himself."

# Character Revealed Through Dialogue

Robert Di Yanni

Robert Di Yanni identifies three functions of dialogue in plays: to advance the plot, to establish the setting, and, most important, to reveal character. The examples he cites from Shakespeare's *Othello* focus on character qualities of Desdemona, her maid Emilia, Iago, and Othello. Di Yanni explains how the content and choice of words in the dialogue show that Desdemona is more innocent than her maid, that Iago is coarse and wicked, and that Othello changes, information the reader or audience learns without direct explanation.

Ezra Pound, the modern American poet, once described drama as "persons moving about on a stage using words"—in short, people talking. Listening to their talk we hear identifiable, individual voices. In their presence we encounter persons, for dialogue inevitably brings us back to character, drama's human center. And though dialogue in plays typically has three major functions—to advance the plot, to establish setting (the time and place of the action), and to reveal character, its most important and consistent function is the revelation of character. . . .

## DESDEMONA AND HER MAID

Consider first the following conversation between Desdemona (wife of the military hero Othello) and Emilia (maid to Desdemona and wife of Othello's lieutenant, Iago). They are talking about adultery:

DESDEMONA. Dost thou in conscience think, tell me, Emilia,
That there be women do abuse their husbands
In such gross kind?

EMILIA. There be some such, no question.

DESDEMONA. Wouldst thou do such a deed for all the world?

Excerpted from *Literature* by Robert DiYanni; © 1986 by Random House, Inc. Reprinted by permission of The McGraw-Hill Companies.

EMILIA. Why, would not you?

DESDEMONA.                    No, by this heavenly light!

EMILIA. Nor I either by this heavenly light.
     I might do 't as well i' the dark.

DESDEMONA. Wouldst thou do such a deed for all the world?

EMILIA. The world's a huge thing; it is a great price for a small
     vice.

DESDEMONA.                    In troth, I think thou wouldst not.

EMILIA. In troth, I think I should; and undo 't when I had done.
     Marry, I would not do such a thing for a joint-ring, nor
     for measures of lawn,[1] nor gowns, petticoats, nor caps,
     nor any petty exhibition, but for all the whole world?
     Why, who would not make her husband a cuckold[2] to
     make a monarch? I should venture purgatory for 't.

DESDEMONA. Beshrew me if I would do such a wrong for the
     whole world.

EMILIA. Why, the wrong is but a wrong i' th' world; and having
     the world for your labor, 'tis wrong in your own world,
     and you might quickly make it right.

Desdemona. I do not think there is any such woman.

In this dialogue we not only see and hear evidence of a rad-
ical difference of values, but we observe a striking difference
of character. Desdemona's innocence is underscored by her
unwillingness to be unfaithful to her husband; her naiveté, by
her inability to believe in any woman's infidelity. Emilia is
willing to compromise her virtue and finds enough practical
reasons to assure herself of its correctness. Her joking tone
and bluntness also contrast with Desdemona's solemnity and
inability to name directly what she is referring to: adultery.

## IAGO REVEALS HIS CHARACTER

And now listen to Iago working on Desdemona's father, Brabantio, to tell him about his daughter's elopement with Othello
(Act I, Scene I):

     Zounds, sir y'are robbed! For shame. Put on your gown.
     Your heart is burst, you have lost half your soul.
     Even now, now, very now, an old black ram
     Is tupping[3] your white ewe. Arise, arise!
     Awake the snorting citizens with the bell,
     Or else the devil will make a grandsire of you. . . .
     I am one sir, that comes to till you your daughter
     and the Moor are making the beast with two backs.

1. a light, cotton fabric. 2. a man married to an unfaithful wife. 3. covering.

Iago's language reveals his coarseness; he crudely reduces sexual love to animal copulation. It also shows his ability to make things happen: he has infuriated Brabantio. The remainder of the scene shows the consequences of his speech, its power to inspire action. Iago is thus revealed as both an instigator and a man of crude sensibilities.

His language is cast in a similar mold in Act II, Scene I, when he tries to convince Roderigo, a rejected suitor of Desdemona, that Desdemona will tire of Othello and turn to someone else for sexual satisfaction. Notice how Iago's words stress the carnality of sex and reveal his violent imagination:

> Her eye must be fed. And what delight
> shall she have to look on the devil? When the
> blood is made dull with the act of sport, there
> should be a game to inflame it and to give
> saiety a fresh appetite, loveliness in favor,
> sympathy in years, manners, and beauties; all
> which the Moor is defective in. Now for want of
> these required conveniences, her delicate tenderness will find
> itself abused, begin to heave the gorge, disrelish and
> abhor the Moor. Very nature will instruct her in it
> and compel her to some second choice. . . .

## OTHELLO'S LANGUAGE REVEALS HIS FALL

Othello's language, like Iago's, reveals his character and his decline from a courageous and confident leader to a jealous lover distracted to madness by Iago's insinuations about his wife's infidelity. The elegance and control, even the exaltation of his early speeches, give way to the crude degradation of his later remarks. Here is Othello in Act I, Scene II, responding to a search party out to find him:

> Hold your hands,
> Both you of my inclining and the rest,
> Were it my cue to fight, I should have known it
> Without a prompter. Whither will you that I go
> To answer this your charge?

The language of this speech is formal, stately, and controlled. It bespeaks a man in command of himself, one who assumes authority naturally and easily.

In Act I, Scene III, Othello speaks to the political authorities and to Brabantio, Desdemona's enraged father:

> Most potent, grave, and reverend signiors,
> My very noble and approved good masters,
> That I have ta'en away this old man's daughter,
> It is most true; true I have married her.
> The very head and front of my offending
> Hath this extent, no more. . . .

From these few lines alone we can sense Othello's stature, his dignity, his self-confidence, and his courtesy. Coupled with other passages from the first two acts of the play, we come away impressed with Othello's gravity and grandeur. His language in large part accounts for our sympathetic response to him, for our admiration, not only for his military exploits, but for his measure of control, poise, and equanimity.

---

## ASIDES AND SOLILOQUIES

*Besides conversation among players, dramatists reveal character through asides and soliloquies. In an aside, a character speaks a few lines of his or her thoughts directly to the audience, lines that other characters on stage supposedly do not hear. Soliloquies are longer speeches in which a character, alone on stage, reveals thoughts and feelings as if thinking out loud. George R. Price comments on the Elizabethan use of asides and soliloquies in* Reading Shakespeare's Plays.

Self-revelation carries over into the Elizabethan drama. It is found, obviously, in asides and in soliloquies; and the student should remember that because soliloquies set forth the character's own conception of his motives they demand very careful study. . . . A dramatic character uses no conscious concealment in soliloquy. . . .

The dramatic advantage of self-revelation is its economy. With the minimum of lines and time, the dramatic relation of the character is set in the minds of the audience. The play can then move on to development of the situation. Though we are accustomed by both fiction and modern drama to a slower, "realistic" process of revelation of character, we need not assume that the older method is less artistic.

George R. Price, *Reading Shakespeare's Plays.* Woodbury, NY: Barron's Educational Series, 1962.

---

By the middle of Act III, however, this view of Othello is no longer tenable. Othello is reduced by Iago to an incoherent babbler, to a man at odds with himself, one who has lost his equilibrium. In Act IV, Scene I, we see the Othello Iago has created by suggesting that Desdemona has been unchaste with Othello's lieutenant, Michael Cassio:

OTHELLO. Lie with her? Lie on her?—We say lie on her when they belie her—Lie with her! Zounds, that's fulsome[1]. Handkerchief—confession—handkerchief—To confess, and be hanged for his labor—first to be hanged, and then to

1. disgusting.

confess! I tremble at it. . . . It is not words that shake me
thus.—Pish! Noses, ears, and lips? Is't possible?—Confess?—Handkerchief?—O devil.

In the language of both Iago and Othello we see meaning
enacted as well as expressed. The verbal dimension of their dialogue is reinforced by action, gesture, movement. We can observe in these brief excerpts and throughout the play not only
how language reveals character, advances the action, and es-
tablishes the setting, but how it also makes things happen and
in effect itself becomes action.

# The Engaging Qualities of *Othello*

Louis B. Wright and Virginia A. LaMar

Louis B. Wright and Virginia A. LaMar identify qualities in *Othello* that particularly engaged Elizabethan audiences and have appealed to audiences and readers ever since. Wright and LaMar contend that the play appeals because it depicts emotions common to every person; it portrays a villain in Venice, a city reputed for its wickedness; it pits good against evil; and it has an exotic foreign character, a Moor. The authors refer to *Othello* as a perfect play, though not a tragedy in the classic Greek sense, in part because it presents its theme without extraneous scenes designed to appease a portion of the audience, be it the monarch or the poor paying customers standing on the ground around the stage, those called groundlings.

Shakespeare's tragedy *Othello* has enjoyed popularity on the stage from the author's time to our own. It has remained a living drama over the centuries because it treats emotions that are universal and persistent in human nature. Its characters do not exist on a plane far removed from ordinary life; we are not asked to witness the conflict of kings and conspirators beyond the experience of everyday people; we are not involved in the consequences of disasters on a cosmic scale; what we witness is a struggle between good and evil, the demonstration of love, tenderness, jealousy, and hate in terms that are humanly plausible.

*Othello* is a drama of pathos [possessing qualities that arouse sympathy] and pity rather than a tragedy of character in which some tragic flaw brings about the doom of the hero. The latter concept was the Greek ideal of pure tragedy. *Othello* does not conform to this classic definition of tragedy, which had for its protagonist some noble hero of high birth, a king

Excerpted from Louis B. Wright and Virginia A. LaMar's Introduction to *The Tragedy of Othello, the Moor of Venice* by William Shakespeare. Copyright © 1957 by Simon & Schuster, Inc. Reprinted by permission of Simon & Schuster, Inc.

or a prince, in a contest with gods or supermen. Though Shakespeare follows tradition sufficiently to make both the hero and the heroine of his play personages of prominence, they are human rather than superhuman, and their reactions are the reactions understood by any spectator in the audience. The concentration upon elemental emotions presented in moving and poetic language has given *Othello* its great popularity, both as a play to be seen and a book to be read by men and women, for nearly four centuries.

*Othello* has been described as Shakespeare's most perfect play. Critics of dramatic structure have praised it for its attention to the main theme without irrelevant distractions. Many Elizabethan plays had rambling subplots and much extraneous detail to amuse the groundlings [rowdies who stood on the ground around the stage]. *Othello* avoids all irrelevancies and the action moves swiftly from the first scene to the denouement [falling action at end of play]. We never get lost in a multiplicity of incidents or a multitude of characters. Our attention remains centered on the arch villainy of Iago and his plot to plant in Othello's mind a corroding belief in his wife's faithlessness. In the working out of this plot, the author maintains suspense until the very end. The characters are distinctly drawn and the contrasts are clear and vivid. No obscurity in language, characterization, or presentation befuddles the spectator or the reader. In *Othello*, Shakespeare displayed the skill of a genius in play construction, a skill that he himself did not always take the trouble to exert. It is no wonder that *Othello* is a favorite of playgoers and readers alike.

## FASCINATION WITH EVIL

Elizabethan dramatists were fond of portraying characters of consummate evil, and if they could lay the scenes in Italy, all the better, because the literature and legend of the day were filled with stories of the wickedness of Italy. Garbled interpretations of Machiavelli [author of *The Prince* and the philosophy that the end justifies the means] were quoted in proof of cynical ruthlessness. The deeds of Alexander VI [formerly Rodrigo Borgia, a corrupt pope], Cesare Borgia [son of Pope Alexander VI, who served as model for Machiavelli's *The Prince*], Lucrezia Borgia [daughter of Pope Alexander VI, the duchess of Ferrara], and many others were a stock in trade of storytellers fascinated with sensational iniquity. To Englishmen, both those who traveled and those who stayed at home and listened, Renaissance Italy possessed a hypnotic fascination. Venice especially

had a glamor and an interest beyond the normal. Every returning traveler had a tall tale to tell about the beauty and complai-
sance of Venetian women, the passion, jealousy, and quick
anger of Venetian men, and the bloody deeds of Venetian
bravoes. For Shakespeare to give his play an initial setting in
Venice was to gain immediate interest. Every Elizabethan spectator was ready to expect some sensational revelation.

---

### BLACK AND WHITE SYMBOLS IN *OTHELLO*

*Though critics have written much about Othello's heritage as a
Moor and about the color of his skin, Othello works more
poignantly as a symbol than as a character with a particular
heritage or color. According to Mary Ann Frese Witt, black and
white ironically and symbolically decipher the inner and outer
natures of both Othello and Iago.*

It was then something of a feat for Shakespeare, and a testimony to his genius, to present a black man as the hero of a
tragedy. Playing upon his audience's preconceptions, Shakespeare makes an original, rich use of black and white symbolism throughout the play. It is the black man who is inwardly
pure, and it is a seemingly honest white man (and a soldier, a
type usually portrayed as genuinely honest) who is inwardly
evil. The difficulty of distinguishing being from seeming is a
major theme in the play, brought out in part by the black-
white symbolism. The alleged supersexuality of Africans also
figures in the play: Iago calls Othello the "lusty Moor," de-
scribing him with images of animal sexuality. Other characters reflect similar prejudice. But, again, the popular stereo-
type is turned around. Othello loves his Venetian wife
Desdemona (though by no means platonically) with romantic
devotion; Iago is totally unable to understand that love is not
simple lust. Othello's overriding concern with sex appears
only when he has been infected by Iago's "poison" (another
important type of image in the play). This gradual mental and
emotional poisoning of Othello by Iago is the motivating force
of the tragedy.

Mary Ann Frese Witt et al., eds., *The Humanities: Cultural Roots and Continu-
ities.* Vol. 1. Lexington, MA: D.C. Heath, 1985.

---

Iago at once captures the attention of the spectator. He is the
personification of the villain that Elizabethans had come to expect from Italian short stories and from Machiavellian commentary. Villains of this type, as well as those of domestic origin, had long been popular on the stage. From the days of the
mystery and morality plays, the characters personifying evil

invariably had gripped the attention of audiences, for iniquity always stirs more popular excitement than virtue. The preacher who paints a vivid picture of wickedness has a larger congregation than one who discourses on the beauties of Paradise. Shakespeare had already achieved success in the portrayal of villains, notably in the characterization of King Richard III, with whom one should compare Iago because of his conscious preference for evil ways to gain his desires. To give some shadow of plausibility to Iago's wickedness, Shakespeare has him declare his hatred of Othello for passing him over and promoting Cassio, and he has Iago hint that Othello may have been intimate with his wife, Emilia, but this latter suggestion is almost an afterthought of Iago's to rationalize a hate and envy that are part of his nature. To make the irony deeper, Shakespeare gives Iago an outward appearance of honest virtue and has Othello call him "honest Iago." Othello himself is by nature courageous, open, generous, unsuspecting—and naïve. Desdemona is warmhearted, tender, faithful, and much in love with her husband. No thought is further from her mind than the infidelity that Iago suggests to Othello. The suspense of the play increases as we watch Iago subtly poison Othello's mind and witness Desdemona's bewilderment, despair, and ultimate death, and this suspense is retained until the last lines when the spectator is left to imagine the tortures awaiting Iago, who is dragged off the stage to judgment. . . .

The best modern opinion is that the first performance of the play was probably in 1604 and that it was composed between 1601 and the date of performance. The play was immediately popular and records of its performance show that its popularity continued through the seventeenth century, except for the period when plays were outlawed during the Puritan regime. . . .

## FASCINATION WITH AN EXOTIC MOOR

Much ink has been spilled in the debate over the color of Othello and what physical characteristics Shakespeare attributed to a "Moor." Actors who have portrayed the part have also shown much concern over their make-up. There is little to indicate that Shakespeare or his contemporaries would have interpreted the union of Othello and Desdemona as a problem in mixed marriage or would have regarded the racial differences as of vital interest. To the Elizabethans, Othello was an exotic, and such interest as always attaches to exotics attached to him. . . .

To an Elizabethan, a Moor was a swarthy man. Shakespeare and his contemporaries were not anthropologists and they were not concerned with questions of "race." The debate as to whether Shakespeare intended Othello to be a Berber [North African Moroccan people] or a Negro [sub-Saharan African people] is beside the point. Shakespeare neither knew nor cared. To him a Moor was a dark, exotic man, and he might call him "black," for he once declared that his brunette ladylove in Sonnet 147 was "as black as hell." In using this descriptive phrase Shakespeare was reacting against the convention of the period which attributed the height of beauty to fair skin and golden hair. Actors who chose to play Othello as a coal-black man, however, were probably taking Shakespeare's words too literally. Shakespeare was not trying in *Othello* to emphasize any racial differences between the hero and the heroine, though the differences in their backgrounds provide Iago with plausible suggestions for Desdemona's alleged disaffection. Othello, as Shakespeare characterizes him, is a soldier of fortune from a foreign country, a hero, who wins Desdemona by his bearing and the romantic recital of his adventures in strange lands. When enemies of Othello want to abuse him, they speak opprobriously of his alien looks and wonder that Desdemona could love so strange a man, but that is part of the reality of the characterization, not a hint on Shakespeare's part of "racism." The unhappy times when men would read some suggestion of racial prejudice into every piece of literature concerned with alien characters lay some centuries ahead.

# Two Worldviews Echo Each Other

Francis Fergusson

Splendid language and a powerful story give Shakespeare's *Othello* its status as a masterpiece, concludes Francis Fergusson. Fergusson demonstrates how the characters of Iago and Othello, opposites in morality, stature, and worldview, echo each other. Iago is coarse, devious, and heartless; Othello is noble, honorable, and heroic. In the beginning, the language of the two men reflects their differences. As Iago poisons Othello's mind, they begin to speak alike. Iago's is an immediate world in which he talks of cities, goats, and monkeys; Othello's is a chaste world in which he talks of stars and trumpets. Because both worlds lack human understanding and a traditional social order, Fergusson concludes that one echoes the other.

*Othello*, written in 1604, is one of the masterpieces of Shakespeare's "tragic period." In splendor of language, and in the sheer power of the story, it belongs with the greatest. But some of its admirers find it too savage. . . .

Shakespeare shows the action, now through Iago's eyes, now through Othello's or Desdemona's; and the reader, listening to them, can feel both the reality and the mysteriousness of the tragedy, much as one does in a painful experience of one's own.

## CONTRAST BETWEEN IAGO AND OTHELLO

Thus, for example, the very first scene is dominated by Iago, and we see it chiefly through his sharp eyes. It opens abruptly, in the midst of Iago's quarrel with his silly victim, Roderigo. The situation is soon clear: Iago is using Roderigo, who thinks he loves Desdemona, to make trouble between her father, Brabantio, and Othello, whom she has just married. On the surface, Iago is the tough-minded but "honest" soldier he always pretends to be. But listen to him the moment he has persuaded Roderigo to wake Brabantio with his yells:

IAGO

Do; with like timorous accent, and dire yell
As when, by night and negligence, the fire
Is spied in populous cities.

RODERIGO

What ho! Brabantio, Signior Brabantio, ho!

IAGO

Awake! What ho, Brabantio! Thieves, thieves!
Look to your house, your daughter, and your bags! . . .
Your heart is burst, you have lost half your soul;
Even now, now, very now, an old black ram
Is tupping your white ewe. Arise, arise,
Awake the snorting citizens with the bell,
Or else the devil will make a grandsire of you.

Iago is letting loose the wicked passion inside him, as he does from time to time throughout the play, when he slips his mask aside. At such moments he always resorts to this imagery of money-bags, treachery, and animal lust and violence. So he expresses his own faithless, envious spirit, and, by the same token, his vision of the populous city of Venice—Iago's "world," as it has been called. . . .

And now Othello begins to take command; he seems to be entirely above Iago's excitement. "My parts, my title, and my perfect soul," he tells Iago, "shall manifest me rightly." And when Brabantio's followers threaten to attack his, he can quiet them all with a word: "Keep up your bright swords, for the dew will rust them." Even these few words dispel Iago's nightmare.

The full "Othello music" first resounds in the next scene (Act I, scene 3) when Othello tells the Duke how Desdemona fell in love when he told "my travel's history":

Wherein of antres[1] vast, and deserts idle,
Rough quarries, rocks, and hills whose heads touch heaven,
It was my hint to speak—such was the process;
And of the Cannibals that each other eat,
The Anthropophagi,[2] and men whose heads
Do grow beneath their shoulders.

It is our first sight of Othello's world: empty of human life as we know it, but filled with the sense of far-off, heroic adventure. We shall see it again, whenever Othello expresses his

1. caves. 2. cannibals.

"perfect soul": rock, stars, danger, and triumph, in words that make sad but exhilarating music. It is the opposite of Iago's world.... A sheltered rich girl, Desdemona must have felt that Othello had wakened her to life itself. "She wished," as Othello says, "that heaven had made her such a man." When Othello sums up their innocent infatuation, we must feel that he is more accurate than he knows:

> She loved me for the dangers I had passed,
> And I loved her that she did pity them.

Othello and Desdemona are so attractive that we tend to see them only as they see each other: the noble Moor, the pure white maiden. But Shakespeare shows their love, even here at the very beginning, as dreamy, utterly defenseless in a world that contains Iago....

Iago himself certainly has plenty of reason. His picture of human motivation as essentially animal is like that of some kinds of disillusioned rationalists [those who rely on reason as a guide to belief and action] who were common in his time, as they are in ours. And he can control his own wicked passions when his reason tells him he must, in order to appear trustworthy. But that does not mean, as some of his critics have thought, that he lacks passion. On the contrary, in the "world" of his philosophy and his imagination, where his spirit lives, there is no cure for passion. He is, behind his mask, as restless as a cage of those cruel and lustful monkeys that he mentions so often. It has been pointed out that he has no intelligible plan for destroying Othello, and he never asks himself what good it will do him to ruin so many people. It is enough for him that he "hates" the Moor....

The main conflict of the play is a strange one, for Othello cannot see his opponent until too late. But the audience sees with extraordinary clarity. In Act II Iago tricks Cassio into disgracing himself, and then takes advantage of the guileless affection between Cassio and Desdemona to create, for Othello, the appearance of evil. He explains this scheme to the audience, with mounting pleasure, as it develops; and by Act III he is ready to snare Othello himself....

## IAGO WATCHES AND IMPLEMENTS HIS DEVIOUS PLAN

The beginning of this scene, when Othello sees Cassio pleading with Desdemona, and then, after Iago has hinted at his "suspicions," listens to Desdemona's insistent urging that he see Cassio, is one of the more painful sequences in the play. How can Desdemona insist, when every word puzzles and torments Othello? It shows her perfect trust, her pride in Othello's love for her; her blind faith in the Othello of her dreams. And when she leaves, Othello expresses the same faith, "perfect," but blind and helpless, in the Desdemona he loves:

> Perdition[1] catch my soul
> But I do love thee; and when I love thee not,
> Chaos is come again.

So we see what Iago has already explained, that Othello may be "had" through his dependence on Desdemona; and we are ready for the first round.

Iago starts very cautiously, wearing his most sympathetic mask. He reasonably and regretfully assembles all the false evidence, while warning Othello not to be troubled, or jump to conclusions. But when he feels that Othello is suffering, he permits himself the triumphant irony of his warning against jealousy:

> O beware my lord of jealousy;
> It is the green-eyed monster, which doth mock
> The meat it feeds on.

He is of course gloating, but he too must feel the teeth of such a monster. He speaks as one who *knows* jealousy, or envy. Perhaps envy is the hidden passion which drives him to assault Othello and try to reduce him to his own level. Othello does not understand this, but he feels very sharply what his danger is:

> Exchange me for a goat,
> When I shall turn the business of my soul
> To exsufflicate[2] and blown surmises,
> Matching thy inference.

He is in fact being exchanged for a goat; his soul is slowly being turned to Iago's world of animal lust and strife. This is the climax of the first round, and we can see already that Iago's spirit is forcing its vision upon Othello's spirit. But Iago, having gone so far, resumes his mask of reason. He contents himself with making Desdemona's adultery look probable: Venetian women are like that; Cassio is attractive; Othello is getting old, and he is a Moor. Poor Othello has had enough; he mutters, "Farewell, farewell," and Iago lets him go.

There follows the short interlude in which Desdemona drops her handkerchief while wiping Othello's brow, Emilia picks it up, and Iago gets it from her. This new piece of false evidence gives Iago another inspiration. When he sees Othello wandering back for the second round, he murmurs:

---

1. damnation. 2. to blow up like a bubble.

Look where he comes. Not poppy, nor mandragora[1],
Nor all the drowsy syrups of the world
Shall ever medicine thee to that sweet sleep
Which thou owedst yesterday.

The melody of these famous lines gives a wonderfully intimate sense of Othello's inner being. It is quite unlike Iago's usual harsh sounds and abrupt rhythms, as though, at the moment when the mastery passes to him, he were acquiring the magic of Othello's own music. Othello, when he sees Iago, instinctively wants to fight him: "Avaunt [away], be gone!" he cries. Perhaps he threatens him; but he can't throw off the evil vision Iago fastened on him, or see Iago as he really is. He sees his own world leaving him:

O now, for ever
Farewell the tranquil mind; farewell content;
Farewell the plumed troops and the big wars,
That makes ambition virtue. O farewell
... Othello's occupation's gone.

Now Iago feels that he is really inside Othello's defenses, and from this point onward he can more frankly surround his victim with his own hatred and lewdness:

Where's satisfaction?
It is impossible you should see this,
Were they as prime as goats, as hot as monkeys,
As salt as wolves in pride, and fools as gross
As ignorance made drunk.

So, as he wins, he hypnotizes Othello with the same nightmare as that with which he had startled old Brabantio in the first scene of the play.

Iago subjugates Othello with his illusions, but Iago himself is a victim of the same hellish sense of life. And when Othello dedicates himself to murder he shows, as before, bigger and stronger than Iago. "Like to the Pontic sea [Black Sea]," says Othello,

Whose icy current and compulsive course
Never retiring ebbs, but keeps due on
To the Propontic, and the Hellespont;
Even so my bloody thoughts, with violent pace,
Shall ne'er look back, ne'er ebb to humble love.

Othello is one of those characters in Shakespeare, like Timon of Athens or Angelo in *Measure for Measure,* who cannot endure any self-doubt, remorse, or knowledge of their own failings. If Othello can't be "perfect" in his love, he will be perfect

---

1. a plant believed to have magic powers and a poisonous root.

in vengeance; and now he starts for hell with the same exciting military music, and the same magnificent, cold, and far-
away imagery with which he used to pursue ambition, love,
and virtue. Iago is carried away, and as he falls on his knees
with Othello, once more echoes the "Othello music":

> Witness you ever-burning lights above,
> You elements that clip us round about,
> Witness that here Iago doth give up
> The execution of his wit, hands, heart,
> To wronged Othello's service.

When Iago says, "I am your own forever," he again reveals the
truth more completely than he knows. He and Othello are, in
fact, tied together in the blind passion of envy and hatred
which can only destroy them. So Shakespeare ends the decisive struggle of the play.

## IAGO GAINS CONTROL OF OTHELLO

In the fourth act we explore the results of Iago's strange victory. All he has to do, to keep control of Othello, is to show Cassio with the handkerchief, or laughing with his courtesan
Bianca. He sees Othello at his feet, in "lethargy"; he can torment him at will. Iago seems to have the power, the satisfaction
of his hatred or envy, which he wanted all along. Yet we know
that the whole effect is based on delusion: Othello's, of course,
but Iago's too, for the end is not yet. Othello has yet to act.

During Act IV Desdemona also acts the very part which Iago
had devised for her. She insists yet again (Act IV, scene 1) that
Othello pardon Cassio, which is "fire and brimstone" for Othello. Thus she blindly forces the Moor to see Iago's nightmare in
her ( Act IV, scene 2), "a cistern for foul toads," as Othello cries,

> there where I have garnered up my heart,
> Where either I must live, or bear no life,
> The fountain from which my current runs,
> Or else dries up.

She does not know what Othello thinks she has done, since he
can't bear to name Cassio. She does not recognize the Othello
she thought she knew, and she cannot imagine what has
changed him. But she, like Othello, must live by their love, or
"bear no life," and she feels that love is going. So, by the end of
the act, she feels death coming, and welcomes it. The famous
scene (Act IV, scene 3) when Emilia helps her prepare for bed,
light, familiar, even joking as it is on the surface, is full of Desdemona's ghostly and unresisting sense of death—a triumph
of Shakespeare's delicate theater-poetry.

Thus Act IV is filled (as always, in Shakespeare's tragedies) with the sufferings, and the partly deluded visions, which are the aftermath of the terrible conflict of Act III. But Act V quickly brings the denouement which none of the characters can quite foresee or control. Iago is carried down in the rush, for all his agility: he fails to get Cassio killed (Act V, scene 1), and Cassio knows his own and Desdemona's innocence. Soon Emilia, too, will see the truth.

## OTHELLO CARRIES OUT IAGO'S TERRIBLE DESTRUCTION

Othello moves to kill Desdemona (Act V, scene 2) with that "icy current and compulsive course" which he had felt at the end of Act III, scene 3. We hear once more the music and the cold, magnificent images that express his "perfect soul":

> Yet I'll not shed her blood,
> Nor scar that whiter skin of hers than snow,
> And smooth as monumental alabaster.

He tells himself that he is sacrificing Desdemona to "justice"; but we see how clumsily (like a great baby) he fumbles to get Desdemona smothered at the second try; how he roars and blubbers when it's over. When Emilia yells at him, "O gull! O dolt!" she only puts a name to what we have seen, even while the great Othello music was in our ears. Shakespeare does nothing to soften this discord; even Othello's last melodious speech, when he stabs himself, hardly wipes out the impression of grotesque horror.

Iago also does nothing to mitigate the starkness of the end. He lets the mischief he has accomplished express his vision of life, and meaning of his motives:

> What you know, you know.
> From this time forth, I never will speak word.

Lodovico gives us a final image of Iago: "O Spartan dog, / More fell than anguish, hunger, or the sea," but the mystery of Iago's evil, like the mystery of Othello's and Desdemona's helpless purity, is allowed to stand in all its bleakness.

It is easy to understand what those critics mean who speak of the intolerable cruelty of *Othello*, and point out that it expresses only part of Shakespeare's sense of human life. But it appears that Shakespeare wanted it that way; as usual, he knew what he was doing. One can see (thinking over the play) that it is extraordinarily consistent, both as psychology and as poetry.

Othello is at the center, the clue to everyone's motives. Venice relies on him as the state's greatest military servant. The innocent bystanders, soldiers, Senators, Cassio, even

Roderigo, depend on his calm leadership. He is the center of Desdemona's life, and, for equal and opposite reasons, of Iago's. His large, noble spirit gives meaning to the lives around it, and to the movement of the play. But, if so, it is because there is little else in the scene which could command loyalty, love, or, for that matter, hatred. Cyprus is a barren military post which isolates the main characters, but as we see in the first act, they are isolated in Venice too. Othello and Iago are mercenary servants of the Venetian oligarchy, with little interest in what it stands for. Desdemona finds nothing to love there, either, until Othello appears. Shakespeare saw no nourishment for the spirit in the commercial republics which he used as settings: Athens, in *Timon*, and Venice. . . .

## POETRY REVEALS THE DEEP MEANINGS

But it is by means of poetry that Shakespeare reveals the deeper meanings he saw both in the motives and in the setting of his play. If one listens to the verse, one may see the play as a conflict between two views of the world, Iago's eternally restless city of goats and monkeys, and Othello's empty scene of stars and trumpets. In the early parts of the play the contrast between the two visions is unresolved. But after the intimate struggle in Act III, when Iago and Othello in their emotional utterances begin to echo each other, we begin to see how the two visions imply each other. In the foreground is the heartless game of the city, behind it the majestic machinery of Iago's "ever-burning lights," or Othello's "chaste stars." What is absent from this "scene" is human understanding, and the kind of love which can only come, take root, and grow through understanding.

If one remembers *Lear* or *Hamlet*, one can see how consciously Shakespeare defined the bleak scene of *Othello*. In both other plays there are characters who understand—or at least learn to understand—what is going on. In both of them the tragic action occurs in a traditional social order which, however shaken, does embody a sane view of human life. Both plays are full of symbols which command love and loyalty. But in order to make [Italian writer Giraldi] Cinthio's story [written forty years before *Othello*, and the basis of *Othello*'s plot] understandable, and to bring out the meaning he saw in it, Shakespeare must show his people as lost. The brilliant but mysterious sharpness of the story, and the unrelieved blackness of the end, are consistent with the wonderful but heartless "scene" which the poetry builds; and all, together, define the meaning of the play.

# *Othello:* A Tragedy of Beauty and Fortune

Helen Gardner

Helen Gardner asserts that Shakespeare's *Othello* is supreme in three kinds of beauty: poetic, intellectual, and moral. She identifies Othello as an extraordinary man who speaks beautiful language—a hero like those of the ancient world, a free man who left his kin and country behind for freely chosen duties as a professional military officer. Desdemona falls in love with this military man. Othello's love for Desdemona is a "great venture of faith," which fails under Iago's calculated attacks. Structurally, all parts of the play focus on the story of Othello and Desdemona's love and its destruction. As a tragedy of fortune, Gardner argues, the play ends heroically when Othello recovers his faith in love and in himself.

Among the tragedies of Shakespeare *Othello* is supreme in one quality: beauty. Much of its poetry, in imagery, perfection of phrase, and steadiness of rhythm, soaring yet firm, enchants the sensuous imagination. This kind of beauty *Othello* shares with *Romeo and Juliet* and *Antony and Cleopatra*; it is a corollary of the theme which it shares with them. But *Othello* is also remarkable for another kind of beauty. Except for the trivial scene with the clown, all is immediately relevant to the central issue; no scene requires critical justification The play has a rare intellectual beauty, satisfying the desire of the imagination for order and harmony between the parts and the whole. Finally, the play has intense moral beauty. It makes an immediate appeal to the moral imagination, in its presentation in the figure of Desdemona of a love which does not alter 'when it alteration finds', but 'bears it out even to the edge of doom'. These three kinds of beauty are interdependent, since all arise from the nature of the hero. Othello's vision of the

Excerpted from Helen Gardner, "The Noble Moor," British Academy Lectures, no. 9, 1955.

world expresses itself in what [writer and critic] Wilson Knight has called the 'Othello music'; the 'compulsive course' of his nature dominates the action, driving it straight on to its conclusion; Othello arouses in Desdemona unshakeable love. . . .

## THE NATURE OF OTHELLO AS HERO

Othello is like a hero of the ancient world in that he is not a man like us, but a man recognized as extraordinary. He seems born to do great deeds and live in legend. He has the obvious heroic qualities of courage and strength, and no actor can attempt the role who is not physically impressive. He has the heroic capacity for passion. But the thing which most sets him apart is his solitariness. He is a stranger, a man of alien race, without ties of nature or natural duties. His value is not in what the world thinks of him, although the world rates him highly, and does not derive in any way from his station. It is inherent. He is, in a sense, a 'self-made man', the product of a certain kind of life which he has chosen to lead. . . .

*Othello* presents a vision of man free. The past, whose claim upon the present is at the heart of *Hamlet*, is in *Othello* a country which the hero has passed through and left behind, the scene of his 'travels' history'. The ancestors of royal siege, the father and mother, between whom the handkerchief passed and from whom it came to him, have no claim upon him. His status in Venice is contractual. The Senate are his 'very noble and approv'd good masters' because he and they have chosen it should be so. His loyalties are not the tangle of inherited loyalties, but the few and simple loyalties of choice. His duties are not the duties of his station, but the duties of his profession. Othello is free as intensely as Hamlet is unfree, and the relation which fails to establish itself in *Hamlet* is the one relation which counts here, the free relation of love. It is presented in its more extreme, that is in heroic, form, as a relation between individuals, owing nothing to, and indeed triumphing over, circumstances and natural inclination. The universality of the play lies here, in its presentation of man as freely choosing and expressing choice by acts: Desdemona crossing the Senate floor to take her place beside her husband, Othello slaying her and slaying himself, Emilia crying out the truth at the cost of her life. *Othello* is particularly concerned with that deep, instinctive level where we feel ourselves to be free, with the religious aspect of our nature, in its most general sense. (This is why a theological interpretation seems so improper.) Othello's nobility lies in his capacity to worship: to feel wonder and give service.

## OTHELLO EVOKES WONDER

Wonder is the note of Othello's greatest poetry, felt in the concreteness of its imagery and the firmness of its rhythms. Wonder sharpens our vision and things, so that we see them, not blurred by sentiment, or distorted by reflection, but in their own beautiful particularity. The services which he has done he speaks of at his first appearance as in his dying speech. He has taken service with the state of Venice. When it calls upon him on his marriage night he accepts, not merely without hesitation, but with alacrity: "Tis well I am found by you.' This is the 'serious and great business' of his life, his 'occupation', source of his disciplined dignity and self-control. He is dedicated to the soldier's life of obedience and responsibility. The 'hardness' of his life gives to his sense of his own worth an impersonal dignity and grandeur. It is grounded in his sense of the worth of the life and the causes he has chosen. It is consistent with humility. This appears in the serious simplicity with which he lays before the Senate the story of his wooing, and later asks their permission, as a favour, to take his wife with him; for he is their servant and will not demand what in their need they could hardly refuse. It appears more movingly in his acknowledgement of his own 'weak merits' as a husband; and finally, most poignantly, in his image of himself as supremely fortunate, through no merit of his own stumbling upon a pearl. It is fitting that the word 'cause' should come to his lips at the crisis of his life. He has always acted for a cause. Othello is often spoken of as a man of action, in tones which imply some condescension. He is primarily a man of faith, whose faith has witnessed to itself in his deeds.

## OTHELLO: A DRAMA OF LOVE, PASSION, AND MARRIAGE

The love between Othello and Desdemona is a great venture of faith. He is free; she achieves her freedom, and at a great cost. Shakespeare, in creating the figure of her wronged father, who dies of grief at her revolt, sharpened and heightened, as everywhere, the story in the source. Her disobedience and deception of him perhaps cross her mind at Othello's ominous 'Think on thy sins.' If so, she puts the thought aside with 'They are loves I bear you.'. . . *Othello* is a drama of passion and runs to the time of passion; it is also a drama of love which, failing to sustain its height of noon, falls at once to night. To borrow [novelist and critic] Edwin Muir's distinction, the long time belongs to the Story, the short belongs to the Fable.

*Othello* is also a drama of marriage. As the hero is more

than a Homeric doer of great deeds, he is more than a lover; he is a husband. Desdemona is not only the 'cunning'st pattern of excelling nature' and the girl who 'saw Othello's visage in his mind'; she is his 'true and loyal wife'. Her soul and fortunes are 'consecrated' to him. The play is not only concerned with passion and love, but with what [French essayist Michel Eyquem de] Montaigne and other experienced observers have thought incompatibles: love and constancy. . . .

---

### OTHELLO FULFILLS TRAGEDY'S PURPOSES

*In* Characters of Shakespear's Plays, *published in 1817, William Hazlitt enumerates purposes that tragedy is said to fulfill.* Othello, *he says, achieves them and evokes sympathy in the audience and reader.*

It has been said that tragedy purifies the affections by terror and pity. That is, it substitutes imaginary sympathy for mere selfishness. It gives us a high and permanent interest, beyond ourselves, in humanity as such. It raises the great, the remote, and the possible to an equality with the real, the little, and the near. It makes man a partaker with his kind. It subdues and softens the stubbornness of his will. It teaches him that there are and have been others like himself, by showing him as in a glass what they have felt, thought, and done. It opens the chambers of the human heart. It leaves nothing indifferent to us that can affect our common nature. It excites our sensibility by exhibiting the passions wound up to the utmost pitch by the power of imagination or the temptation of circumstances; and corrects their fatal excesses in ourselves by pointing to the greater extent of sufferings and of crimes to which they have led others. Tragedy creates a balance of the affections. It makes us thoughtful spectators in the lists of life. It is the refiner of the species; a discipline of humanity. The habitual study of poetry and works of imagination is one chief part of a well-grounded education. . . . —'Othello' furnishes an illustration of these remarks. It excites our sympathy in an extraordinary degree. The moral it conveys has a closer application to the concerns of human life than that of almost any other of Shakespear's plays.

William Hazlitt, *Lectures on The Literature of the Age of Elizabeth, and Characters of Shakespear's Plays.* London: Bell & Daldy, 1870.

---

I cannot resist adapting some Johnsonian expressions [expressions of British writer Samuel Johnson] and saying this is 'sad stuff': 'the man is a liar and there's an end on't.' What Iago injects into Othello's mind, the poison with which he charges him, is either false deductions from isolated facts—she deceived her father—and from dubious generalizations—Venetian women deceive their husbands—or flat lies. Whatever from our more melancholy experiences we choose to call the facts of life, in this play there is one fact which matters, upon which the plot is built and by which all generalizations are tested:

Moor, she was chaste; she lov'd thee, cruel Moor.          (v. ii.)

## IAGO'S CRAFTY DESTRUCTION

. . . Iago ruins Othello by insinuating into his mind the question, 'How do you know?' The tragic experience with which this play is concerned is loss of faith, and Iago is the instrument to bring Othello to this crisis of his being. His task is made possible by his being an old and trusted companion, while husband and wife are virtually strangers, bound only by passion and faith; and by the fact that great joy bewilders, leaving the heart apt to doubt the reality of its joy. The strange and extraordinary, the heroic, what is beyond nature, can be made to seem the unnatural, what is against nature. This is one of Iago's tricks. But the collapse of Othello's faith before Iago's hints, refusals, retreats, reluctant avowals, though plausible and circumstantiated, is not, I believe, ultimately explicable; nor do I believe we make it so by searching for some psychological weakness in the hero which caused his faith to fail, and whose discovery will protect us from tragic experience by substituting for its pleasures the easier gratifications of moral and intellectual superiority to the sufferer. There is only one answer to Iago's insinuations, the answer Othello made to Brabantio's warning: 'My life upon her faith.' It is one thing to retort so to open enmity; more difficult to reply so to the seemingly well-meant warnings of a friend. That Othello does not or cannot reply so to Iago, and instead of making the venture of faith, challenges him to prove his wife false, is his tragic error.

Tragic suffering is suffering which a nature, by reason of its virtues, is capable of experiencing to the full, but is incapable of tolerating, and in which the excellencies of a nature are in conflict with each other. The man of conscience suffers the torment of confusion of conscience, the man of loving heart the torment of love spurned and of invasion by the passion of hatred. The one finds himself 'marshalled to knavery', the other driven to bitter curses. The man of moral imagination and human feeling will suffer the extremity of moral despair and human isolation. The man of faith is most able to experience what loss of faith is: but he is also unable to endure existence in a world where faith is dead. Othello has known 'ecstasy', which doth 'unperplex'. The loss of that leaves him 'perplexed in the extreme' and conscious of sex and sex only as, [in John Donne's words,] 'what did move'. He has seen Desdemona as his 'soul's joy'. It is intolerable to be aware in her of only what 'the sense aches at'. . . .

*Othello* is not a study in pride, egoism, or self-deception: its subject is sexual jealousy, loss of faith in a form which involves the whole personality at the profound point where body meets spirit. The solution which Othello cannot accept is Iago's: 'Put up with it.' This is as impossible as that Hamlet should, like Claudius, behave as if the past were done with and only the present mattered. . . .

## HEROISM IN DEATH

[Tragic responsibility]shows itself in Othello's destruction of an idol, his decision to regain his freedom by destroying what he must desire, but cannot honour. That baser passions are mingled with this imperative to sacrifice, that in the final moment Othello kills his wife in rage, only means that in presenting man as 'an animal that worships', Shakespeare, keeping to 'the truth of human passions' presents both terms. But, in its mixture of primitive animality and agonizing renunciation, the murder of Desdemona has upon it the stamp of the heroic. It has what [Irish poet William Butler] Yeats saw in the Easter Rising, which neither his moral nor his political judgement approved, and one of whose leaders he had disliked and despised: a 'terrible beauty', contrasting with the 'casual comedy' of daily life.

The act is heroic because Othello acts from inner necessity. Although the thought of social dishonour plays a part in his agony, it has no place in this final scene. He kills her because he cannot [in the words of Adriana in *The Comedy of Errors*] 'digest the poison of her flesh', and also to save her from herself, to restore meaning to her beauty. The act is also heroic in its absoluteness, disinterestedness, and finality. Othello does not look beyond it. It must be done. The tragic hero usurps the functions of the gods and attempts to remake the world. This *hubris* [overbearing pride], which arouses awe and terror, appears in an extreme form in Othello's assumption of the role of a god who chastises where he loves, and of a priest who must present a perfect victim. He tries to confess her, so that in her last moment she may be true, and suffering the death of the body as expiation may escape the death of the soul. Her persistence in what he believes to be a lie and her tears at the news of Cassio's death turn the priest into the murderer. The heroic is rooted in reality here: the godlike is mingled with the brutal, which [Greek philosopher and writer] Aristotle saw as its true opposite, and Desdemona, love's martyr, dies like a frightened child, pleading for 'but half an hour' more of life. . . .

Emilia's silence while her mistress lived is fully explicable in terms of her character. She shares with her husband the generalizing trick and is well used to domestic scenes. The jealous, she knows,

> are not ever jealous for the cause
> But jealous for they are jealous.                    (III. iv.)

If it was not the handkerchief it would be something else. Why disobey her husband and risk his fury? It would not do any good. This is what men are like. But Desdemona dead sweeps away all such generalities and all caution. At this sight, Emilia though 'the world is a huge thing' finds that there is a thing she will not do for it. By her heroic disregard for death she gives the only 'proof' there can be of Desdemona's innocence: the testimony of faith. For falseness can be proved, innocence can only be believed. Faith, not evidence, begets faith.

The revival of faith in Othello which rings through his last speech overrides that sense of his own guilt which we have been told he ought to be dwelling on. His own worth he sees in the services he has rendered. It is right that he should be conscious of what has given his life value when he is about to take it, as he was conscious of her beauty when about to sacrifice that. His error he cannot explain. He sees it in an image which asserts her infinite value and his supreme good fortune, which in ignorance he did not realize, accepting and translating into his own characteristic mode of thought Emilia's characteristic 'O gull! O dolt! As ignorant as dirt!' The tears he weeps now are not 'cruel tears', but good tears, natural and healing. He communicates this by an image drawn from his life of adventure. Perhaps the Arabian trees come to his mind because in that land of marvels 'the Phoenix [a mythological bird that perishes in flames and rises again from the ashes] builds her spicy nest'. Then, as he nerves himself to end everything, there flashes across his mind an image from his past which seems to epitomize his whole life and will 'report him and his cause aright'; an act of suicidal daring, inspired by his chosen loyalty to Venice. With the same swiftness he does justice on himself, traducer [one who makes false statements] and murderer of his Venetian wife. As, at their reunion, after the tempest, his joy stopped his speech, so now his grief and worship express themselves finally in an act, the same act: he dies 'upon a kiss'. . . .

## *OTHELLO:* A TRAGEDY OF FORTUNE

Each of Shakespeare's great tragedies has its own design. The ground plan of the tragedy of *Othello* is that of a tragedy of fortune, the fall of a great man from a visible height of happiness to utter loss. This is not at all the shape the story has in the source; but this is how Shakespeare saw [Italian writer Giraldi] Cinthio's powerful but sordid story of a garrison intrigue. He spent his first two acts in presenting wonder great as content, and content that is absolute, delaying the opening of his tragic conflict until his third act. The design of the tragedy of fortune has a very different effect from the design of what may be called the tragedy of dilemma. . . .

In its simplest form the tragedy of fortune cannot be rationalized. It takes man out of the realm of natural causality, the steady course which birth holds on to death, showing him as the victim of the illogical, what can neither be avoided nor foreseen. To achieve its effect it glorifies human life, displaying the capacity of the human heart for joy and leaving on the mind an ineffaceable impression of splendour, thus contradicting the only moral which can be drawn from it: *Vanitas vanitatum* [vanity of vanities]. *Othello* has this in common with the tragedy of fortune that the end in no way blots out from the imagination the glory of the beginning. But the end here does not merely by its darkness throw up into relief the brightness that was. On the contrary, beginning and end chime against each other. In both the value of life and love is affirmed. . . .

Should the course of his [Othello's] life be described as a pilgrimage to a goal, or is it a straying from a centre which he finds again in death? Such straying is of the essence of life, whose law is change. Failures and recoveries of faith are the rhythm of the heart, whose movement is here objectified and magnified for our contemplation. If the old saying is true 'Qui non zelat non amat' [He who does not feel jealous does not love], then the greater love is, the greater jealousy will be. Perfect love casts out fear; but beneath the moon, mistress of change, only in death can

> Beauty, truth, and rarity,
> Grace in all simplicity,

be safe from mistaking, and constancy find its true image. The close of *Othello* should leave us at peace, for [according to a poem attributed to Shakespeare, entitled "The Phoenix and Turtle"]

Death is now the phoenix' nest;
And the turtle's loyal breast
To eternity doth rest.

The significance of *Othello* is not to be found in the hero's nobility alone, in his capacity to know ecstasy, in his vision of the world, and in the terrible act to which he is driven by his anguish at the loss of that vision. It lies also in the fact that the vision was true. I cannot agree to find lacking in meaning this most beautiful play which seems to have arisen out of the same mood as made [British poet John] Keats declare: 'I am certain of nothing but of the holiness of the Heart's affections and the truth of Imagination.'

# The Juxtaposition of Opposites in *Macbeth*

John Jay Chapman

John Jay Chapman focuses on the multiple uses of contrast in *Macbeth*. This single dramatic element of placing two opposite effects beside each other dramatizes both thought and emotion. Chapman cites quiet scenes set beside bloody actions, Macbeth's hesitation set beside Lady Macbeth's brazenness, the terror of night set beside the ghastly reality of day. According to Chapman, the contrast between Macbeth's speeches in which he conjures up courage for bloody acts and his speeches envisioning a quiet life most poignantly heighten the tragic nature of the play.

There are so many reasons why Shakespeare's greater plays affect us powerfully, that it seems like fatuity [utter foolishness] to point out special good qualities in any one of them; yet, as a great many people have tried their hand at this, and the practice never seems to have injured the plays, I will hazard a few remarks upon the nature of dramatic writing, and illustrate them with the play of "Macbeth."

## THE CONTRAST OF OPPOSITES

The main point about dramatic writing is that everything must be made obvious. A man who writes a book may state his idea and develop it and adorn it at leisure. He may even hide it with charms, and compensate the reader in a hundred ways for his obscurity. But in a theatre ideas must be delivered through a series of shocks. Shakespeare's method of doing this is by the contrast of opposites. He places two effects beside one another, and causes the idea to jump out by the contact. This is true as to his great effects of element with element, conception with conception, scene with scene. It is true also of his dramatis personæ [characters]. He must have kings

Excerpted from *A Glance Toward Shakespeare* by John Jay Chapman (Atlantic Monthly Press, 1922).

and beggars, good angels and devils. It is true also of the give-and-take of his dialogue. The dazzling play of opposites throughout Shakespeare, whether in adjectives, phrases, scenes, characters, or climaxes, is what makes him stageable. Say "Heaven" to him, he says "Hell"; "Black,"—"White"; "To be,"—"Not to be." He shadows each impression with a double that has been refracted from the thing itself, and causes an idea to stand in the air vividly, like an apparition.

This double-flash in Shakespeare is to be found in his earliest and in his latest work. There is a famous *emendation* [revision intended to improve] of his text which shows up this action of his mind in a startling manner. In "Love's Labor's Lost" the professed love-hater, Biron, gives a whimsical description of Cupid, calling him "a wimpled, whining, purblind, wayward boy," "a regent of love-rhymes, lord of folded arms," etc. One of the lines in the folio text reads as follows:—

This signior Iunio's giant dwarf don Cupid.

After the commentators had wearied themselves with trying to identify "Iunio," or "Junio," with one Junius, a Roman captain in a play by [Francis] Beaumont and [John] Fletcher; after they had amended "Junio" to "Julio" and had imagined a reference to Giulio Romano—someone at last suggested the reading,—

This senior-junior, giant-dwarf, Dan Cupid,—

and learned and unlearned alike shouted "Shakespeare!"

I mention in passing this passion of Shakespeare for the antithetical. It is his habit, a part of his dramatic technique, and it runs all through his work. But we must not fix our attention on it, or try to fathom it; for many shimmers of fancy are at play, some of them small and silvery as aspen leaves, and others as large as the shadow cast by a mainsail. He sometimes enhances a great effect of gorgeous eloquence by placing in front of it a bank of gloomy foreboding and quiet talk. He does this in "Henry V," where he introduces Henry's magnificent poetry about the responsibility of kings with a dark, muttering, introspective scene in prose—a sort of antechamber to Apollo's temple.

## CALM BETWEEN DRAMATIC ACTIONS

In "Macbeth" there is a notable case of great blanket-work, or heavy cloud-rolling and premonitory muffled gloom, almost of stupidity. Between the witch-and-murder beginnings of the play and the battle-scenes at the end of it, there falls a long scene at the English court, which is one of the dullest scenes in Shakespeare (Act IV, Sc. 3). Malcolm and Macduff are discovered: they declare that they will seek out some desolate shade and weep their sad bosoms empty. Both the characters seem to be half asleep, and to be talking about their dreams. Nothing could rest us better from the murders we have just been witnessing, or better set off the turmoil in Scotland that

### THE REALITY OF DAYLIGHT

*After Macbeth has murdered Duncan, and Lady Macbeth has returned the daggers and smeared blood on the guards, persistent knocking at the gate heightens the tension of the already nervous couple. The knocking signals morning and brings the horror of their deeds into daylight's reality.*

MACB.                                            I'll go no more.
I am afraid to think what I have done;
Look on't again I dare not.
     LADY.                                  Infirm of purpose!
Give me the daggers. The sleeping and the dead
Are but as pictures. 'Tis the eye of childhood
That fears a painted devil. If he do bleed,
I'll gild the faces of the grooms withal,
For it must seem their guilt.
                              *Exit. Knocking within.*
     MACB.                       Whence is that knocking?
How is't with me when every noise appals me?
What hands are here? Ha! they pluck out mine eyes!
Will all great Neptune's ocean wash this blood
Clean from my hand? No. This my hand will rather
The multitudinous seas incarnadine,
Making the green one red.
                    *Enter* LADY MACBETH.
     LADY. My hands are of your colour, but I shame
To wear a heart so white. [*Knock.*] I hear a knocking
At the south entry. Retire we to our chamber.
A little water clears us of this deed.
How easy is it then! Your constancy
Hath left you unattended. [*Knock.*] Hark! more knocking.
Get on your nightgown, lest occasion call us
And show us to be watchers. Be not lost
So poorly in your thoughts.
     MACB. To know my deed, 'twere best not know myself.
                                        [*Knock.*]
Wake Duncan with thy knocking! I would thou couldst!
                                    *Exeunt.*

Shakespeare, *The Tragedy of Macbeth*, act 2, scene 2.

is to follow immediately, than the stupor of this scene.

It is idle to inquire how far Shakespeare was conscious of his lights and shades, of his contrasted settings and antithetical characters. Falstaff is a fat old man, the Prince, a thin young man [*King Henry IV*, Part One]; Caliban balances Ariel [*The Tempest*]; Malvolio is a prig, Toby Belch, a scapegrace [*Twelfth Night*]. Such types appeared to him in pairs and are somehow parts of each other. So also in a single character there are often contrasts that give it brilliancy; for example, the wisdom of fools, the fierceness of the gentle, the jests of gravediggers, the pomposity of the empty-minded. It is always a hiatus [a break in continuity] that makes us laugh or cry on the stage. In "Hamlet" the drama arises, as we have seen, out of the heart-piercing emergency-calls of fate, and Hamlet's heartrending incapacity to meet them.

In "Macbeth" the contrasts are gigantic and Rembrandt-esque. The drama is an old-fashioned, blood-and-thunder, boys' play, and its merit lies in the way it is done. The terror it inspires is due to the abyss that lies between the inner natures of Macbeth and Lady Macbeth, and the murder which they perpetrate. Recite the facts of the play as if done by the kind of persons who usually do such deeds, and the story will have little interest. It would be a foolish task for us to prove that such sensitive, high-keyed, metaphysical natures as Macbeth and Lady Macbeth—persons who tremble at shadows and are haunted by nightmares—seldom commit murders—as foolish as proving that the practical, hardened villains of the world do not discourse wittily and gayly, and enjoy the drama of their own existence as Richard III and Iago [*Othello*] seem to do. Such characters are dramatic devices; and we must accept the hypersensitiveness of Macbeth and Lady Macbeth as one of Shakespeare's greatest strokes of genius.

## MACBETH AND LADY MACBETH AS A SINGLE DRAMATIC ELEMENT

When Macbeth first comes on the stage, he is already unhinged, because the thought of murder has been flitting through his head. His wife and he have lived so long together that they are exactly in tune with one another. It makes no difference which of them first had the idea of a murder, for together they make up the picture of the terrified person. In their conversations they often exchange rôles, now one of them taking the lead, and now the other. Although it has been customary since Mrs. Siddons's [Sarah Siddons, British actress famous for her performance as Lady Macbeth] time to regard

Lady Macbeth as the worse criminal of the two, there is really little to choose between them, and Macbeth plots the murder of Banquo without confiding in his wife. To my mind they appear as a single dramatic element. Lady Macbeth actually dies of remorse and mental trouble, while Macbeth, although he has a fighting rôle to distract his mind, gibbers with metaphysical terrors till the end. He identifies the sickness of Lady Macbeth with his own remorse, and says to the doctor, in regard to Lady Macbeth's "thick coming fancies,"—

> Cure her of that.
> Canst thou not minister to a mind diseased,
> Pluck from the memory a rooted sorrow,
> Raze out the written troubles of the brain,
> And with some sweet oblivious antidote
> Cleanse the stuff'd bosom of that perilous stuff
> Which weighs upon the heart?

Even at his final meeting with Macduff, he is obsessed by the witches and their prophecies: he is living the inner life of terror and remorse.

> Accursed be that tongue that tells me so,
> For it hath cow'd my better part of man!
> And be these juggling fiends no more believ'd,
> That palter with us in a double sense;
> That keep the word of promise to our ear,
> And break it to our hope.

Thus, only two minutes before he is killed, Macbeth is seen reviewing the story of their crime, just as his wife reviews that story in her sleep-walking. In "Macbeth," Shakespeare appears to have doubled his leading character, just as he doubled his whole plot in "King Lear."

## FIERCE LIGHTS AND BLACK SHADOWS

Let us glance rapidly through the play and recall its fierce lights and black shadows, its plunges from mood to mood, from crashing tempest to ominous and horrible spots of calm. The witches in the opening are almost pure allegory. Macbeth doubts whether he has really seen them or not, and we ourselves see them as portions of his mood. Then comes Lady Macbeth with the letter, and we see that both she and her lord are in the coils of an obsession. They are both frightfully excited. The look on Macbeth's face confirms his wife's doubt as to his capacity. Both of them are, from the beginning, very much afraid that they will be found out. Murder is a business foreign to their natures, and they know that they will do it bunglingly. The unsuspecting Duncan and his train enter immediately, and a wafture of æolian music [a rush of verse music] accompanies his step on the threshold of the rude, bleak, forbidding Scotch castle from which he is never to emerge alive.

> BANQUO.                    This guest of summer,
> The temple-haunting martlet, does approve
> By his loved mansionry that the heaven's breath
> Smells wooingly here: no jutty, frieze,
> Buttress, nor coign of vantage, but this bird
> Hath made his pendent bed and procreant cradle:
> Where they most breed and haunt, I have observ'd
> The air is delicate.

Surely this is a dramatic introduction to a coarse, feudal, uncomfortable, gloomy, and bare-walled piece of butchery.

I shall not recite the murder itself. The physical blood and grime of the thing is as awful to the gentle natures of Macbeth and his wife as is the horror of the crime itself, and the terror, always present, of being discovered.

After the realism of the truly dreadful and most lifelike scenes between Macbeth and his wife during the murder, they stand shivering, and ask what o'clock it is, and listen for the owl and the cricket.

The audience at this point receives a shock as of blank emptiness. Everything has stopped: we see the very boards of the stage. Then, as if from another world, comes the knocking of the porter,—daylight,—and the noisy, innocent, leisurely obscenity of the porter.

This plunge from the imaginative terrors of midnight into the cruel facts of common day is perhaps the most sudden transition in drama. It is the daylight that makes the murder so ghastly in review; and it is the natural goodness of Macbeth and of his lady, their domestic quality, their spiritual remoteness from the thing in hand, that makes us shudder.

## THE NATURE OF MACBETH'S SOUL

Of all the horror-breeding passages in the drama, the most telling are the two speeches that give us a glimpse into Macbeth as a poetic, introspective, soulful person. At the very moment when he is encouraging himself and lashing himself up to be as bloody as possible there comes to him a vision of the quiet life.

> We have scotch'd the snake, not kill'd it:
> She'll close and be herself. . . .
>
>                    Better be with the dead,
> Whom we, to gain our peace, have sent to peace,

Than on the torture of the mind to lie
In restless ecstasy. Duncan is in his grave;
After life's fitful fever he sleeps well;
Treason has done his worst: nor steel, nor poison,
Malice domestic, foreign levy, nothing,
Can touch him further.

Again when the servant announces that the English forces are upon him, Macbeth is seized with an access of sentiment—a vision of lost happiness.

SERVANT.    The English force, so please you.

MACBETH.    Take thy face hence.
                    Seyton!—I am sick at heart
            When I behold—Seyton, I say!—This push
            Will cheer me ever, or disseat me now.
            I have liv'd long enough: my way of life
            Is fall'n into the sere, the yellow leaf,
            And that which should accompany old age,
            As honor, love, obedience, troops of friends,
            I must not look to have; but, in their stead,
            Curses, not loud but deep, mouth-honor, breath,
            Which the poor heart would fain deny, and dare not.
            Seyton!

To no other dramatist but Shakespeare did nature reveal these climaxes of antiphonal [alternating] feeling—a devil rushing in where a god is called, or *vice versa.*

# Macbeth Tempts Fate

Cleanth Brooks

Cleanth Brooks explores the significance and richness of clothing imagery in *Macbeth*. Brooks says that Macbeth, though proud to wear the mantle of Thane of Cawdor, is uncomfortable in his kingly robes because he stole them. Brooks cites other symbolic uses of clothing images that sharpen the contrast between the horror of the murder and the nature of what rightfully should have been. According to Brooks, ambition moves Macbeth to commit the first murder, but, despite his discomfort in the clothes he wears, Macbeth's desire to control the future drives him to murder those who threaten to wear kingly robes in the future.

One of the most startling things which has come out of [Caroline F.E.] Spurgeon's book on Shakespeare's imagery is her discovery of the "old clothes" imagery in *Macbeth*. As she points out: "The idea constantly recurs that Macbeth's new honours sit ill upon him, like a loose and badly fitting garment, belonging to someone else." And she goes on to quote passage after passage in which the idea is expressed. But, though we are all in Spurgeon's debt for having pointed this out, one has to observe that Spurgeon has hardly explored the full implications of her discovery. Perhaps her interest in classifying and cataloguing the imagery of the plays has obscured for her some of the larger and more important relationships. At any rate, for reasons to be given below, she has realized only a part of the potentialities of her discovery.

Her comment on the clothes imagery reaches its climax with the following paragraphs:

> And, at the end, when the tyrant is at bay at Dunsinane, and the English troops are advancing, the Scottish lords still have this image in their minds. Caithness sees him as a man vainly trying to fasten a large garment on him with too small a belt:
>
>> He cannot buckle his distemper'd cause
>> Within the belt of rule;

Excerpts from *The Well Wrought Urn* by Cleanth Brooks. Copyright 1947; renewed 1975 by Cleanth Brooks. Reprinted by permission of Harcourt Brace & Company.

while Angus, in a similar image, vividly sums up the essence of what they all have been thinking ever since Macbeth's accession to power:

> now does he feel his title
> Hang loose about him, like a giant's robe
> Upon a dwarfish thief.

This imaginative picture of a small, ignoble man encumbered and degraded by garments unsuited to him, should be put against the view emphasized by some critics (notably [British poet and critic Samuel Taylor] Coleridge and [British critic A.C.] Bradley) of the likeness between Macbeth and [British poet John] Milton's Satan in grandeur and sublimity.

## CLOTHES SIGNIFY MACBETH'S NEW ROLES

Undoubtedly Macbeth . . . is great, magnificently great. . . . But he could never be put beside, say, Hamlet or Othello, in nobility of nature; and there *is* an aspect in which he is but a poor, vain, cruel, treacherous creature, snatching ruthlessly over the dead bodies of kinsman and friend at place and power he is utterly unfitted to possess. It is worth remembering that it is thus that Shakespeare, with his unshrinking clarity of vision, repeatedly *sees* him.

But this is to make primary what is only one aspect of the old-clothes imagery! And there is no warrant for interpreting the garment imagery as used by Macbeth's enemies, Caithness and Angus, to mean that *Shakespeare* sees Macbeth as a poor and somewhat comic figure.

The crucial point of the comparison, it seems to me, lies not in the smallness of the man and the largeness of the robes, but rather in the fact that—whether the man be large or small—these are not *his* garments; in Macbeth's case they are actually stolen garments. Macbeth is uncomfortable in them because he is continually conscious of the fact that they do not belong to him. There is a further point, and it is one of the utmost importance; the oldest symbol for the hypocrite is that of the man who cloaks his true nature under a disguise. Macbeth loathes playing the part of the hypocrite—and actually does not play it too well. If we keep this in mind as we look back at the instances of the garment images which Spurgeon has collected for us, we shall see that the pattern of imagery becomes very rich indeed. Macbeth says in Act I:

> The Thane of Cawdor lives: why do you dress me
> In borrow'd robes?

Macbeth at this point wants no honors that are not honestly

his. Banquo says in Act I:

> New honors come upon him,
> Like our strange garments, cleave not to their mold,
> But with the aid of use.

But Banquo's remark, one must observe, is not censorious [highly critical]. It is indeed a compliment to say of one that he wears new honors with some awkwardness. The observation becomes ironical only in terms of what is to occur later.

Macbeth says in Act 1:

> He hath honor'd me of late; and I have bought
> Golden opinions from all sorts of people,
> Which would be worn now in their newest gloss,
> Not cast aside so soon.

Macbeth here is proud of his new clothes: he is happy to wear what he has truly earned. It is the part of simple good husbandry not to throw aside these new garments and replace them with robes stolen from Duncan.

But Macbeth has already been wearing Duncan's garments in anticipation, as his wife implies in the metaphor with which she answers him:

> Was the hope drunk,
> Wherein you dress'd yourself?

(The metaphor may seem hopelessly mixed, and a full and accurate analysis of such mixed metaphors in terms of the premises of Shakespeare's style waits upon some critic who will have to consider not only this passage but many more like it in Shakespeare.) For our purposes here, however, one may observe that the psychological line, the line of the basic symbolism, runs on unbroken. A man dressed in a drunken hope is garbed in strange attire indeed—a ridiculous dress which accords thoroughly with the contemptuous picture that Lady Macbeth wishes to evoke. Macbeth's earlier dream of glory has been a drunken fantasy merely, if he flinches from action now.

But the series of garment metaphors which run through the play is paralleled by a series of masking or cloaking images which—if we free ourselves of Spurgeon's rather mechanical scheme of classification—show themselves to be merely variants of the garments which hide none too well his disgraceful self. He is consciously hiding that self throughout the play.

"False face must hide what the false heart doth know," he counsels Lady Macbeth before the murder of Duncan; and later, just before the murder of Banquo, he invokes night to "Scarf up the eye of pitiful day."

## SYMBOLIC CLOTHES DEEPEN THE MEANING OF THE PLAY

One of the most powerful of these cloaking images is given to
Lady Macbeth in the famous speech in Act I:

> Come, thick night,
> And pall thee in the dunnest smoke of hell,
> That my keen knife see not the wound it makes,
> Nor heaven peep through the blanket of the dark,
> To cry, "Hold, Hold!"

I suppose that it is natural to conceive the "keen knife" here as
held in her own hand. Lady Macbeth is capable of wielding it.
And in this interpretation, the imagery is thoroughly significant. Night is to be doubly black so that not even her knife may
see the wound it makes. But I think that there is good warrant
for regarding her "keen knife" as Macbeth himself. She has
just, a few lines above, given her analysis of Macbeth's character as one who would "not play false, / And yet [would]
wrongly win." To bring him to the point of action, she will
have to "chastise [him] with the valor of [her] tongue." There
is good reason, then, for her to invoke night to become black-
er still—to pall itself in the "dunnest smoke of hell." For night
must not only screen the deed from the eye of heaven—conceal it at least until it is too late for heaven to call out to Macbeth "Hold, Hold!" Lady Macbeth would have night blanket the
deed from the hesitant doer. The imagery thus repeats and re-
inforces the substance of Macbeth's anguished aside uttered in
the preceding scene:

> Let not light see my black and deep desires;
> The eye wink at the hand; yet let that be
> Which the eye fears, when it is done, to see.

I do not know whether "blanket" and "pall" qualify as garment metaphors in Spurgeon's classification: yet one is the
clothing of sleep, and the other, the clothing of death—they are
the appropriate garments of night; and they carry on an important aspect of the general clothes imagery. It is not necessary to attempt to give here an exhaustive list of instances of
the garment metaphor; but one should say a word about the
remarkable passage in II.iii.

Here, after the discovery of Duncan's murder, Banquo says

> And when we have our naked frailties hid,
> That suffer in exposure, let us meet,
> And question this most bloody piece of work—

that is, "When we have clothed ourselves against the chill
morning air, let us meet to discuss this bloody piece of work."
Macbeth answers, as if his subconscious mind were already

taking Banquo's innocent phrase, "naked frailties," in a deeper, ironic sense:

> Let's briefly put on manly readiness. . . .

It is ironic; for the "manly readiness" which he urges the other lords to put on, is, in his own case, a hypocrite's garment: he can only pretend to be the loyal, grief-stricken liege who is almost unstrung by the horror of Duncan's murder.

But the word "manly" carries still a further ironic implication: earlier, Macbeth had told Lady Macbeth that he dared

> do all that may become a man;
> Who dares do more is none.

Under the weight of her reproaches of cowardice, however, he *has* dared do more, and has become less than a man, a beast. He has already laid aside, therefore, one kind of "manly readiness" and has assumed another: he has garbed himself in a sterner composure than that which he counsels to his fellows—the hard and inhuman "manly readiness" of the resolved murderer.

The clothes imagery, used sometimes with emphasis on one aspect of it, sometimes on another, does pervade the play. And it should be evident that the daggers "breech'd with gore"—though Spurgeon does not include the passage in her examples of clothes imagery—represent one more variant of this general symbol. Consider the passage once more:

> Here lay Duncan,
> His silver skin lac'd with his golden blood;
> And his gash'd stabs look'd like a breach in nature
> For ruin's wasteful entrance: there, the murderers,
> Steep'd in the colors of their trade, their daggers
> Unmannerly breech'd with gore. . . .

The clothes imagery runs throughout the passage; the body of the king is dressed in the most precious of garments, the blood royal itself; and the daggers too are dressed—in the same garment. The daggers, "naked" except for their lower parts which are reddened with blood, are like men in "unmannerly" dress—men, naked except for their red breeches, lying beside the red-handed grooms. The figure, though vivid, is fantastic; granted. But the basis for the comparison is *not* slight and adventitious. The metaphor fits the real situation on the deepest levels. As Macbeth and Lennox burst into the room, they find the daggers wearing, as Macbeth knows all too well, a horrible masquerade. They have been carefully "clothed" to play a part. They are not honest daggers, honorably naked in readiness to guard the king, or, "mannerly" clothed in their own sheaths. Yet the disguise which they wear will enable Macbeth to assume the robes of Duncan—robes to which he is no more entitled than are the daggers to the royal garments which they now wear, grotesquely. . . .

The stimulus to Duncan's murder, as we know, was the prophecy of the Weird Sisters. But Macbeth's subsequent career of bloodshed stems from the same prophecy. Macbeth was to have the crown, but the crown was to pass to Banquo's children. The second part of the prophecy troubles Macbeth from the start. It does not oppress him, however, until the crown has been won. But from this point on, the effect of the prophecy is to hurry Macbeth into action and more action until he is finally precipitated into ruin.

## SYMBOL OF HYPOCRISY

*In* Shakespeare the Professional and Related Studies, *Kenneth Muir professes that the images of Macbeth's unsuitable clothes symbolize the king's hypocrisy.*

The contrast between the man and his clothes is a symbol of the hypocrisy to which Macbeth is committed. He has to 'look like the innocent flower, But be the serpent under't'; he has to 'mock the time with fairest show' and make his face a vizard to his heart; and in the last act he complains of the hypocritical loyalty—the mouth-honour—he receives from his own subjects. Life itself, he declares, is a walking shadow, a poor player,

> That struts and frets his hour upon the stage
> And then is heard no more. It is a tale
> Told by an idiot, full of sound and fury,
> Signifying nothing.

This is a bitterer version of Prospero's lines when he interrupts the masque. 'We are such stuff as dreams are made on'.

Kenneth Muir, *Shakespeare the Professional and Related Studies.* Totowa, NJ: Rowman and Littlefield, 1973.

We need not spend much time in speculating on whether Macbeth, had he been content with Duncan's murder, had he tempted fate no further, had he been willing to court the favor of his nobles, might not have died peaceably in bed. We are dealing, not with history, but with a play. Yet, even in history the usurper sometimes succeeds; and he sometimes succeeds on the stage. Shakespeare himself knew of, and wrote plays about, usurpers who successfully maintained possession of the crown. But, in any case, this much is plain: the train of murders into which Macbeth launches aggravates suspicions of his guilt and alienates the nobles.

Yet, a Macbeth who could act once, and then settle down to enjoy the fruits of this one attempt to meddle with the future would, of course, not be Macbeth. For it is not merely his great imagination and his warrior courage in defeat which redeem him for tragedy and place him beside the other great tragic protagonists: rather, it is his attempt to conquer the future, an attempt involving him, like Oedipus, in a desperate struggle with fate itself. It is this which holds our imaginative sympathy, even after he has degenerated into a bloody tyrant and has become the slayer of Macduff's wife and children.

To sum up, there can be no question that Macbeth stands at the height of his power after his murder of Duncan, and that the plan—as outlined by Lady Macbeth—has been relatively successful. The road turns toward disaster only when Macbeth decides to murder Banquo. Why does he make this decision? Shakespeare has pointed up the basic motivation very carefully:

> Then prophet-like,
> They hail'd him father to a line of kings.
> Upon my head they plac'd a fruitless crown,
> And put a barren scepter in my gripe,
> Thence to be wrench'd with an unlineal hand,
> No son of mine succeeding. If't be so,
> For Banquo's issue have I fil'd my mind;
> For them the gracious Duncan have I murder'd;
> Put rancors in the vessel of my peace
> Only for them; and mine eternal jewel
> Given to the common enemy of man,
> To make them kings, the seed of Banquo kings!

Presumably, Macbeth had entered upon his course from sheer personal ambition. Ironically, it is the more human part of Macbeth—his desire to have more than a limited personal satisfaction, his desire to found a line, his wish to pass something on to later generations—which prompts him to dispose of Banquo. There is, of course, a resentment against Banquo, but that resentment is itself closely related to Macbeth's desire to found a dynasty. Banquo, who has risked nothing, who has remained upright, who has not defiled himself, will have kings for children; Macbeth, none. Again, ironically, the Weird Sisters who have given Macbeth, so he has thought, the priceless gift of knowledge of the future, have given the real future to Banquo.

So Banquo's murder is decided upon, and accomplished. But Banquo's son escapes, and once more, the future has eluded Macbeth. The murder of Banquo thus becomes almost meaningless. This general point may be obvious enough, but we shall do well to note some of the further ways in which Shakespeare has pointed up the significance of Macbeth's war with the future.

When Macbeth, at the beginning of Scene vii, Act I, contemplates Duncan's murder, it is the future over which he agonizes:

If it were done, when 'tis done, then 'twere well
It were done quickly; if the assassination
Could trammel up the consequence, and catch
With his surcease success, that but this blow
Might be the be-all and the end-all here. . . .

But the continuum of time cannot be partitioned off; the future is implicit in the present. There is no net strong enough to trammel up the consequence—not even in this world.

# Major Symbols in *Macbeth*

Kenneth Muir

Kenneth Muir opens his essay with a quotation by Belgian poet and dramatist Maurice Maeterlinck, who suggests that while the dialogue moves the action in Shakespeare's *Macbeth*, the images penetrate the listener's or reader's soul. Recurring images of sleep, blood, and time are among the most significant ones that move the audience; Muir suggests that collectively the images contribute symbolically to the underlying theme of the play. Muir contends that the audience senses that Macbeth's act of murdering Duncan disrupts nature's order—breaks a link in the chain of being—which cannot be restored until Macbeth is overthrown.

It is the countless presence, the uninterrupted swarm of all those images that form the profound life, the secret and almost unlimited first existence of [*Macbeth*]. Upon its surface floats the dialogue necessary to the action. It seems to be the only one that our ears seize; but, in reality, it is to the other language that our instinct—our unconscious sensibility, our soul—listens; and if the spoken words touch us more deeply than those of any other poet, it is because they are supported by a great host of hidden powers writes [Belgian poet and dramatist Maurice Maeterlinck in an excerpt from *Fortnightly Review*, 1910]

The 'hidden powers' are not supernatural but the images used, consciously or unconsciously, by the poet. . . .

## SLEEP AS A SYMBOL

The Master of the [ship] *Tiger*, whose wife has offended the First Witch, is threatened with the punishment of insomnia:

Sleep shall neither night nor day
Hang upon his penthouse lid;
He shall live a man forbid.

Excerpted from *Shakespeare the Professional and Related Studies* by Kenneth Muir (London: William Heinemann, 1973). Copyright © 1973 by Kenneth Muir.

This is the first statement of a theme which acquires great significance later in the play. After the murder of Duncan, Macbeth complains of the way he and his wife

> sleep
> In the affliction of these terrible dreams
> That shake us nightly.

They lie 'on the torture of the mind ... In restless ecstasy', while Duncan in his grave 'After life's fitful fever ... sleeps well'. Lady Macbeth tells her husband after the banquet:

> You lack the season of all natures, sleep.

The anonymous Lord (III. vi) looks forward to the time when, with the overthrow of the tyrant, they may give 'sleep to our nights'. Macbeth thinks that if he kills Macduff he will 'sleep in spite of thunder'. Lady Macbeth, because of 'a great perturbation in nature' and 'slumbery agitation' walks in her sleep and re-enacts the murders of Duncan, Banquo and Lady Macduff.

> She is troubled with thick-coming fancies,
> That keep her from her rest.

The key passage in the theme of sleeplessness occurs just after the murder of Duncan, and it was suggested to Shakespeare by a passage in Holinshed's *Chronicles* [a history of England begun in 1577], a few pages before the account of Macbeth. After King Kenneth had slain his nephew, he lived in continual fear, 'for so commeth it to passe, that such as are pricked in conscience for anie [any] secret offense committed, have ever an unquiet mind'. A voice 'was heard as he was in bed in the night time to take this rest', telling him that his sin was known to God and that he and his issue would be punished for it.

> For even at this present are there in hand secret practises to dispatch both thee and thy issue out of the waie, that other maie injoy this kingdome which thou doost indevour to assure unto thine issue. The king, with this voice being stricken into great dread and terror, passed that night without anie sleep comming in his eies.

So Macbeth, after the murder, tells his wife:

> Methought I heard a voice cry, 'Sleep no more!
> Macbeth does murther Sleep',—the innocent Sleep;
> Sleep, that knits up the ravell'd sleave of care,
> The death of each day's life, sore labour's bath,
> Balm of hurt minds, great Nature's second course,
> Chief nourisher in life's feast ...
> Still it cried, 'Sleep no more!' to all the house:
> 'Glamis hath murther'd Sleep, and therefore Cawdor
> Shall sleep no more, Macbeth shall sleep no more!'

The voice which Macbeth thinks comes from without is

really the echo of his own conscience. As [critic A.C.] Bradley commented, the voice 'denounced on him, as if his three names gave him three personalities to suffer in, the doom of sleeplessness'; and, as [critic John] Murry says, 'we are straightway plunged into an abyss of metaphysical horror'. The murder of a sleeping guest, of a sleeping king, of a saintly old man, the murder, as it were, of sleep itself, carries with it the appropriate retribution of insomnia. . . .

## BLOOD AS A SYMBOL

[British poet] John Masefield once remarked that the subject of *Macbeth* is blood; and from the appearance of the bloody sergeant in the second scene of the play to the last scene of all, we have a continual vision of blood. Macbeth's sword in the battle 'smok'd with bloody execution'; he and Banquo seemed to 'bathe in reeking wounds'; the Sergeant's 'gashes cry for help'. The second Witch comes from the bloody task of killing swine. The visionary dagger is stained with 'gouts of blood'. Macbeth, after the murder, declares that not all great Neptune's ocean will cleanse his hands:

> this my hand will rather
> The multitudinous seas incarnadine,
> Making the green one red.

Duncan is spoken of as the fountain of his sons' blood; his wounds

> look'd like a breach in nature
> For ruin's wasteful entrance.

The world had become a 'bloody stage'. Macbeth, before the murder of Banquo, invokes the 'bloody and invisible hand' of night. We are told of the twenty trenched gashes on Banquo's body and his ghost shakes his 'gory locks' at Macbeth, who is convinced that 'blood will have blood'. At the end of the banquet scene, he confesses wearily that he is 'stepp'd so far' in blood, that

> should I wade no more,
> Returning were as tedious as go o'er.

The Second Apparition, a bloody child, advises Macbeth to be 'bloody, bold, and resolute'. Malcolm declares that Scotland bleeds,

> and each new day a gash
> Is added to her wounds.

Lady Macbeth, sleep-walking, tries in vain to remove the 'damned spot' from her hands:

> Here's the smell of the blood still. All the perfumes of Arabia
> will not sweeten this little hand.

In the final scene, Macbeth's severed head is displayed on a
pole. As [critic] Jan Kott has recently reminded us in *Shakespeare Our Contemporary*, the subject of the play is murder,
and the prevalence of blood ensures that we shall never forget
the physical realities in metaphysical overtones.

## THE SIGNIFICANCE OF TIME

*Macbeth* is not the only one of Shakespeare's works in which
time is particularly significant. It is the main theme of the *Sonnets*, where it is regarded as the enemy of love and beauty; it is
the subject of Lucrece's tirade [in the poem "The Rape of Lucrece"]; and it is relevant to the interpretation of *Troilus and
Cressida*. As several critics have recognized, Time is of central
importance in *Macbeth*. He is promised by the Weird Sisters
that he will be king 'hereafter' and Banquo wonders if they 'can
look into the seeds of time'. Macbeth, tempted by the thought of
murder, declares that 'Present fears / Are less than horrible
imaginings' and decides that 'Time and the hour runs through
the roughest day'. Lady Macbeth says she feels 'The future in
the instant'. In his soliloquy in the last scene of Act I, Macbeth
speaks of himself as 'here upon this bank and shoal of time',
time being contrasted with the sea of eternity. He pretends that
he would not worry about the future, or about the life to come,
if he could be sure of success in the present; and his wife implies that the conjunction of time and place for the murder will
never recur. Just before the murder, Macbeth reminds himself
of the exact time and place, so that he can relegate (as [poet
and critic] Stephen Spender suggests) 'the moment to the past
from which it will never escape into the future'. Macbeth is
troubled by his inability to say amen, because he dimly realizes
he has forfeited the possibility of blessing and because he
knows that he has become 'the deed's creature'. The nightmares of the guilty pair and the return of Banquo from the
grave symbolize the haunting of the present by the past. When
Macbeth is informed of his wife's death, he describes how life
has become for him a succession of meaningless days, the futility he has brought upon himself by his crimes:

> To-morrow, and to-morrow, and to-morrow,
> Creeps in this petty pace from day to day
> To the last syllable of recorded time,
> And all our yesterdays have lighted fools
> The way to dusty death.

At the very end of the play, Macduff announces that with the death of the tyrant 'The time is free' and Malcolm promises, without 'a large expense of time' to do what is necessary ('which would be planted newly with the time') and to bring back order from chaos 'in measure, time, and place'.

## ORDER DISRUPTED AND RESTORED

From this last speech, it can be seen that *Macbeth* can be regarded as a play about the disruption of order through evil, and its final restoration [a theme suggested by G. Wilson Knight and other critics]. It begins with what the witches call a hurly-burly and ends with the restoration of order by Malcolm. Order is represented throughout by the bonds of loyalty; and chaos is represented by the powers of darkness with their upsetting of moral values ('Fair is foul and foul is fair'). The witches can raise winds to fight against the churches, to sink ships and destroy buildings: they are the enemies both of religion and of civilization. Lady Macbeth invokes the evil spirits to take possession of her; and, after the murder of Duncan, Macbeth's mind begins to dwell on universal destruction. He is willing 'to let the frame of things disjoint, both the worlds suffer' merely to be freed from his nightmares. Again, in his conjuration of the witches in the cauldron scene, he is prepared to risk absolute chaos, 'even till destruction sicken' through surfeit [excessive amount], rather than not obtain an answer. In his last days, Macbeth is 'aweary of the sun' and he wishes 'the estate of the world' were undone. Order in Scotland, even the moral order in the universe, can be restored only by his death. [Critic] G.R. Elliott contrasts the threefold hail with which Malcolm is greeted at the end of the play with the threefold hail of the witches on the blasted heath: they mark the destruction of order and its restoration.

All through the play ideas of order and chaos are juxtaposed. When Macbeth is first visited by temptation his 'single state of man' is shaken and 'nothing is but what is not'. In the next scene Shakespeare presents ideas of loyalty, duty, and the reward of faithful service, in contrast both to the treachery of the dead Thane of Cawdor, and to the treacherous thoughts of the new thane. Lady Macbeth prays that 'no compunctious visitings of nature' shall prevent her fell purpose; and in the next scene in which Duncan appears he describes the beautiful setting of Macbeth's castle. The main purpose of this description is for dramatic irony—the setting contrasting with the deed which the audience know is about to be enacted there—but it also

## DARKNESS DISRUPTED BY THE PORTER'S KNOCK

*In his 1823 essay "On the Knocking at the Gate in* Macbeth,*" British essayist Thomas De Quincey observes that Macbeth and Lady Macbeth become fiends in a dark, isolated world within the castle when Macbeth kills Duncan. The porter's knock at the gate symbolically represents a return of the human world where the repercussions of the night's deeds will be felt.*

[In *Macbeth*,] the retiring of the human heart, and the entrance of the fiendish heart was to be expressed and made sensible. Another world has stept in; and the murderers are taken out of the region of human things, human purposes, human desires. They are transfigured: Lady Macbeth is "unsexed"; Macbeth has forgot that he was born of woman; both are conformed to the image of devils; and the world of devils is suddenly revealed. . . . Hence it is, that when the deed is done, when the work of darkness is perfect, then the world of darkness passes away like a pageantry in the clouds: the knocking at the gate is heard; and it makes known audibly that the reaction has commenced; the human has made its reflux upon the fiendish; the pulses of life are beginning to beat again; and the re-establishment of the goings-on of the world in which we live, first makes us profoundly sensible of the awful parenthesis that had suspended them.

Thomas De Quincey. "On the Knocking at the Gate in *Macbeth*," in G.B. Harrison, ed., *Shakespeare: The Complete Works*. New York: Harcourt, Brace and Company, 1952.

links up with the natural images of growth used by Duncan in the previous scene. We are reminded, as Lady Macbeth welcomes the King, of the duties of hospitality soon to be violated.

Before the murder, Macbeth reminds himself that he is the kinsman, the subject and the host of his intended victim; Duncan sends a diamond to his 'most kind hostess'; and Banquo speaks of his franchised bosom and clear allegiance. The vision of the dagger repeats in a more intense form the experience that in the first act had shaken Macbeth's single state of man; and later he is afraid that the stones will cry out against the unnaturalness of the murder. At the moment when the murder is being committed, there is a violent storm:

Lamentings heard i' the air, strange screams of death,
And prophesying with accents terrible
Of dire combustion and confused events
New hatch'd to the woeful time—

possibly an allusion to dire the combustion of the gunpowder plot [the plot of a few Roman Catholics to blow up the Houses of Parliament on November 5, 1605], but carrying also a more universal significance—an unnatural darkness hides the sun, a falcon is killed by an owl, and Duncan's horses eat each other. As Ross emphasizes, the deed is against nature.

The third act is devoted to the murder of Banquo and the appearance of his ghost at the banquet. In the first scene he is invited as the chief guest to the solemn supper, the great feast, with which Macbeth's coronation is being celebrated.

In the second scene Macbeth's mind begins to dwell on universal destruction. He is willing to 'let the frame of things disjoint, both the worlds suffer', rather than endure the terrible dreams that shake him every night; and he envies Duncan in his grave, safe from treachery and foreign invasion. In the Banquet scene, stress is laid on its ceremoniousness. In the very first line Macbeth refers to the 'degrees' of the guests, and this contrasts with his wife's abrupt dismissal of the guests when the feast is broken up: 'Stand not upon the order of your going'. Lady Macbeth reminds her husband that 'the sauce to meat is ceremony'. The 'twenty trenched gashes' on Banquo's head are each 'a death to nature'—enough to kill him and to upset the natural order. As soon as Macbeth pretends to wish that Banquo were present, the ghost appears on two occasions. When her guests are dismissed, Lady Macbeth tells her husband:

> You have displac'd the mirth, broke the good meeting
> With most admir'd disorder.

The anonymous Lord who discusses the state of the realm with Lennox prays for the return of normal conditions of life, disrupted by Macbeth's tyranny:

> Give to our tables meat, sleep to our nights,
> Free from our feasts and banquets bloody knives,
> Do faithful homage and receive free honours:
> All which we pine for now.

In the scene in England Malcolm's self-accusations—in particular his pretence of wishing to uproar the universal peace and confound all unity on earth—are disorders contrasted with the virtues he pretends not to have, with the virtues he does have, and with the miraculous powers of the pious Edward. Order is restored by the overthrow of the tyrant.

# The Character of Macbeth

William Hazlitt

William Hazlitt approaches the protagonist in Shakespeare's *Macbeth* from three angles. He focuses on Macbeth as a man carried along by a violent fate which, Hazlitt says, Macbeth has too much conscience to follow. Hazlitt highlights Macbeth's perplexity by contrasting his hesitancy with Lady Macbeth's unflinching determination. Finally, by comparing Macbeth to Richard III, Hazlitt makes the strong case that Macbeth possesses many human qualities deserving of sympathy.

William Hazlitt, a British essayist who wrote during the first quarter of the nineteenth century, is best known for his essays on art and drama, essays on everyday subjects, and his literary criticism concerning Shakespeare's characters, English poets, and English comic writers.

[*Macbeth* is] distinguished for the lofty imagination it displays, and for the tumultuous vehemence of the action; and the one is made the moving principle of the other. The overwhelming pressure of preternatural [supernatural] agency urges on the tide of human passion with redoubled force. Macbeth himself appears driven along by the violence of his fate like a vessel drifting before a storm: he reels to and fro like a drunken man; he staggers under the weight of his own purposes and the suggestions of others; he stands at bay with his situation; and from the superstitious awe and breathless suspense into which the communications of the Weird Sisters throw him, is hurried on with daring impatience to verify their predictions, and with impious and bloody hand to tear aside the veil which hides the uncertainty of the future.

Excerpted from *Lectures on the Literature of the Age of Elizabeth* by William Hazlitt (London: Bell & Dalby, 1870).

## MACBETH'S DETERMINATION AND HESITATION

He [Macbeth] is not equal to the struggle with fate and conscience. He now "bends up each corporal agent to this terrible feat;" [I, vii]; at other times his heart misgives him, and he is cowed and abashed by his success. "The attempt, and not the deed, confounds us." His mind is assailed by the stings of remorse, and full of "preternatural solicitings." His speeches and soliloquies are dark riddles on human life, baffling solution, and entangling him in their labyrinths. In thought he is absent and perplexed, sudden and desperate in act, from a distrust of his own resolution. His energy springs from the anxiety and agitation of his mind. His blindly rushing forward on the objects of his ambition and revenge, or his recoiling from them, equally betrays the harassed state of his feelings.

This part of his character is admirably set off by being brought in connection with that of Lady Macbeth, whose obdurate strength of will and masculine firmness give her the ascendancy over her husband's faltering virtue. She at once seizes on the opportunity that offers for the accomplishment of all their wished—for greatness, and never flinches from her object till all is over. The magnitude of her resolution almost covers the magnitude of her guilt. She is a great bad woman, whom we hate, but whom we fear more than we hate. She does not excite our loathing and abhorrence like Regan and Goneril [older daughters of King Lear]. She is only wicked to gain a great end, and is perhaps more distinguished by her commanding presence of mind and inexorable self-will, which do not suffer her to be diverted from a bad purpose, when once formed, by weak and womanly regrets, than by the hardness of her heart or want of natural affections.

## LADY MACBETH'S UNFLINCHING DETERMINATION

The impression which her lofty determination of character makes on the mind of Macbeth is well described where he exclaims,

> Bring forth men-children only;
> For thy undaunted mettle should compose
> Nothing but males! [I, vii]

Nor do the pains she is at to "screw his courage to the sticking-place," the reproach to him, not to be "lost so poorly in himself," the assurance that "a little water clears them of this deed," show anything but her greater consistency in depravity. Her strong-nerved ambition furnishes ribs of steel to "the sides of his intent;" and she is herself wound up to the execution of her baneful project with the same unshrinking fortitude in crime, that in other circumstances she would probably have shown patience in suffering. The deliberate sacrifice of all other considerations to the gaining "for their future days and nights sole sovereign sway and masterdom," by the murder of Duncan, is gorgeously expressed in her invocation on hearing of "his fatal entrance under her battlements:"—

> Come, you spirits
> That tend on mortal thoughts, unsex me here:
> And fill me, from the crown to the toe, top-full
> Of direst cruelty! make thick my blood,
> Stop up th' access and passage to remorse,
> That no compunctious visitings of nature
> Shake my fell purpose, nor keep peace between
> Th' effect and it. Come to my woman's breasts,
> And take my milk for gall, you murdering ministers,
> Wherever in your sightless substances
> You wait on nature's mischief! Come, thick night!
> And pall thee in the dunnest smoke of hell,
> That my keen knife see not the wound it makes,
> Nor heav'n peep through the blanket of the dark,
> To cry, Hold, hold!—                                    [I, v]

When she first hears that "the king [Duncan] comes her to-night," [I, v] she is so overcome by the news, which is beyond her utmost expectations, that she answers the messenger, "Thou'rt mad to say it:" and on receiving her husband's account of the predictions of the Witches, conscious of his instability of purpose, and that her presence is necessary to goad him on to the consummation of his promised greatness, she exclaims—

> ——Hie thee hither,
> That I may pour my spirits in thine ear,
> And chastise with the valour of my tongue
> All that impedes thee from the golden round,
> Which fate and metaphysical aid doth seem
> To have thee crown'd withal.                          [I, v]

This swelling exultation and keen spirit of triumph, this uncontrollable eagerness of anticipation, which seems to dilate her form and take possession of all her faculties, this solid, substantial flesh-and-blood display of passion, exhibit a striking contrast to the cold, abstracted, gratuitous, servile malignity of the Witches, who are equally instrumental in urging Macbeth to his fate for the mere love of mischief, and from a disinterested delight in deformity and cruelty. They are hags of mischief, obscene panders to iniquity, malicious from their impotence of enjoyment, enamoured of destruction, because they are themselves unreal, abortive, half-existences: who become sublime from their exemption from all human sympathies and contempt for all human affairs; as lady Macbeth does by the force of passion!

Her fault seems to have been an excess of that strong principle of self-interest and family aggrandisement, not amenable to the common feelings of compassion and justice, which is so marked a feature in barbarous nations and times. A passing reflection of this kind, on the resemblance of the sleeping king to her father, alone prevents her from slaying Duncan with her own hand. . . .

## *MACBETH:* A CONTRAST OF EXTREMES

*Macbeth* (generally speaking) is done upon a stronger and more systematic principle of contrast than any other of Shakespear's plays. It moves upon the verge of an abyss, and is a constant struggle between life and death. The action is desperate and the reaction is dreadful. It is a huddling together of fierce extremes, a war of opposite natures which of them shall destroy the other. There is nothing but what has a violent end or violent beginnings. The lights and shades are laid on with a determined hand; the transitions from triumph to despair, from the height of terror to the repose of death, are sudden and startling; every passion brings in its-fellow-contrary, and the thoughts pitch and jostle against each other as in the dark. The whole play is an unruly chaos of strange and forbidden things, where the ground rocks under our feet. . . .

The leading features in the character of Macbeth are striking enough, and they form what may be thought at first only a bold, rude, Gothic outline. By comparing it with other characters of the same author we shall perceive the absolute truth and identity which is observed in the midst of the giddy whirl and rapid career of events. Macbeth in Shakespear no more loses his identity of character in the fluctuations of fortune or the storm of passion, than Macbeth in himself would have lost the identity of his person.

## MACBETH'S CHARACTER CLARIFIED BY COMPARISON WITH RICHARD III

Thus he is as distinct a being from Richard III as it is possible to imagine, though these two characters in common hands, and indeed in the hands of any other poet, would have been a repetition of the same general idea, more or less exaggerated. For both are tyrants, usurpers, murderers, both aspiring and ambitious, both courageous, cruel, treacherous.

## A Harsher View of Macbeth

*In his book* Shakespere, *Edward Dowden describes Macbeth as a harsher and bloodier man and Lady Macbeth as a more delicate woman than Hazlitt describes them. Dowden emphasizes Macbeth's brutality and describes Lady Macbeth as a helpful wife and a woman too sensitive to kill a king who reminds her of her father.*

The contrast between Macbeth and Lady Macbeth, united by their affections, their fortunes, and their crime, is made to illustrate and light up the character of each. Macbeth has physical courage, but moral weakness, and is subject to excited imaginative fears. His faint and intermittent loyalty embarrasses him: he would have the gains of crime without its pains. But when once his hands are dyed in blood, he hardly cares to withdraw them; and the same fears which had tended to hold him back from murder now urge him on to double and treble murders, until slaughter, almost reckless, becomes the habit of his reign. At last the gallant soldier of the opening of the play fights for his life with a wild and brutelike force. His whole existence has become joyless and loveless, and yet he clings to existence.

Lady Macbeth is of a finer and more delicate nature. Having fixed her eye upon an end,—the attainment for her husband of Duncan's crown,—she accepts the inevitable means; she nerves herself for the terrible night's work by artificial stimulants; yet she cannot strike the sleeping King, who resembles her father. Having sustained her weaker husband, her own strength gives way; and in sleep, when her will cannot control her thoughts, she is piteously afflicted by the memory of one stain of blood upon her little hand. At last her thread of life snaps suddenly. Macbeth, whose affection for her was real, has sunk too far into the apathy of joyless crime to feel deeply her loss.

Edward Dowden, in Franklin Thomas Baker, Introduction to *The Tragedy of Macbeth*, by William Shakespeare. New York: American Book Company, 1898.

But Richard is cruel from nature and constitution. Macbeth becomes so from accidental circumstances. Richard is from his birth deformed in body and mind, and naturally incapable of good. Macbeth is full of "the milk of human kindness," is frank, sociable, generous. He is tempted to the commission of guilt by golden opportunities, by the instigations of his wife, and by prophetic warnings. Fate and metaphysical aid conspire against his virtue and his loyalty. Richard on the contrary needs no prompter, but wades through a series of crimes to the height of his ambition from the ungovernable violence of his temper and a reckless love of mischief. He is never gay but in the prospect or in the success of his villainies: Macbeth is full of horror at the thoughts of the murder of Duncan, which he is with difficulty prevailed on to commit, and of remorse after its perpetration. Richard has no mixture of common humanity in his composition, no regard to kindred or posterity, he owns no fellowship with others, he is "himself alone."

Macbeth is not destitute of feelings of sympathy, is accessible to pity, is even made in some measure the dupe of his uxoriousness [excessive devotion to one's wife], ranks the loss of friends, of the cordial love of his followers, and of his good name, among the causes which have made him weary of life, and regrets that he has ever seized the crown by unjust means, since he cannot transmit it to his posterity—

> For Banquo's issue have I fil'd my mind;
> For them the gracious Duncan have I murder'd, ...
> To make them kings, the seed of Banquo kings.                [III, i]

In the agitation of his mind, he envies those whom he has sent to peace—

> ———Duncan is in his grave;
> After life's fitful fever he sleeps well.                [III, ii]

It is true, he becomes more callous as he plunges deeper in guilt.

> ———I have supp'd full with horrors;
> Direness, familiar to my slaughterous thoughts,
> Cannot once start me—                [V, v]

And he in the end anticipates his wife in the boldness and bloodiness of his enterprises, while she for want of the same stimulus of action, "is troubled with thick-coming fancies that keep her from her rest," [V, iii] goes mad and dies. Macbeth endeavours to escape from reflection on his crimes by repelling their consequences, and banishes remorse for the past by the meditation of future mischief. This is not the principle of Richard's cruelty, which displays the wanton malice of a fiend as much as the frailty of human passion.

Macbeth is goaded on to acts of violence and retaliation by necessity; to Richard, blood is a pastime. There are other decisive differences inherent in the two characters. Richard may be regarded as a man of the world, a plotting, hardened knave, wholly regardless of everything but his own ends, and the means to secure them. Not so Macbeth. The superstitions of the age, the rude state of society, the local scenery and customs, all give a wildness and imaginary grandeur to his character. From the strangeness of the events that surround him, he is full of amazement and fear; and stands in doubt between the world of reality and the world of fancy. He sees sights not shown to mortal eye, and hears unearthly music. All is tumult and disorder within and without his mind; his purposes recoil upon himself, are broken and disjointed; he is the double thrall of his passions and his evil destiny. Richard is not a character either of imagination or pathos, but of pure self-will. There is no conflict of opposite feelings in his breast. The apparitions which he sees only haunt him in his sleep; nor does he live like Macbeth in a waking dream.

Macbeth has considerable energy and manliness of character; but then he is "subject to all the skyey influences." He is sure of nothing but the present moment. Richard in the busy turbulence of his projects never loses his self-possession, and makes use of every circumstance that happens as an instrument of his long-reaching designs. In his last extremity we can only regard him as a wild beast taken in the toils: while we never entirely lose our concern for Macbeth; and he calls back all our sympathy by that fine close of thoughtful melancholy,

——My way of life
Is fallen into the sear, the yellow leaf;
And that which should accompany old age,
As honour, love, obedience, troops of friends,
I must not look to have; but in their stead
Curses not loud but deep, mouth-honour, breath,
Which the poor heart would fain deny, and dare not.       [V, iii]

# The Greatness of *King Lear*

Edward Dowden

Edward Dowden calls Shakespeare's *King Lear* the greatest poetry of all north European genius and analyzes the reasons for his conclusion. In this play, according to Dowden, Shakespeare addresses life's most mysterious questions about the existence of suffering and good and evil, and he has the wisdom to know he cannot answer them. The play portrays great evil, in Gloucester's son Edmund and Lear's daughters Goneril and Regan; great suffering, in Gloucester and Lear; and great good, in Cordelia, Edgar, and Kent. Shakespeare does not explain why evil and suffering and goodness exist. He does, however, oppose evil, as Dowden demonstrates, not by denying it, but by asserting the presence of its opposites—virtue, loyalty, and love.

*King Lear* is, indeed, the greatest single achievement in poetry of the Teutonic, or Northern, genius. By its largeness of conception and the variety of its details, by its revelation of a harmony existing between the forces of nature and the passions of man, by its grotesqueness and its sublimity, it owns kinship with the great cathedrals of Gothic architecture. . . .

## SHAKSPERE ADDRESSES LIFE'S DEEPEST MYSTERIES

In *King Lear*, more than in any other of his plays, Shakspere stands in presence of the mysteries of human life. A more impatient intellect would have proposed explanations of these. A less robust spirit would have permitted the dominant tone of the play to become an eager or pathetic wistfulness respecting the significance of these hard riddles in the destiny of man. Shakspere checks such wistful curiosity, though it exists discernibly; he will present life as it is. If life proposes inexplica-

Excerpted from *Shakspere: A Critical Study of His Mind and Art* by Edward Dowden (New York: Harper & Bros., 1880).

ble riddles, Shakspere's art must propose them also. But, while Shakspere will present life as it is, and suggest no inadequate explanations of its difficult problems, he will gaze at life not only from *within*, but, if possible, also from an extra-mundane, extra-human [beyond human] point of view, and, gazing thence at life, will try to discern what aspect this fleeting and wonderful phenomenon presents to the eyes of gods. Hence a grand irony in the tragedy of *Lear*; hence all in it that is great is also small; all that is tragically sublime is also grotesque. Hence it sees man walking in a vain shadow; groping in the mist; committing extravagant mistakes; wandering from light into darkness; stumbling back again from darkness into light; spending his strength in barren and impotent rages; man in his weakness, his unreason, his affliction, his anguish, his poverty and meanness, his everlasting greatness and majesty. . . .

The ethics of the play of *King Lear* are Stoical [unaffected by pleasure or pain] ethics. Shakspere's fidelity to the fact will allow him to deny no pain or calamity that befalls man. "There was never yet philosopher that could endure the toothache patiently" [from *Much Ado About Nothing*]. He knows that it is impossible to

Fetter strong madness in a silken thread,
Charm ache with air, and agony with words.

He admits the suffering, the weakness, of humanity; but he declares that in the inner law there is a constraining power stronger than a silken thread; in the fidelity of pure hearts, in the rapture of love and sacrifice, there is a charm which is neither air nor words, but indeed, potent enough to subdue pain and make calamity acceptable. Cordelia, who utters no word in excess of her actual feeling, can declare, as she is led to prison, her calm and decided acceptance of her lot:

We are not the first
Who, with best meaning, have incurred the worst;
For thee, oppressed king, I am cast down;
Myself could else out-frown false fortune's frown.

[Compare also, as expressing the mood in which calamity must be confronted, the words of Edgar:

Men must endure
Their going hence, even as their coming hither;
Ripeness is all.]

## *Lear* Presents Vision, Not Doctrine

But though ethical principles radiate through the play of *Lear*, its chief function is not, even indirectly, to teach or inculcate moral truth, but rather, by the direct presentation of a vision of human life and of the enveloping forces of nature, to "free, arouse, dilate." We may be unable to set down in words any set of truths which we have been taught by the drama. But can we set down in words the precise moral significance of a fugue of Handel or a symphony of Beethoven? We are kindled and aroused by them; our whole nature is quickened; it passes from the habitual, hard, encrusted, and cold condition into "the fluid and attaching state"—the state in which we do not seek truth and beauty, but attract and are sought by them; the state in which "good thoughts stand before us like free children of God, and cry 'We are come.'"[Goethe's "Conversations with Eckermann," Feb. 24, 1824.] The play or the piece of music is not a code of precepts or a body of doctrine; it is "a focus where a number of vital forces unite in their purest energy."

In the play of *King Lear* we come into contact with the imagination, the heart, the soul of Shakspere, at a moment when they attained their most powerful and intense vitality.... Shakspere, in accordance with his dramatic method, drove forward across the intervening accidents towards the passion of Lear in all its stages, his wild revolt against humanity, his conflict with the powers of night and tempest, his restoration through the sacred balm of a daughter's love.

## THE CHARACTERS OF LEAR, GONERIL, AND REGAN

Nevertheless, though its chief purpose be to get the forces of the drama into position before their play upon one another begins, the first scene cannot be incoherent. In the opening sentence Shakspere gives us clearly to understand that the partition of the kingdom between Albany and Cornwall is already accomplished. In the concluding sentences we are reminded of Lear's "inconstant start," of "the unruly waywardness that infirm and choleric years bring with them." It is evidently intended that we should understand the demand made upon his daughters for a profession of their love to have been a sudden freak of self-indulged waywardness, in which there was something of jest, something of unreason, something of the infirmity which requires demonstrations of the heart. Having made the demand, however, it must not be refused. Lear's will must be opposeless. It is the centre and prime force of his little universe. To be thrown out of this passionate wilfulness, to be made a passive thing, to be stripped first of affection, then of power, then of home or shelter, last, of reason itself, and finally, to learn the preciousness of true love only at the moment

## *LEAR:* BETTER TO READ THAN TO SEE

*In 1811, when British Victorian essayist Charles Lamb wrote his famous essay* On the Tragedies of Shakespeare, Considered with Reference to Their Fitness for Stage Representation, *Shakespeare's characters had become so familiar that Lamb and many others thought of them as real human beings, almost like friends. Consequently, Lamb resented any actor's trying to impersonate his image of the real Lear.*

To see Lear acted—to see an old man tottering about the stage with a walking-stick, turned out of doors by his daughters in a rainy night, has nothing in it but what is painful and disgusting. We want to take him into shelter and relieve him. That is all the feeling which the acting of Lear ever produced in me. But the Lear of Shakespeare cannot be acted.... On the stage we see nothing but corporal infirmities and weakness, the impotence of rage; while we read it, we see not Lear, but we are Lear—we are in his mind, we are sustained by a grandeur which baffles the malice of daughters and storms; in the aberrations of his reason, we discover a mighty irregular power of reasoning, immethodized from the ordinary purposes of life, but exerting its powers, as the wind blows where it listeth, at will upon the corruptions and abuses of mankind.

Charles Lamb, in G.B. Harrison, ed., *Shakespeare: The Complete Works.* New York: Harcourt, Brace and Company, 1952.

when it must be forever renounced—such is the awful and purifying ordeal through which Lear is compelled to pass.

Shakspere "takes ingratitude," [French writer] Victor Hugo has said, "and he gives this monster two heads, Goneril . . . and Regan." The two terrible creatures are, however, distinguishable. Goneril is the calm wielder of a pitiless force, the resolute initiator of cruelty. Regan is a smaller, shriller, fiercer, more eager piece of malice. The tyranny of the elder sister is a cold, persistent pressure, as little affected by tenderness or scruple as the action of some crushing hammer; Regan's ferocity is more unmeasured, and less abnormal or monstrous. Regan would avoid her father, and, while she confronts him alone, quails a little as she hears the old man's curse pronounced against her sister:

O the blest gods! so will you wish on me
When the rash mood is on.

But Goneril knows that a helpless old man is only a helpless old man, that words are merely words. When, after Lear's terrible malediction, he rides away with his train, Goneril, who would bring things to an issue, pursues her father, determined to see matters out to the end. [It is Goneril who first suggests the plucking-out of Gloucester's eyes.] To complete the horror they produce in us, these monsters are amorous. Their love is even more hideous than their hate. The wars of

> Dragons of the prime
> That tare each other in their slime

formed a spectacle less prodigious than their mutual blandishments and caresses.

> *Regan.* I know your lady does not love her husband;
> I am sure of that: and at her late being here
> She gave strange oeillades[1] and most speaking looks
> To noble Edmund.

To the last Goneril is true to her character. Regan is despatched out of life by her sister; Goneril thrusts her own life aside, and boldly enters the great darkness of the grave.

## THE PLOT OF GLOUCESTER, EDMUND, AND EDGAR

Of the secondary plot of this tragedy—the story of Gloucester and his sons—[German critic and translator August Wilhelm von] Schlegel has explained one chief significance: "Were Lear alone to suffer from his daughters, the impression would be limited to the powerful compassion felt by us for his private misfortune. But two such unheard-of examples taking place at the same time would have the appearance of a great commotion in the moral world; the picture becomes gigantic, and fills us with such alarm as we should entertain at the idea that the heavenly bodies might one day fall from their appointed orbits." ["Lectures on Dramatic Art," translated by J. Black, p. 412.] The treachery of Edmund, and the torture to which Gloucester is subjected, are out of the course of familiar experience; but they are commonplace and prosaic in comparison with the inhumanity of the sisters and the agony of Lear. When we have climbed the steep ascent of Gloucester's mount of passion, we see still above us another *via dolorosa* [way of sorrow] leading to that

> Wall of eagle-baffling mountain,
> Black, wintry, dead, unmeasured,

to which Lear is chained. Thus the one story of horror serves as a means of approach to the other, and helps us to conceive its magnitude. The two, as Schlegel observes, produce the impression of a great commotion in the moral world. The

1. loving looks.

thunder which breaks over our head does not suddenly cease
to resound, but is reduplicated, multiplied, and magnified, and
rolls away with long reverberation.

Shakspere also desires to augment the moral mystery, the
grand inexplicableness of the play. We can assign causes to explain the evil in Edmund's heart. His birth is shameful, and the
brand burns into his heart and brain. He has been thrown
abroad in the world, and is constrained by none of the bonds
of nature or memory, of habit or association. A hard, sceptical
intellect, uninspired and unfed by the instincts of the heart,
can easily enough reason away the consciousness of obligations the most sacred. Edmund's thought is "active as a viru-
lent acid, eating its rapid way through all the tissues of human
sentiment." [This and the quotation next following from
George Eliot's novel, *Romola*.] His mind is destitute of dread of
the Divine Nemesis. [Greek goddess of vengeance]. Like Iago,
like Richard III., he finds the regulating force of the universe
in the *ego*—in the individual will. But that terror of the unseen
which Edmund scorned as so much superstition is "the initial
recognition of a moral law restraining desire, and checks the
hard bold scrutiny of imperfect thought into obligations which
can never be proved to have any sanctity in the absence of feeling." We can, therefore, in some degree account for Edmund's
bold egoism and inhumanity. What obligations should a child
feel to the man who, for a moment's selfish pleasure, had degraded and stained his entire life? In like manner, Gloucester's
sufferings do not appear to us inexplicably mysterious.

> The gods are just, and of our pleasant vices
> Make instruments to plague us;
> The dark and vicious place where thee he got
> Cost him his eyes.

But, having gone to the end of our tether, and explained all
that is explicable, we are met by enigmas which will not be
explained. We were, perhaps, somewhat too ready, [as Lear
says,] to

> Take upon us the mystery of things
> As if we were God's spies.

Now we are baffled, and bow the head in silence. Is it, indeed,
the stars that govern our condition? Upon what theory shall
we account for the sisterhood of a Goneril and a Cordelia? And
why is it that Gloucester, whose suffering is the retribution for
past misdeeds, should be restored to spiritual calm and light,
and should pass away in a rapture of mingled gladness and
grief,

> His flaw'd heart,
> Alack! too weak the conflict to support,
> 'Twixt two extremes of passion, joy and grief,
> Burst smilingly;

while Lear, a man more sinned against than sinning, should be robbed of the comfort of Cordelia's love, should be stretched to the last moment upon "the rack of this tough world," and should expire in the climax of a paroxysm [an outburst of emotion] of unproductive anguish?

Shakspere does not attempt to answer these questions. The impression which the facts themselves produce, their influence to "free, arouse, dilate," seems to Shakspere more precious than any proposed explanation of the facts which cannot be verified. The heart is purified not by dogma, but by pity and terror. But there are other questions which the play suggests. If it be the stars that govern our conditions; if that be, indeed, a possibility which Gloucester, in his first shock and confusion of mind, declares,

> As flies to wanton boys are we to the gods;
> They kill us for their sport;

if, measured by material standards, the innocent and the guilty perish by a like fate—what then? Shall we yield ourselves to the lust for pleasure? shall we organize our lives upon the principles of a studious and pitiless egoism?

## SHAKSPERE'S CLEAR VIEWS ON GOOD AND EVIL

To these questions the answer of Shakspere is clear and emphatic. Shall we stand upon Goneril's side or upon that of Cordelia? Shall we join Edgar or join the traitor? Shakspere opposes the presence and the influence of evil not by any transcendental denial of evil, but by the presence of human virtue, fidelity, and self-sacrificial love. In no play is there a clearer, an intenser manifestation of loyal manhood, of strong and tender womanhood. The devotion of Kent to his master is a passionate, unsubduable devotion, which might choose for its watchword the saying of [German writer Johann Wolfgang von] Goethe, "I love you; what is that to you?" Edgar's nobility of nature is not disguised by the beggar's rags; he is the skilful resister of evil, the champion of right to the utterance. And if Goneril and Regan alone would leave the world unintelligible and desperate, there is

> One daughter,
> Who redeems nature from the general curse
> Which twain have brought her to.

We feel throughout the play that evil is abnormal; a curse which brings down destruction upon itself; that it is without any long career; that evil-doer is at variance with evil-doer. But good is normal; for it the career is long; and "all honest and good men are disposed to befriend honest and good men, as such,"

> *Cordelia.* O thou good Kent, how shall I live, and work,
> To match thy goodness! My life will be too short,
> And every measure fail me.
> *Kent.* To be acknowledged, madam, is o'erpaid.
> All my reports go with the modest truth;
> Nor more, nor clipped, but so.

Nevertheless, when everything has been said that can be said to make the world intelligible, when we have striven our utmost to realize all the possible good that exists in the world, a need of fortitude remains.

## PRINCIPAL CHARACTERS CONFRONT GREATER POWER

It is worthy of note that each of the principal personages of the play is brought into presence of those mysterious powers which dominate life and preside over human destiny; and each, according to his character, is made to offer an interpretation of the great riddle. Of these interpretations, none is adequate to account for all the facts. Shakspere (differing in this from the old play) placed with the story in heathen times, partly, we may surmise, that he might be able to put the question boldly, "What are the gods?" Edmund, as we have seen, discovers no power or authority higher than the will of the individual and a hard trenchant intellect. In the opening of the play he utters his ironical appeal:

> I grow; I prosper—
> Now gods stand up for bastards.

It is not until he is mortally wounded, with his brother standing over him, that the recognition of a moral law forces itself painfully upon his consciousness, and he makes his bitter confession of faith:

> The wheel is come full circle, I am here.

His self-indulgent father is, after the manner of the self-indulgent, prone to superstition; and Gloucester's superstition affords some countenance to Edmund's scepticism. "This is the excellent foppery of the world, that when we are sick in fortune—often the surfeit of our own behavior—we make guilty of our disasters the sun, the moon, and the stars, as if we were villains by necessity; fools by heavenly compulsion;

knaves, thieves, and treachers by spherical predominance; drunkards, liars, and adulterers by an enforced obedience of planetary influence; and all that we are evil in by a divine thrusting-on."

Edgar, on the contrary, the champion of right, ever active in opposing evil and advancing the good cause, discovers that the gods are upon the side of right, are unceasingly at work in the vindication of truth and the execution of justice. His faith lives through trial and disaster, a flame which will not be quenched. And he buoys up, by virtue of his own energy of soul, the spirit of his father, which, unprepared for calamity, is staggering blindly, stunned from its power to think, and ready to sink into darkness and a welter [jumble] of chaotic disbelief. Gloucester, in his first confusion of spirit, exclaims bitterly against the divine government:

As flies to wanton boys are we to the gods;
They kill us for their sport.

But before the end has come he "shakes patiently his great affliction off;" he will not quarrel with the "great opposeless wills" of the gods; nay, more than this, he can identify his own will with theirs, he can accept life contentedly at their hands, or death. The words of Edgar find a response in his own inmost heart:

Thou happy father,
Think that the clearest gods, who make them honors
Of men's impossibilities, have preserved thee.

And as Edgar, the justiciary, finds in the gods his fellow-workers in the execution of justice, so Cordelia, in whose heart love is a clear and perpetual illumination, can turn for assistance and co-operancy in her deeds of love to the strong and gentle rulers of the world:

O you kind gods,
Cure this great breach in his abused nature.

Kent possesses no vision, like that which gladdens Edgar, of a divine providence. His loyalty to right has something in it of a desperate instinct, which persists, in spite of the appearances presented by the world. Shakspere would have us know that there is not any devotion to truth, to justice, to charity, more intense and real than that of the man who is faithful to them out of the sheer spirit of loyalty, unstimulated and unsupported by any faith which can be called theological. Kent, who has seen the vicissitude of things, knows of no higher power presiding over the events of the world than fortune. Therefore, all the more, Kent clings to the passionate instinct of right-doing, and to the hardy temper, the fortitude which makes evil, when it happens to come, endurable. It is Kent who utters his thought in the words—

> Nothing almost sees miracles
> But misery.

And the miracle he sees, in his distress, is the approaching succor from France, and the loyalty of Cordelia's spirit. It is Kent, again, who, characteristically making the best of an unlucky chance, exclaims, as he settles himself to sleep in the stocks,

> Fortune, good night; smile once more, turn thy wheel.

And again:

> It is the stars,
> The stars above us, govern our conditions.

And again (of Lear):

> If Fortune brag of two she loved and hated,
> One of them we behold.

Accordingly, there is at once an exquisite tenderness in Kent's nature, and also a certain roughness and hardness, needful to protect, from the shocks of life, the tenderness of one who finds no refuge in communion with the higher powers, or in a creed of religious optimism.

But Lear himself—the central figure of the tragedy—what of him? What of suffering humanity that wanders from the darkness into light, and from the light into the darkness? Lear is grandly passive—played upon by all the manifold sources of nature and of society. And though he is in part delivered from his imperious self-will, and learns, at last, what true love is, and that it exists in the world, Lear passes away from our sight, not in any mood of resignation or faith or illuminated peace, but in a piteous agony of yearning for that love which he had found only to lose forever. Does Shakspere mean to contrast the pleasure in a demonstration of spurious affection in the first scene with the agonized cry for real love in the last scene, and does he wish us to understand that the true gain from the bitter discipline of Lear's old age was precisely this—his acquiring a supreme need of what is best, though a need which finds, as far as we can learn, no satisfaction?

We guess at the spiritual significance of the great tragic facts of the world, but, after our guessing, their mysteriousness remains.

Our estimate of this drama as a whole . . . depends very much on the view we take of the Fool; . . . "I know not how I can better describe the Fool than as the soul of pathos in a sort of comic masquerade; one in whom fun and frolic are sublimed and idealized into tragic beauty. . . . His 'laboring to outjest Lear's heart-struck injuries' tells us that his wits are set a-dancing by grief; that his jest bubble up from the depths of a heart struggling with pity and sorrow, as foam enwreathes the face of deeply troubled water. . . . There is all along a shrinking, velvet-footed delicacy of step in the Fool's antics, as if awed by the holiness of the ground; and he seems bringing diversion to the thoughts, that he may the better steal a sense of woe into the heart. And I am not clear whether the inspired antics that sparkle from the surface of his mind are in more impressive contrast with the dark, tragic scenes into which they are thrown, like rockets into a midnight tempest, or with the undercurrent of deep tragic thoughtfulness out of which they falteringly issue and play." [*Shakespeare's Life, Art, and Characters*, vol. ii.]

Of the tragedy of *King Lear* a critic wishes to say as little as may be; for, in the case of this play, words are more than ordinarily inadequate to express or describe its true impression. A tempest or a dawn will not be analyzed in words; we must feel the shattering fury of the gale, we must watch the calm light broadening. And the sensation experienced by the reader of *King Lear* resembles that produced by some grand natural phenomenon. The effect cannot be received at secondhand; it cannot be described; it can hardly be suggested.

# The Double Plot
# of *King Lear*

Jay L. Halio

Jay L. Halio examines the double plot in Shakespeare's *King Lear*. Both Lear and Gloucester suffer
from the cruelty of their children, but Halio explains
that their destinies differ. Gloucester, blinded and
overtaken by despair, learns to "see" in a better, more
feeling way. A determined Lear, who defies nature's
elements, turns foolish and mad before his senses are
restored when he is reunited with his daughter
Cordelia. Both men die. Halio argues that, in a terrifying way, Gloucester's blindness and death and Lear's
profound anguish and death symbolize the passage of
what is finite and mortal and the endurance of immortal hope and love.

*King Lear* is Shakespeare's most successful and sustained use
of the double plot in his tragedies. The Lear story, gathered
from the ancient legend (recorded, for example, in Holinshed's *Chronicles*) and already made into the chronicle play of
*King Leir* by the early 1590s, is paralleled by the Gloster plot,
for which Shakespeare borrowed from Sidney's *Arcadia*. But
the function of the double plot is obviously more than an un-
derscoring, by analogy, of the main themes.

## THE DOUBLE DESTINIES OF GLOSTER AND LEAR

At key points, the destinies of Lear and Gloster contrast, particularly as they meet their fate: Lear with a wished-for Ti-
tanism ("I will endure"), Gloster with despair ("a man may rot
even here"). The treachery of Gloster's bastard son makes the
cruelty of Lear's legitimate daughters all the more intense for
this irony. But the double plot structure along with the imagery makes the play expand spatially and temporally: set in
pre-Roman times but infused with allusions to the Gospels

From Jay L. Halio, Introduction to *King Lear* (Edinburgh: Oliver & Boyd, 1973).
Reprinted by permission of the author.

both verbally and symbolically, *King Lear* assumes the dimensions of a cosmic drama played out on the bare boards of our common human experience, searching the depths of the most primitive sources of our being and questioning, in the process, the nature and justice of the gods to whom we owe our origin and from whom only, as Gloster learns, we can expect deliverance.

But what kind of deliverance? And from what? The [German] philosopher Karl Jaspers has said [in *Tragedy Is Not Enough*]:

> A yearning for deliverance has always gone hand in hand with the knowledge of the tragic. When man encounters the hard fact of tragedy, he faces an inexorable limit. At this limit, he finds no guarantee of general salvation. Rather, it is in acting out his own personality, in realizing his selfhood even unto death, that he finds redemption and deliverance.

Both Lear and Gloster are compelled by their initial actions to continue acting out their own personalities, to realise their selfhoods "even unto death". One would have expected men of such advanced age to have already made the discoveries about themselves that Lear and Gloster are forced now to make; but this is part of the terror, the awe, of Shakespeare's drama. Lear cries in Act III, "Then let them anotomise Regan", but it is Lear—and through him, mortality—that is anatomised: and there we find all three daughters as extensions of the king. "The darke and vitious place where thee he gotte, / Cost him his eies", Edgar says to the dying Edmund; but before he dies Gloster has learned to see "feelingly", a better way of seeing than he has hitherto known. The play repeatedly and insistently adumbrates [suggests] such paradoxes, determined as it is not only to discover "any cause in nature that makes these hard hearts", but also to show the love that brings Cordelia back from France to go about her father's business. The discovery that it makes is that for some acts there is "No cause, no cause".

## *LEAR* PORTRAYS REALITY AND CONSEQUENCES NOT CAUSES

For at bottom, rationalism must give way; or rather, any rational knowing. Why does Cordelia respond as she does in Scene I? Is acting out her selfhood, maintaining her integrity, as we would say, so important to her? Should it be? At this particular point? Behold the consequences. Knowing so much— recognising, with Kent, the real nature of her sisters—surely with them she also knows her father's nature. Then what makes her both love and oppose him? And he, on the sudden,

to cast her out with such dire comparisons as to the "barbarous Scythyan [ancient nomadic people], / Or he that makes
his generation messes / To gorge his appetite [he that feeds
gluttonously on his own children]"—*she* who was his youngest
and dearest? We may rationalise the cause as we will: Shakespeare simply presents "the thing itselfe". Only for Kent's returning to serve Lear as Caius do we find an explanation, such
as it is:

LEAR. . . . . what would'st thou?

KENT. Service.

LEAR. Who would'st thou serve?

KENT. You.

LEAR. Do'st thou know me fellow?

KENT. No sir, but you have that in your countenance, which I
would faine call Maister.

LEAR. Whats that?

KENT. Authoritie.                                        (I. IV.)

The mystery remains—the source of that "Authoritie". But it is
there, the vagaries of the foolish, rash old King notwithstand-
ing, and Kent knows it. Nor can he break away from it, even
when it disowns him, or at the end when it dies from him.

By contrast, Edmund attempts in his soliloquy in I. II to give
us a completely rationalised basis for his behaviour. A child of
nature, he will make "Nature" his goddess. But in so doing he
must violate some of the most natural impulses that man is
heir to: the filial devotion of a child to its parent, or a brother
to a brother.

Such is the "nature" of this play—contradictory, complex,
cursed, and finally redeeming. In Cordelia the bond of nature
that ties her to her father remains radically unbroken, despite
her pride and his fury at her stubborn honesty. He curses her
from his kingdom eventually to ask *her* blessing and forgiveness. Stunned into a "shipwreck" of the soul that begins with
his defiance of the elements which oppose him during the
storm, Lear comes finally to know himself and nature. "Men
must indure," Edgar tells his regressive father, but he does not
say why. "Ripenes is all [perfect readiness is all]" is not the
reason, but the result. Men must endure so that they may experience the shipwreck of the soul and encounter the fact of
tragedy. For men like Lear and Gloster there remains no other
route to redemption and deliverance.

## LEAR'S RAGE AND THE FOOL'S ADVICE

*In act 3, scene 2, in the storm on the heath, Lear rages at the elements and his daughters, but the fool urges humility and a dry house.*

LEAR: Blow, winds, and crack your cheeks! rage, blow,
You cataracts and hurricanoes[1], spout
Till you have drenched our steeples, drowned the cocks[2]!
You sulphurous and thought-executing[3] fires,
Vaunt-couriers[4] of oak-cleaving thunderbolts,
Singe my white head! And thou, all-shaking thunder,
Strike flat the thick rotundity o'th' world,
Crack Nature's molds[5], all germains[6] spill at once,
That make ingrateful man!

FOOL: O nuncle, court holy water[7] in a dry house is better
than this rain water out o' door. Good nuncle, in, and ask thy
daughters' blessing! Here's a night pities neither wise men nor
fools.

LEAR: Rumble thy bellyfull! Spit, fire; spout, rain!
Nor rain, wind, thunder, fire are my daughters;
I tax[8] not you, you elements, with unkindness;
I never gave you kingdom, called you children;
You owe me no subscription[9]. Then let fall
Your horrible pleasure. Here I stand your slave,
A poor, infirm, weak, and despised old man;
But yet I call you servile ministers,
That will with two pernicious daughters join
Your high-engendered battles 'gainst a head
So old and white as this. O! O! 'tis foul!

FOOL: He that has a house to put's head in has a good headpiece.

Shakespeare, *King Lear.*

Kent tries to head Lear off before embarking on this route but is banished for his pains. The Foole then enters with a new approach and through his nonsense tries to pound sense into the King. But he is too late; or rather, his ministry becomes a kind of scourge which he himself finally repents of as he asks Lear to come back out of the storm and ask his daughters' blessing. It is "a brave night to coole a curtizan", but Lear persists in venting his anguish until, his wits beginning to turn, he allows himself to be led to some shelter. By this time, his self-pity has also begun a transformation into compassion for the "poore naked wretches" throughout his realm that must

1. waterspouts. 2. weather vanes. 3. killing quick as thought. 4. forerunners. 5. the molds in which men are made. 6. seeds of life. 7. flatter the great ones. 8. accuse. 9. submission.

"bide the pelting of this pittiles night". Thus Lear enters the dark night of his soul, touched at first with "noble anger", as he has asked, but now about to undergo descent into a spiritual purgatory from which his recovery is neither certain nor rapid. When, however, he does emerge, he will be so far from demanding love and empire that a prison cage will be space enough from him as long as he is with his loved Cordelia. There he will be content to remain with her as "Gods spies" to take upon themselves "the mistery of things". Though much of the mystery has already been revealed, something remains behind. Cordelia must die.

Again, the question insistently imposes itself: why? The eighteenth century found the ending of this play so terrifying that Nahum Tate's redaction long held the stage. Dr [Samuel] Johnson, editing *King Lear*, found the ending so appalling that he would never look at it again. Indeed, it was not until the mid-nineteenth century that Shakespeare's original began to provide the text for actual performances of the play. The twentieth century has repeatedly revived Shakespeare's play, with excellent performances in the last two decades, including two recent film versions. Is it that we are accordingly tougher-minded than our forebears, and better able to "take it", or that after two world wars we have become inured to horror? Nevertheless, the question remains: why should Cordelia die? Perhaps, as [critic] Robert Speaight says [in *Nature in Shakesperian Tragedy*], "the world of *King Lear* is too monstrous for the reign of innocence. . . . Cordelia's death must remain as a redemption, but also as a reproach."

## GOOD MORTALS PASS; THE LOVE THEY EMBODIED REMAINS

The Foole is already gone, last seen at the end of III. VI.—dead by hanging? of a broken heart? Or, to alter the frame of reference, is his function simply over, as Lear enters the phantasmagoria [fantastic imagery, as in a dream]of his madness? The Foole and Cordelia share more than an affinity or sympathetic relationship, their roles beautifully complement each other; but though they do not overlap, there is some question whether the parts were actually doubled in performance (would Armin play both a woman's role and the Foole's?). In any event, the Foole's terror and hopelessness on the heath must give way to the ministrations of the returned daughter, who nevertheless may not survive the unleashed horror of humanity preying upon itself. Although she lives just long enough to be reconciled with her father, both this reconciliation and her death become necessary in order, in Jaspers' terms, to release the infinite from the finite, the fundamental reality from its particular configuration [arrangement]. In this process, Cordelia, Kent, the Foole, and Lear all play their necessary and important roles. Love endures, however men must abide the transiency of its embodiment as well as their own passing.

By watching the doom of what is finite, man witnesses the reality and truth of the infinite. Being is the background of all backgrounds; it dooms to failure every particular configuration. The more grandiose the hero and the idea he is living with, the more tragic the march of events and the more fundamental the reality that is revealed.

Tragedy is not intended to evaluate morally the justice of the doom of a guilty man who never ought to have become guilty. Crime and punishment are a narrower framework submerged in moralism. It is only when man's moral substance articulates itself into powers which collide that man grows to heroic stature; it is only then that his crime is reduced to a guiltless and necessary result of his character, and it is only then that his doom becomes his restoration, in which the past is included and redeemed. Tragic doom ceases to be meaningless accident and becomes necessity precisely because the absolute has from the outset condemned everything finite. Then the comprehensive reality of the whole process becomes clear—the process for which the individual sacrifices himself precisely because he is great. The tragic hero himself is at one with reality when he goes to meet his doom.

At the end, Lear is on the firm ground of reality, even as he witnesses the death of his beloved child. Though his eyes "are not othe best", he sees more clearly now than ever, despite Albany's disclaimer that he "knowes not what he sees, and vaine it is, / That we present us to him." If Lear cannot or will not make the identification between Kent and Caius, it is because he is intent on the main spectacle of Cordelia:

> Why should a dog, a horse, a rat have life,
> And thou no breath at all? thout come no more,
> Never, never, never, never, never. . . .            (v. iii.)

But his last words, avoiding self-concern finally and forever, are entirely other-directed:

> Do you see this? Looke on her, looke her lips,
> Looke there, looke there.

It is a cry of amazement and of hope. What he has seen—and sees—kills him; but it releases all his love, that of those closest to him, and ours.

# The Plot of Tragedy Best Suits *King Lear*

Sylvan Barnet, Morton Berman, and William Burto

Sylvan Barnet, Morton Berman, and William Burto discuss the original historical version of *King Lear* and the various treatments accorded it. In 1681 Nahum Tate rewrote the closing scenes of Shakespeare's *King Lear* to give it a happy ending and thus avoid the play's brutality. The authors declare that such tampering undermines the play as a tragedy. The authors describe the tragic plot and subplot, in which Gloucester's pain and Lear's anguish mirror each other. As a tragic hero, Lear suffers, learns patience, and dies, the only ending appropriate for Shakespeare's grand theme, according to the authors.

Like the Greeks, the Elizabethans were less insistent that their dramatists devise new stories than that they retell old ones more effectively. [British playwright John] Dryden's description, in 1668, of Shakespeare's contemporary, [playwright] Ben Jonson, is as appropriate to Shakespeare as to Jonson: "He has done his robberies so openly that we may see that he fears not to be taxed by any law. He invades authors like a monarch, and what would be theft in other poets is only victory in him."

The victory which Shakespeare achieved in the creation of *King Lear* is rooted partly in Elizabethan history books and partly in an anonymous Elizabethan play, *King Leir.* The legend of Lear, a king in Britain before the Roman conquest, who had disowned Cordelia, his virtuous daughter, and exposed himself to [the guile of] her two wicked sisters, Goneril and Regan, was sanctified as history. But historical accounts and the anonymous drama are untragic, for their hero was finally restored to the throne by the devotion of the daughter whom he had rejected. Although the old drama of *King Leir* ended

Introduction to *King Lear* in *Eight Great Tragedies,* edited by Sylvan Barnet, Morton Berman, and William Burto (New York: New American Library, 1957). Copyright 1957 by Sylvan Barnet, Morton Berman, and William Burto. Reprinted by permission of the editors.

happily with the king's restoration, history books carried the story further, and related that after his peaceful death Cordelia was deposed and died in prison.

---

### *LEAR* OPENS LIKE A FAIRY TALE

*In an article published in the June 1995 issue of* The World & I, *writer and critic Sam Schoenbaum notes that* Lear *opens like a fairy tale. Like other folktales, it has ungrateful children and bad sisters, elements like those in such stories as the goosegirl-princess and Cinderella.*

A flourish of trumpets heralds the entry of the old king, his three daughters, and other notables and attendants. The king, to express his darker purpose, calls for a map. There is to be, in effect, an auction in which his youngest and favorite daughter, Cordelia, will refuse to take part.

This play opens like nothing so much as an elemental fairy tale: There was once a very old king who wanted to retire from statecraft, so one day he summoned his three daughters before the whole court and asked, "Which of you shall we say does love us most, for she will inherit the most opulent third of the kingdom?" Two of the daughters professed boundless love, but the third and youngest, who most loved and was most loved by him, would say nothing. . . .

If the love test sounds folkloristic, such is indeed the case, as is abundantly recognized: There are many ancient European and Oriental antecedents about good and bad children, and about filial ingratitude. There is the goosegirl-princess, who told her father she "loved him like salt," and Cinderella (the most famous such story, at least in the West), who was mistreated by her ugly sisters. In such universalities lies the heart of the mystery.

Sam Schoenbaum, "The Tragedy of King Lear," *The World & I*, June 1995.

---

Such was the raw material which Shakespeare appropriated, and to it he added a subplot, borrowed from [British writer] Sir Philip Sidney's *Arcadia*, a courtly Elizabethan novel by the ideal gentleman (scholar, poet, soldier) of the age. To the story of Lear and his daughters, Shakespeare joined a tale of a man (Gloucester, in the play) who trusted his wicked son and rejected his loyal one, and he linked these two stories by having the villainous son (Edmund) engage in intrigues with Lear's two ferocious daughters. And, instead of ending (as the old play did) with justice triumphant, Shakespeare so darkened both tales that some of his most perceptive and sympathetic critics have felt that his play is not tragic but pessimistic.

In 1681 [British writer] Nahum Tate, finding Shakespeare's *Lear* "A Heap of Jewels, unstrung and unpolisht," decided to improve it. In his version he not only restored Lear to the throne, but he had Lear's fair daughter, Cordelia, wed to Gloucester's honest son, Edgar. This happy ending held the stage until 1823, when [actor] Edmund Kean reverted to the tragic conclusion; but after three performances Kean took up Tate's ending again, and not until 1838 did [actor and theater manager] William Macready set Shakespeare's own play back on the boards. Even Dr. [Samuel] Johnson, the finest critic of eighteenth-century England and one of the most perceptive students of Shakespeare's plays, found the tragic ending unsatisfactory. Admitting that justice does not always triumph on earth, he insisted nevertheless that a play is not worsened if it conforms to our hopes rather than to our experience. "A play in which the wicked prosper, and the virtuous miscarry, may doubtless be good, because it is a just representation of the common events of human life: but since all reasonable beings naturally love justice, I cannot easily be persuaded that the observation of justice makes a play worse." Johnson's words deserve careful thought, and though few people would now go back to Tate's happier text, many readers have felt that in *Lear* Shakespeare was needlessly brutal.

But the picture in *Lear* is tragic, not brutal, and Johnson somewhat misstated the case when he asserted that "the wicked prosper." True, Goneril and Regan, Lear's "tigers, not daughters," treat the old king barbarously, and Lear and Cordelia die; Gloucester, too, who foolishly relied on Edmund and mistrusted Edgar, dies in the course of the drama. But if the good people perish, so, too, do the wicked, and at the end of the play, though the greatest people are no more, the kingdom returns to the hands of the righteous. The cataclysm [violent upheaval] subsides, and evil has—at least for a while—expired in the holocaust which it created.

## *LEAR*'S TRAGIC PLOT

The play begins with Lear's abdication; portioning out his kingdom to his daughters, he blindly rejects Cordelia, his favorite, when she refuses—or is unable—to publicly pronounce her love for him. Because Kent, a faithful courtier, interposes, Lear banishes him, too, and calls upon the goddess Nature to witness his rejection of Cordelia. But he soon finds that Goneril and Regan, the daughters who freely professed their love, are in reality monsters of ingratitude, and he who gave them a kingdom learns that he has no place to rest his head. Again he calls on Nature, now to make Goneril sterile, and if this time he has indeed been mistreated, we nevertheless perceive that he has not yet learned all that he must before his tragic life is over. Out on the heath he wanders about in the storm, but the rain which beats down on his head is far weaker than the storm which rages in his mind.

Tragedy, Edith Hamilton has said in *The Greek Way*, is the suffering of a soul that can suffer greatly, and Lear's anguish is dramatically counterpoised against Gloucester's pain. The Gloucester subplot parallels the main plot, but Gloucester never reaches Lear's heights. Gloucester's blinding, horrible though it be, is only the physical counterpart to the more painful, yet more noble, suffering of Lear. Still further removed from the tragic hero, Kent—who, with the Fool, sometimes plays a role corresponding to a Greek chorus—is bound in the stocks, but with a patient shrug (which was never Lear's way) he asks simply that Fortune turn her wheel.

It is precisely Lear's *im*patience which makes him potentially tragic. Every inch a king, his curses are cosmic (though as unnatural as the cruel acts which he asks Nature to witness), and his early appeal to the gods is that they should touch him with noble anger. But Lear must acquire patience and wisdom, not anger. As the tragedy progresses he does indeed become a man more sinned against than sinning, and if at the beginning of the play Regan astutely remarks that Lear "hath ever but slenderly known himself," Lear acquires some self-knowledge through his suffering. But the consequences of folly cannot be undone by tardy knowledge, and the evil forces work their course. Cordelia dies, and the hope that she and Lear might dwell in an almost mystical union is shattered. Lear, however, has seen too much of life to remain in this world, and his death is as appropriate as it is inevitable. The best comment on the impertinence of Tate's revised happy ending is [British essayist] Charles Lamb's: "A happy ending!—as if the living martyrdom that Lear had gone through,—the flaying of his feelings alive, did not make a fair dismissal from the stage of life the only decorous thing for him. . . . As if the childish pleasure of getting his gilt robes and sceptre again could tempt him to act over again his misused station—as if, at his years and with his experience, anything was left but to die."

# CHRONOLOGY

**1532**

Henry VIII breaks with Catholic Church

**1557**

John Shakespeare marries Mary Arden

**1558**

Elizabeth I becomes queen of England

**1559**

*Book of Common Prayer* made the official English liturgy

**1561**

Philosopher and statesman Francis Bacon born

**1563**

Thirty-nine Articles formally state the doctrines of the
Church of England

**1564**

Plague at Stratford
William Shakespeare born
Christopher Marlowe born

**1566**

Ovid's *Metamorphoses* translated by Arthur Golding

**1569**

John Shakespeare becomes bailiff of Stratford

**CA. 1570**

Emilia Bassano born

**1572**

Ben Jonson born

**1573**

Architect Inigo Jones born
Poet John Donne born

**1574–1575**

Persecution of Catholics and Anabaptists in England

**1576**

The Theatre built in London

**1577**

The Curtain and Blackfriars theaters open in London
Raphael Holinshed publishes *Chronicles*

**1577–1580**

Sir Francis Drake's voyage around the world

**1582**

Shakespeare marries Anne Hathaway

**1583**

Daughter Susanna born

**1585**

Twins Hamnet and Judith born

**1587**

Holinshed's *Chronicles,* 2nd ed., published
Execution of Mary, Queen of Scots
Marlowe's *1 Tamburlaine*

**1587–1590**

Shakespeare acting and touring

**1588**

Spanish Armada defeated by English navy
Marlowe's *2 Tamburlaine*

**1590**

Sidney's *The Arcadia* published
Spenser's *Faerie Queene* published

**1591**

*1 Henry VI*

**1591–1592**

*2* and *3 Henry VI*

**1592**

Robert Greene's attack on Shakespeare
The Rose theater opens

**1592–1593**

*The Comedy of Errors*
Sonnets
*Richard III*
Plague in London

**1593**

Marlowe dies

*Titus Andronicus*
*The Taming of the Shrew*
*The Two Gentlemen of Verona*
*Love's Labour's Lost*
*Venus and Adonis* published

## 1594

Lord Chamberlain's Company formed
*The Rape of Lucrece* published

## 1594–1595

*A Midsummer Night's Dream*
*Romeo and Juliet*
*Richard II*

## CA. 1595

The Swan theater is built

## 1595–1596

*The Merchant of Venice*

## 1596

Shakespeare applies for and is granted coat of arms for his
    father
Hamnet Shakespeare dies
*King John*

## 1597

Shakespeare buys New Place
*1 Henry IV*

## 1598

The Theatre torn down; timbers used for new Globe
Irish rebellion begins
*2 Henry IV*
*Much Ado About Nothing*

## 1599

Globe theater opens
*Henry V*
*As You Like It*
*Julius Caesar*
*The Merry Wives of Windsor*

## 1600

The Fortune theater opens

## 1600–1601

*Hamlet*

*Twelfth Night*
*Troilus and Cressida*

## 1601

John Shakespeare dies
"The Phoenix and the Turtle"

## 1602

Shakespeare buys land at Stratford
*Othello*

## 1603

Plague in London
Elizabeth I dies
James I becomes king
English conquest of Ireland
Chamberlain's Men become King's Men
*All's Well That Ends Well*

## 1604

*Measure for Measure*

## 1605

Repression of Catholics and Puritans in England
Gunpowder Plot to kill James I and members of Parliament
Shakespeare invests in Stratford tithes

## 1606

Charter granted for Virginia colony
Visit by the king of Denmark
Jonson's *Volpone*
*King Lear*
*Macbeth*

## 1607

Founding of Jamestown in America
Daughter Susanna marries John Hall

## 1607–1609

*Antony and Cleopatra*
*Coriolanus*
*Timon of Athens* (unfinished)
*Pericles* completed

## 1608

Plague in London
King's Men acquire Blackfriars
Granddaughter Elizabeth Hall born
Mary Arden Shakespeare dies

## 1609

King's Men begin acting in Blackfriars theater
Sonnets and "A Lover's Complaint" published by Thomas
    Thorpe

## 1610

*Cymbeline*

## 1610–1611

*The Winter's Tale*

## 1611

*The Maydenhead of the first musicke that ever was printed for
    the Virginalls,* first book of keyboard music in England
The King James Bible published
Shakespeare contributes to Highway Bill
*The Tempest*

## 1612

Shakespeare's brother Gilbert dies

## 1612–1613

*Henry VIII*

## 1613

The Globe theater burns down
Shakespeare's brother Richard dies
Shakespeare buys house in Blackfriars area

## 1616

Daughter Judith marries Thomal Quiney
Shakespeare dies

## 1623

Anne Hathaway Shakespeare dies
Actors Condell and Heminge publish First Folio

# WORKS BY WILLIAM SHAKESPEARE

Note: Many of the dates in this list are approximate. Because no manuscripts identified with the date of writing exist, scholars must decide a most likely date, either of the writing or of the first production, to many plays.

**1591**
*1 Henry VI*

**1591–1592**
*2* and *3 Henry VI*

**1592–1593**
*The Comedy of Errors*
*Richard III*
sonnets

**1593**
*Titus Andronicus*
*The Taming of the Shrew*
*The Two Gentlemen of Verona*
*Love's Labour's Lost*
*Venus and Adonis* published

**1594**
*The Rape of Lucrece* published

**1594–1595**
*A Midsummer Night's Dream*
*Romeo and Juliet*
*Richard II*

**1595–1596**
*The Merchant of Venice*

**1596**
*King John*

**1597**
*1 Henry IV*

**1598**
*2 Henry IV*
*Much Ado About Nothing*

### 1599

*Henry V*
*As You Like It*
*Julius Caesar*
*The Merry Wives of Windsor*
"The Passionate Pilgrim" published

### 1600–1601

*Twelfth Night*
*Hamlet*
*Troilus and Cressida*

### 1601

"The Phoenix and the Turtle"

### 1602

*Othello*

### 1603

*All's Well That Ends Well*

### 1604

*Measure for Measure*

### 1606

*King Lear*
*Macbeth*

### 1607–1609

*Antony and Cleopatra*
*Coriolanus*
*Timon of Athens* (unfinished)
*Pericles* completed

### 1609

sonnets and "A Lover's Complaint" first published by Thomas
Thorpe

### 1610

*Cymbeline*

### 1610–1611

*The Winter's Tale*

### 1611

*The Tempest*

### 1612–1613

*Henry VIII*

# For Further Research

## About William Shakespeare

Janet Adelman, ed., *Twentieth-Century Interpretations of King Lear: A Collection of Critical Essays.* Englewood Cliffs, NJ: Prentice-Hall, 1978.

Peter Alexander, *Shakespeare's Life and Art.* London: James Nisbet and Co., 1939.

James Black, "The Visual Artistry of *Romeo and Juliet,*" *Studies in English Literature* 15 (Spring 1975), 245–56.

A.C. Bradley, *Shakespearean Tragedy: Hamlet, Othello, King Lear, Macbeth.* 1904. Reprint, New York: World Publishing, 1961.

Nicholas Brooke, *Shakespeare's Early Tragedies.* London: Methuen & Co., 1968.

Ivor Brown, *How Shakespeare Spent the Day.* New York: Hill and Wang, 1963.

S.T. Coleridge, *Shakespearean Criticism* (1811–1834). Ed. by T.M. Raysor. Cambridge, MA: Harvard University Press, 1930.

Hardin Craig and David Berington, *An Introduction to Shakespeare.* Rev. ed. Glenview, IL: Scott, Foresman, 1951.

Delora G. Cunningham, *"Macbeth:* The Tragedy of the Hardened Heart," *Shakespeare Quarterly* 14 (1963), 39–46.

Edward Dowden, *Shakespeare: A Critical Study of His Mind and Art.* New York: Harper & Brothers Publishers, 1880.

Harley Granville-Barker and G.B. Harrison, eds., *A Companion to Shakespeare Studies.* New York: Cambridge University Press, 1934.

William Hazlitt, *Characters of Shakespeare's Plays.* 1817. In vol. IV of the *Complete Works,* ed. by P.P. Howe. 21 vols. London: J.M. Dent, 1932–34.

Cyrus Hoy, *Hamlet: An Authoritative Text: Intellectual Backgrounds, Extracts from Sources, Essays in Criticism.* New York: W.W. Norton, 1963.

Dieter Mehl, *Shakespeare's Tragedies: An Introduction.* New York: Cambridge University Press, 1986.

George R. Price, *Reading Shakespeare's Plays.* Woodbury, NY: Barron's Educational Series, 1962.

A.L. Rowse, *Shakespeare the Man.* New York: Harper & Row, 1973.

S. Schoenbaum, *William Shakespeare: A Documentary Life.* New York: Oxford University Press in association with The Scolar Press, 1975.

Edith Sitwell, *A Notebook on William Shakespeare.* Boston: Beacon Press, 1948.

Logan Pearsall Smith, *On Reading Shakespeare.* New York: Harcourt, Brace, 1933.

Robert Speaight, *Nature in Shakespearian Tragedy.* London: Hollis & Carter, 1955.

Theodore Spencer, *Shakespeare and the Nature of Man: Lowell Lectures, 1942.* 2nd ed. London: Collier-Macmillan, 1949.

Caroline F.E. Spurgeon, *Shakespeare's Imagery and What It Tells Us.* New York: Cambridge University Press, 1935.

## ABOUT ELIZABETHAN THEATERS AND TIMES

Joseph Quincy Adams, *Shakespearean Playhouses.* New York: Houghton Mifflin, 1917.

Maurice Ashley, *Great Britain to 1988.* Ann Arbor: University of Michigan Press, 1961.

Arthur Bryant, *Spirit of England.* London: William Collins & Co. 1982.

Elizabeth Burton, *The Pageant of Elizabethan England.* New York: Charles Scribner's Sons, 1958.

Will and Ariel Durant, *The Age of Reason Begins.* Vol. VII of *The Story of Civilization.* New York: Simon and Schuster, 1961.

Alfred Harbage, *Shakespeare's Audience.* New York: Columbia University Press, 1941.

G.B. Harrison, *Elizabethan Plays and Players.* Ann Arbor: University of Michigan Press, 1956.

A.V. Judges, *The Elizabethan Underworld.* New York: Octagon Books, 1965.

Walter Raleigh, ed., *Shakespeare's England: An Account of the Life and Manners of His Age.* 2 vols. Oxford: Clarendon Press, 1916.

*Shakespeare and the Theatre.* London: Shakespeare Association of London, 1927. (This is a series of papers by a variety of critics.)

E.M.W. Tillyard, *The Elizabethan World Picture.* New York: Random House, n.d. (Published by arrangement with The Macmillan Company, 1943.)

George Macaulay Trevelyan, *The Age of Shakespeare and the Stuart Period.* Vol. 2 of *Illustrated English Social History.* London: Longmans, Green, 1950.

# INDEX